CHELTENHAM PUBS

THROUGH TIME

Geoff Sandles

AMBERLEY PUBLISHING

First published 2012

Amberley Publishing
The Hill, Stroud
Gloucestershire, GL5 4EP

www.amberleybooks.com

ISBN 978 1 4456 0399 5

British Library Cataloguing in Publication Data.
A catalogue record for this book is available from the British Library.

Typeset in 9.5pt on 12pt Celeste.
Typesetting by Amberley Publishing.
Printed in the UK.

Introduction

There is no definitive answer to the question, 'How many pubs were there in Cheltenham?' On my website www.gloucestershirepubs.co.uk I have listed an astonishing 339 licensed premises in the town, but the information is sourced from documents spanning from the eighteenth century to modern times. Clearly not all the pubs were operating at the same time and several have changed their identities, thus there are duplications. Then there is the problem of deciding what actually constitutes a pub. *The Pocket Oxford English Dictionary* simply defines a pub as 'a building in which beer and other drinks are served'. Thus wine bars, nightclubs, hotels and restaurants have to be included.

From a personal viewpoint the definition of a pub is straightforward – at least a good pub. First and foremost it has to have good beer. Everything else then usually falls into place: delicious food, enthusiastic staff and friendly locals. Today, however, not every pub can operate to its full potential, restricted by the dictates of large pub companies who set exorbitant rates for their tenants and prevent them from sourcing beers from a brewery of their choice. Allegations have been made against these 'pubcos' (Pub Companies) that they have deliberately run down pubs so that they can claim they are unviable and sell them for lucrative housing development. Property developers have also been guilty of similar scams – recently the Greyhound in Hewlett Road was scandalously reduced to rubble. In 2012 these contentious issues should be addressed by the government.

There is a subtle difference between the beer tie and a tied house. The disadvantage of the modern beer tie has already been discussed, whereas the tied house system can actually be beneficial to pubs. Historically pubs were acquired by the local brewery to guarantee supply. Free houses and those brewing their own beer were bought by family brewers in Victorian times to ensure their beers were always available. In Cheltenham, pubs like the Bayshill Inn and the Caledonian Inn were snapped up by Gardner's Original Brewery in the High Street. Quality control was better in the larger breweries, resulting in a more consistent product for the beer drinker.

However, the tied house system was far from perfect. Through a series of brewery takeovers and amalgamations the Cheltenham Original Brewery gained prominence, eventually supplying three quarters of the town's pubs. By the 1950s the takeover mania was on a regional scale. West Country Breweries had hundreds of pubs extending beyond the Gloucestershire border into Herefordshire, Wiltshire, Worcestershire and parts of Wales. In 1963 ownership of West Country Breweries and the Cheltenham brewery passed to Whitbread. In the 1970s keg beers Trophy and Tankard replaced traditional local brews, with the exception of West Country Pale Ale.

CAMRA, the Campaign for Real Ale, spearheaded the battle against keg beer. From humble beginnings the campaign now boasts 130,000 members and is a respected consumer group. A pub crawl around Cheltenham in the late 1970s might have involved drinking five or six different ales, mostly from national brewers. Today a bewildering variety of ales from small craft and regional breweries would be found in those same pubs. CAMRA can take some credit for this amazing transformation.

In 1989 the large, pub-owning breweries had to dispose of their pubs under the 'Beer Orders'. Whitbread closed their brewery in Cheltenham in 1998. It seemed that the town's brewing history had come to an end. However, Battledown Brewery opened in 2005 followed by Festival Brewery in 2007 and Prescott Brewery in 2009. The last time that Cheltenham had three operating breweries was in the 1880s! Clearly there has never been a better time to enjoy a beer in a Cheltenham pub.

In choosing the selection of images for this book I have consciously tried to arrange them in a rough geographical order. Unfortunately, due to lack of space this has necessitated omitting the pubs of the surrounding villages such as Prestbury and Bishops Cleeve. Similarly there are some superb pubs that don't get a mention either, like the Jolly Brewmaster and Somerset Arms.

The descriptions of Cheltenham pubs on the Gloucestershire Pubs website go into considerable detail and many are accompanied by photographs. I look forward to hearing from you if you can furnish me with any more information or supply any old images.

Finally, may I extend my gratitude to those who have assisted me in the preparation of this book. Particularly to Michael Wilkes, who kindly gave me access to his wonderful collection of colour slides. Also to the anonymous gentleman who generously donated many of the black-and-white images.

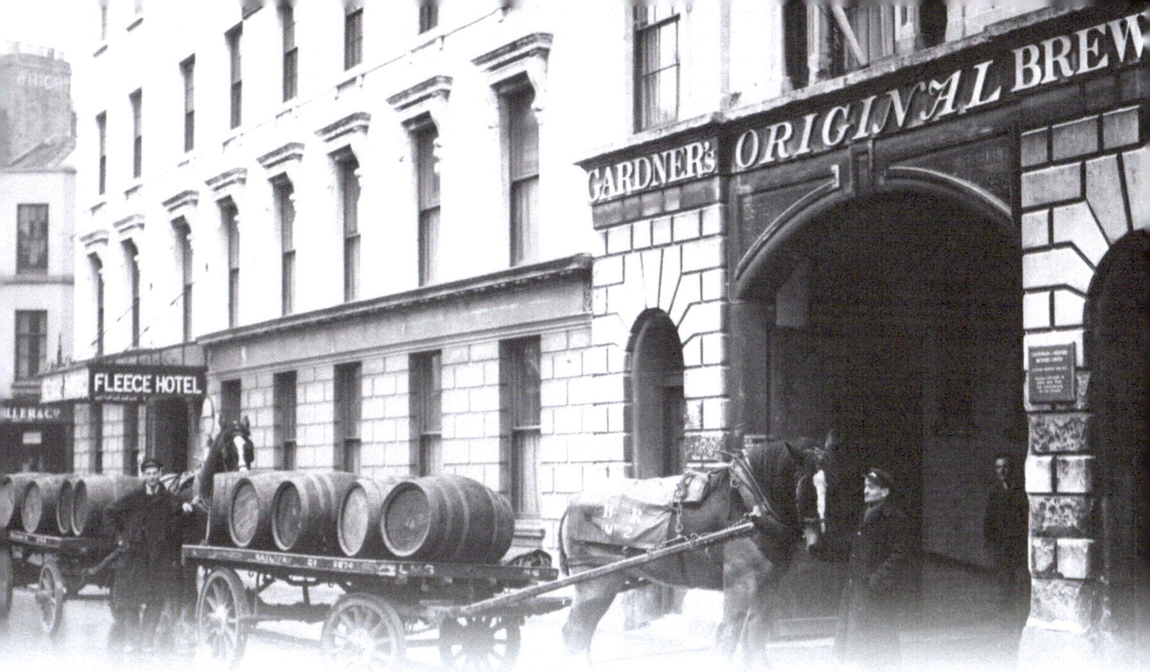

CHAPTER 1

Cheltenham High Street & New Street

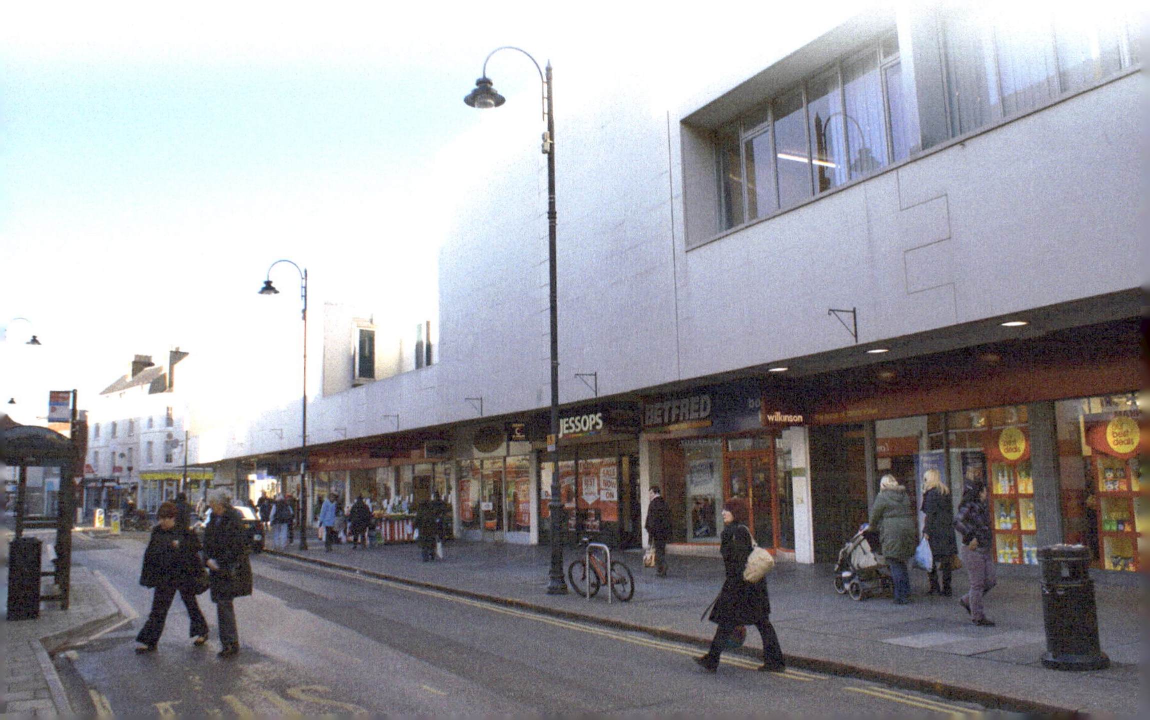

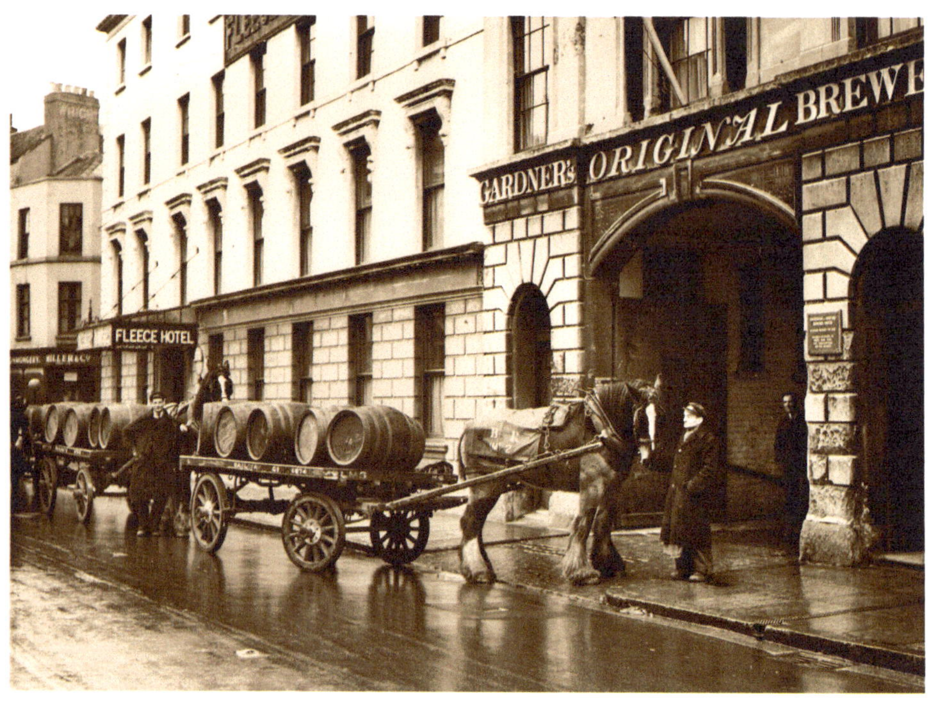

Fleece Hotel and Cheltenham Original Brewery, High Street

The Fleece Hotel, situated in front of the Cheltenham Brewery, and the neighbouring Cheltenham Grammar School, were razed to the ground in 1967 and replaced with an architect's vision of retail utopia, which was actually an ugly concrete shopping precinct. In January 2012 a £20 million scheme was announced to demolish the concrete carbuncle and regenerate the area with shops, a hotel, flats and a pedestrian link into the brewery retail centre. (Photograph courtesy Alan Brant)

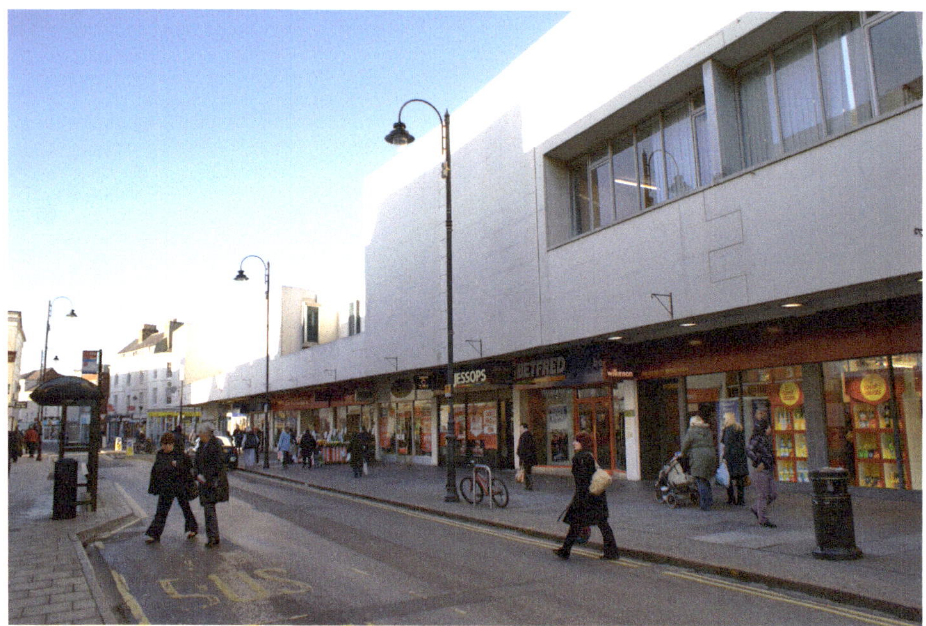

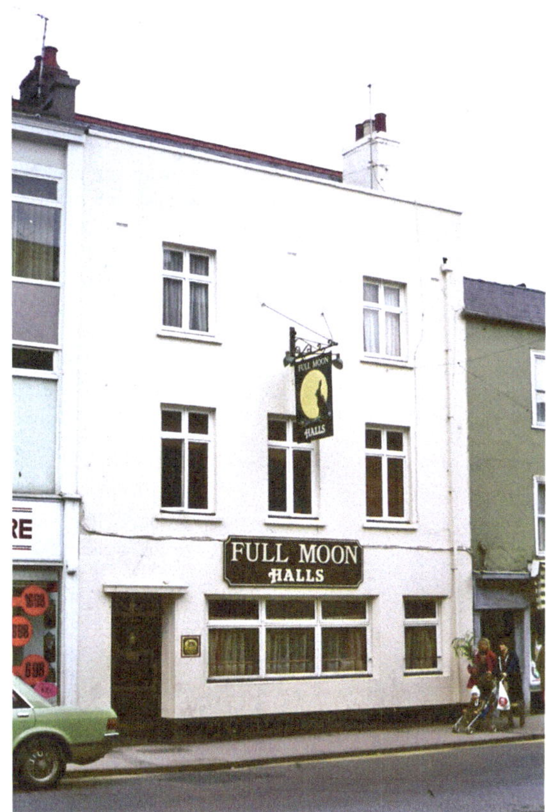

Full Moon, Lower High Street

Not all pubs in Cheltenham sold beer from the local Original Brewery. For a long time the Full Moon was owned by Ind Coope of Burton upon Trent (Allied Breweries). Latterly they brewed Double Diamond, but it didn't work wonders for the Full Moon as it closed in the early 1980s. In more recent times it has been a video shop and is now in use as a Polish restaurant.

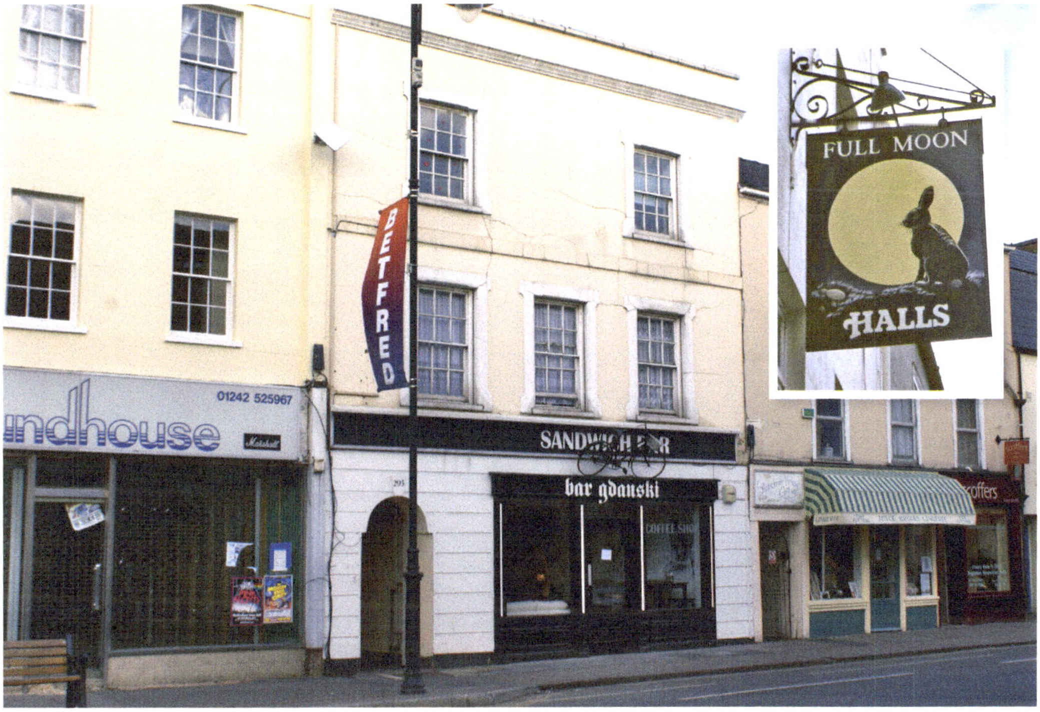

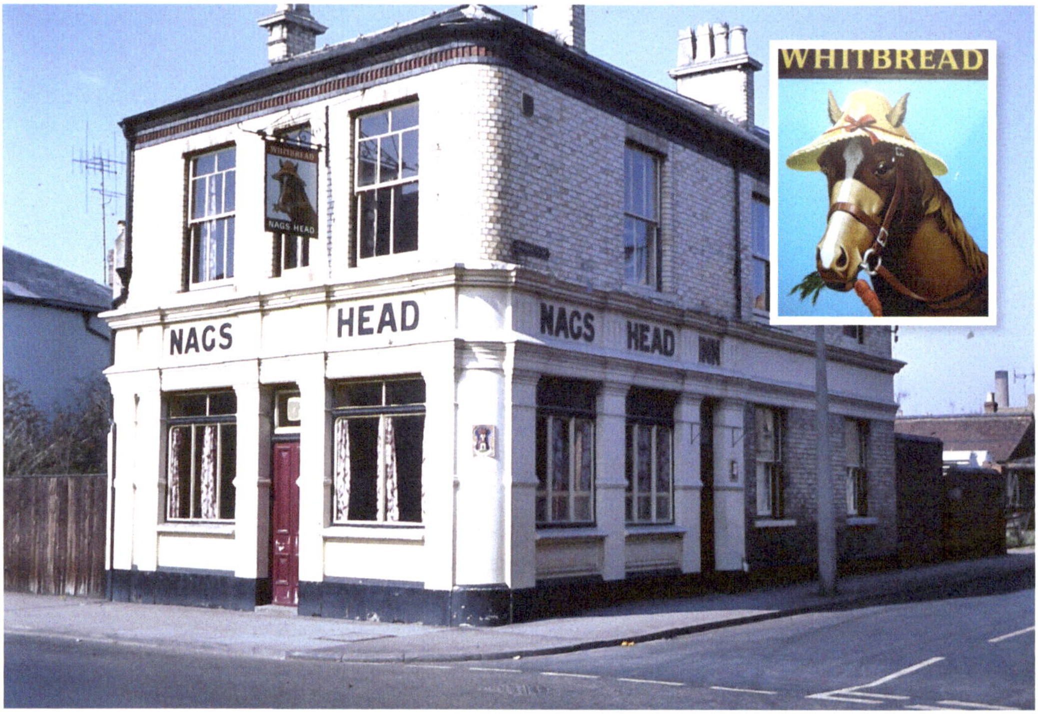

Nags Head, Lower High Street

The Nags Head, on the western corner of Granville Street, served its last pints in the mid-1970s. The building was then put to commercial use but has now been converted to residential use. Panelling now obscures the wording 'Nags Head' in raised lettering on the front of the building. It would cost nothing to remove these panels and expose the façade of the Nags Head, restoring it to its original splendour.

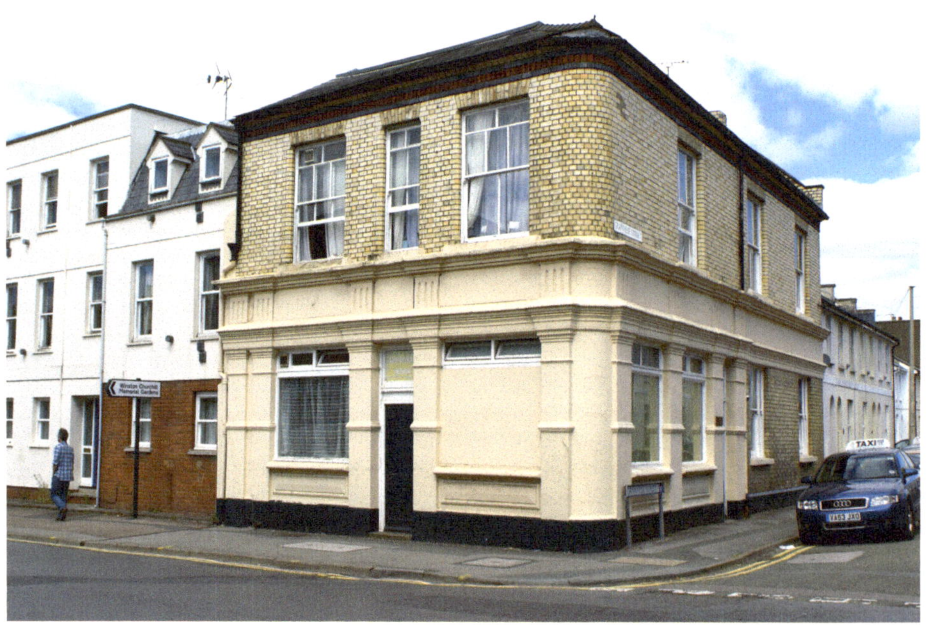

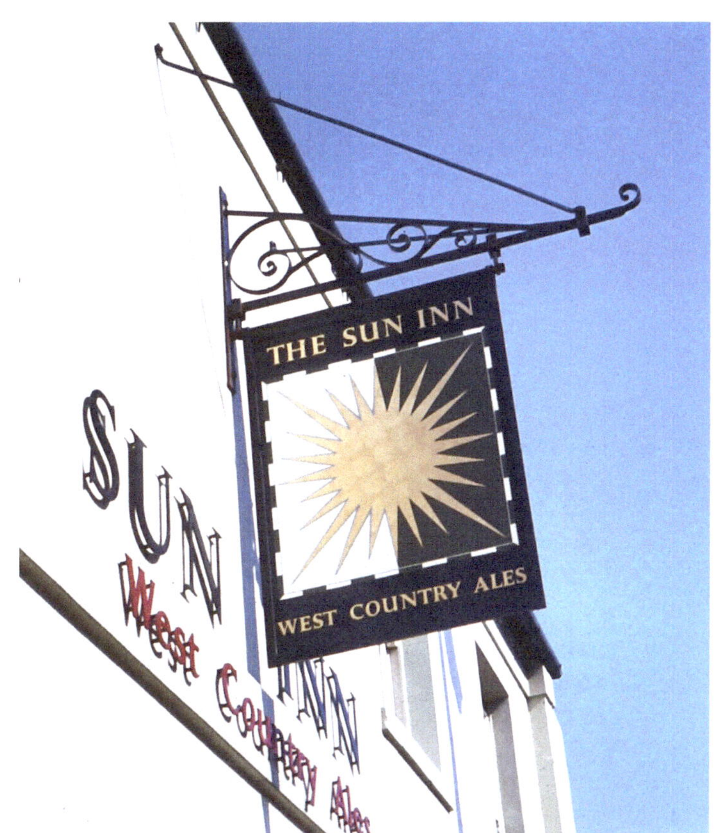

Sun Inn, Lower High Street

The Sun Inn was located midway between Granville Street and Swindon Street on the northern side of the High Street. The West Country Ales branding was still *in situ* on the Sun Inn in the late 1970s when it eventually ceased trading; somehow it had escaped the ubiquitous Whitbread corporate signage. Residential flats now occupy the site.

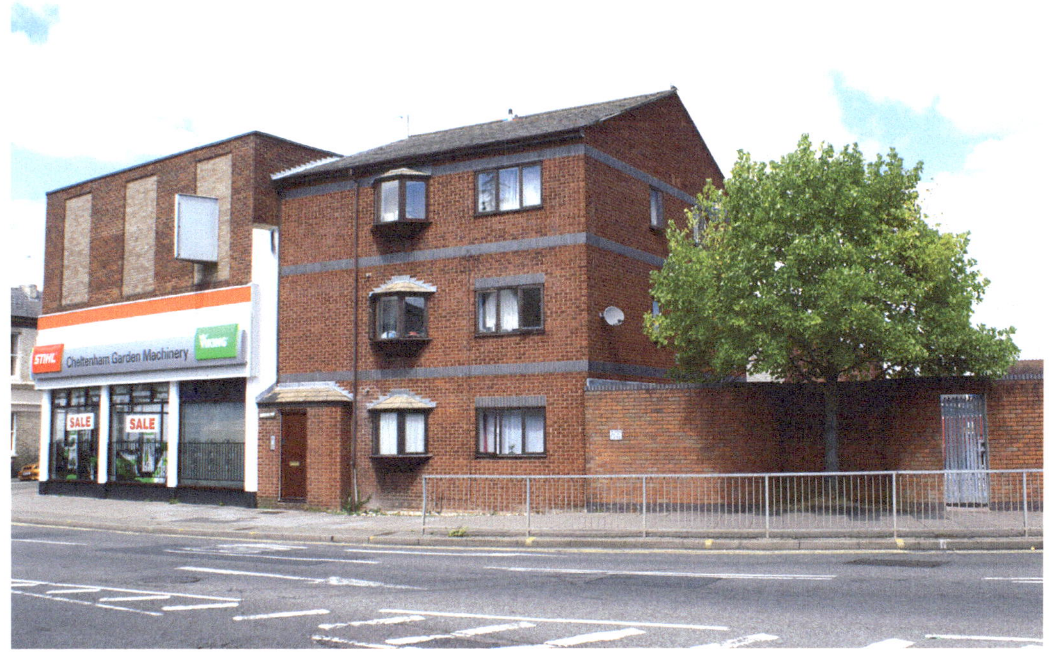

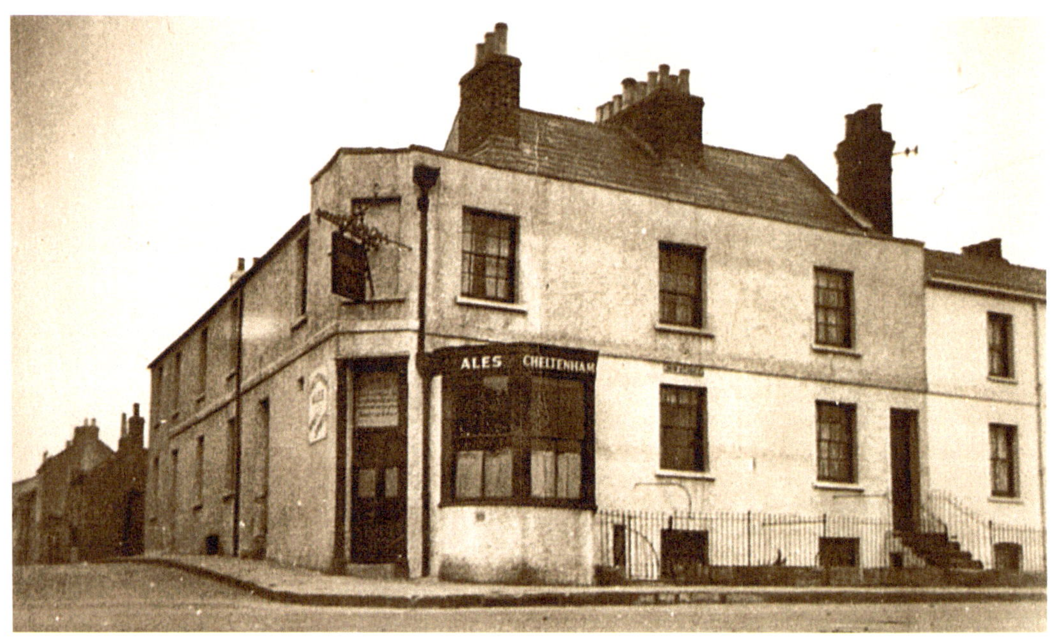

Compasses Inn, New Street

Standing on the corner of Park Street and New Street, the Compasses changed its identity to the Cavern in October 1995. Seven years later the name had changed to Nostalgia, but during the last years of it trading as a pub the name reverted back to the Cavern. An old painted advertisement for 'Cheltenham Ales, Wines & Spirits' can still be seen on the side of the old building.

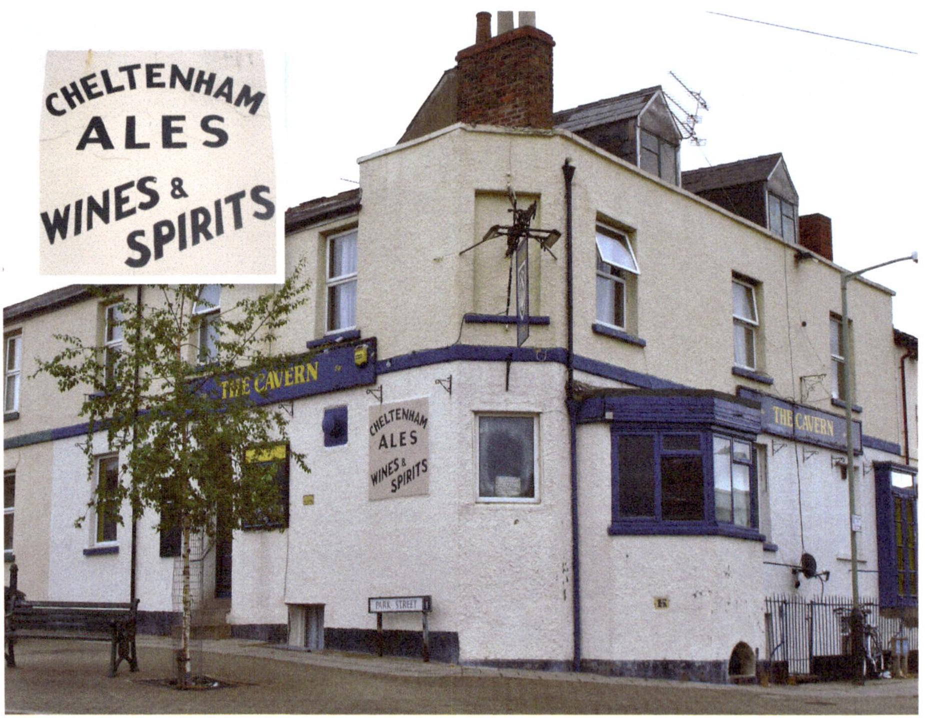

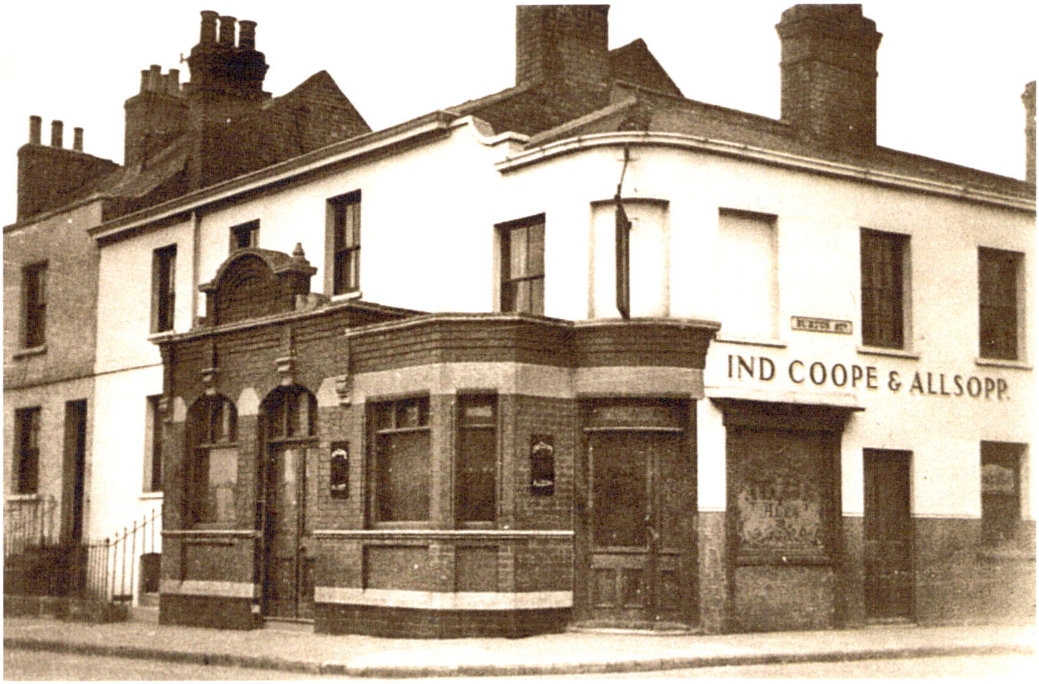

Welsh Harp, New Street

At one time there were three pubs side-by-side: the Dove & Rainbow, the Welsh Harp and the Compasses. The Welsh Harp closed down in August 1996 and languished for a period with boarded-up windows. After a brief incarnation as an Irish-themed pub, the Flute & Jig, the pub reopened as the Bath House. It had closed by January 2008, and is now in residential use.

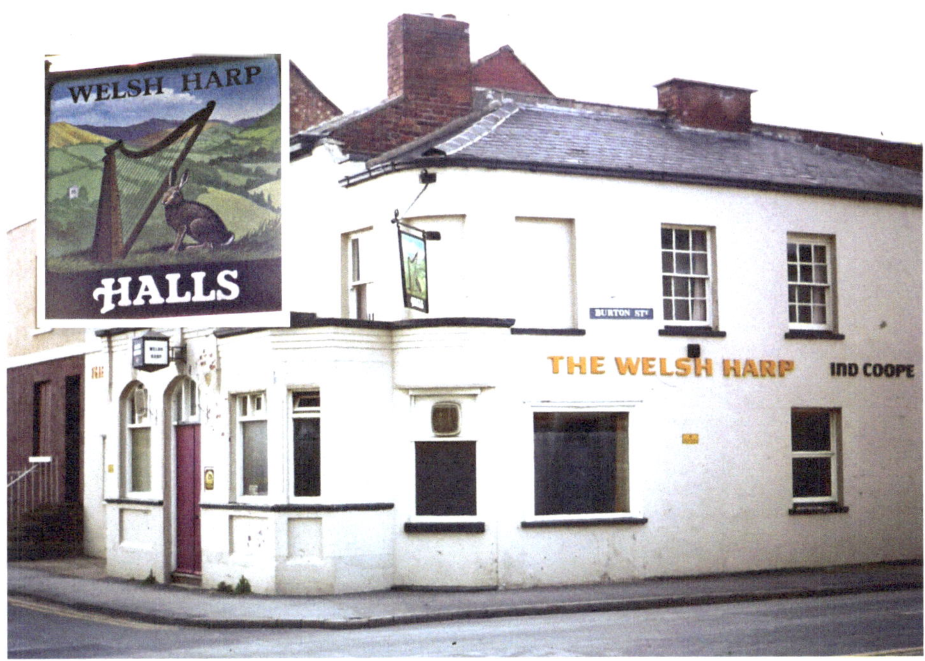

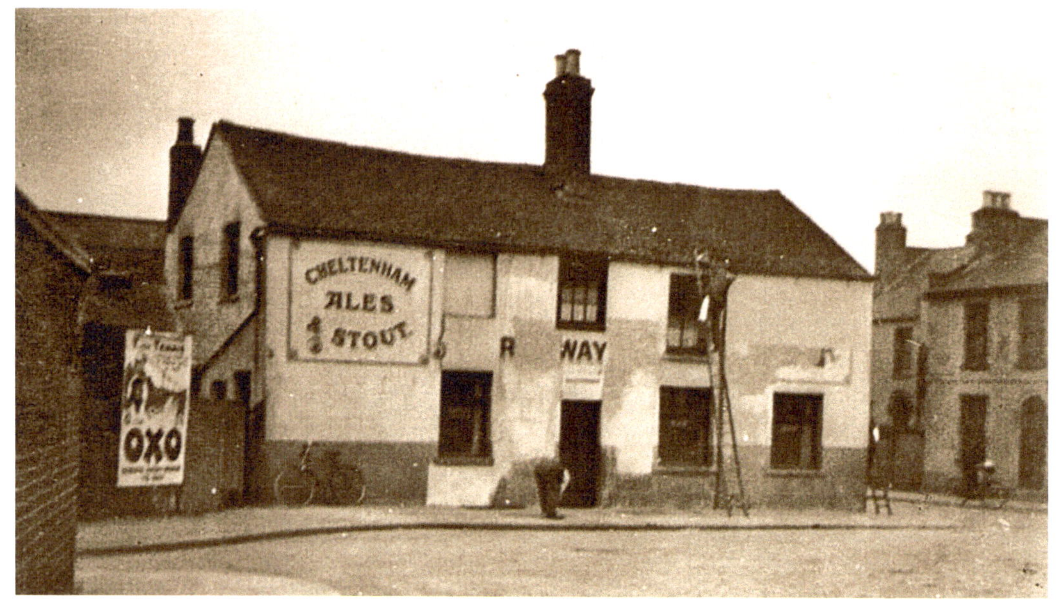

Railway Inn, New Street

The Railway Inn is situated on the junction with New Street and Knapp Road. It took its name from the Great Western Railway spur which first opened from Cheltenham Lansdown to St James on 23 October 1847. The sites of the station and railway yards have since been redeveloped, leaving the Railway Inn as a sole reminder of this once-busy railway terminus. The Railway Inn was acquired by Banks' Brewery of Wolverhampton in 1991.

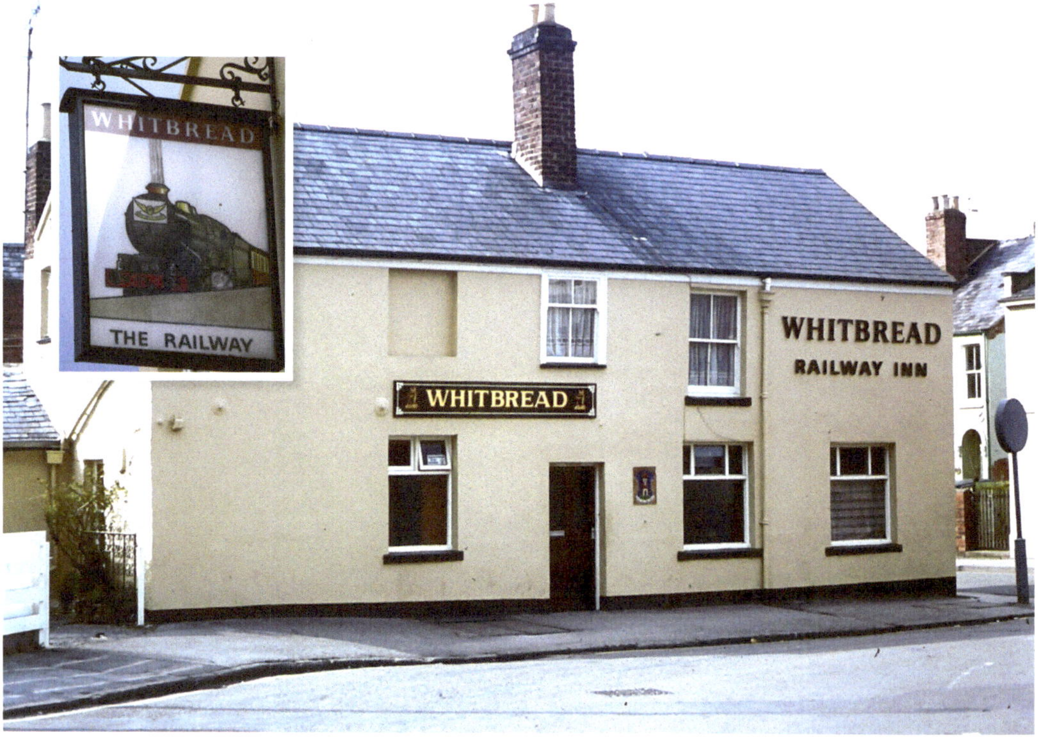

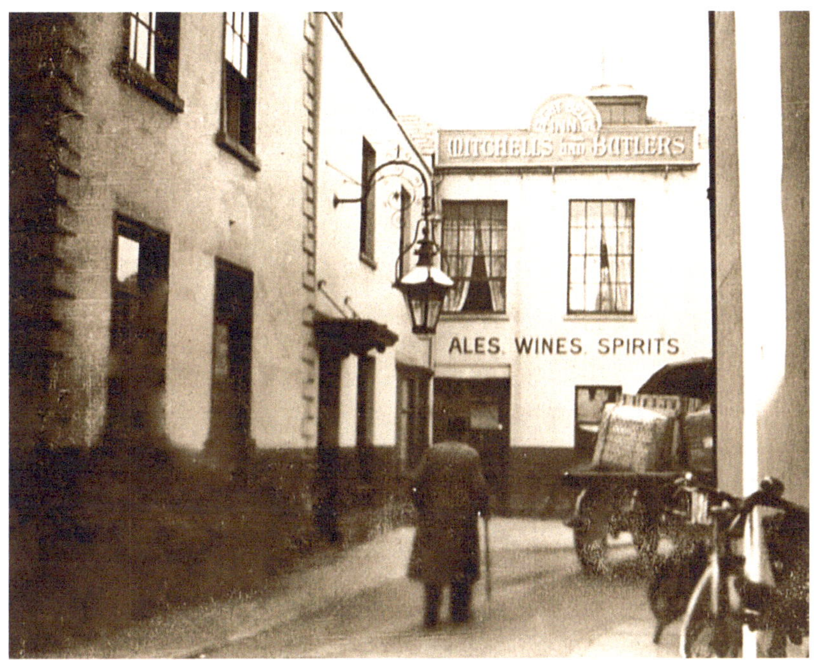

Eight Bells, Church Street

The premises have been a young persons' live music venue for at least four decades. Now known as the 2 Pigs it has had previous incarnations as Copperfields and, before that, Kings. A newspaper article from June 1975 proclaimed 'Topless dancers of Church Street ... lunchtime sessions of boobs and beer have arrived in Cheltenham – at a new pub in the shadow of the parish church – where topless Go-Go dancers are attracting customers at lunchtime and in the evening'.

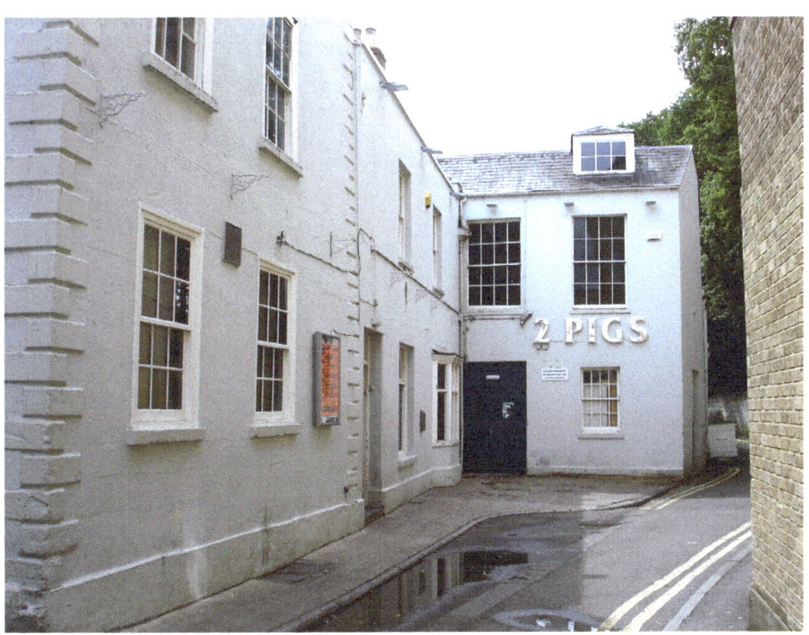

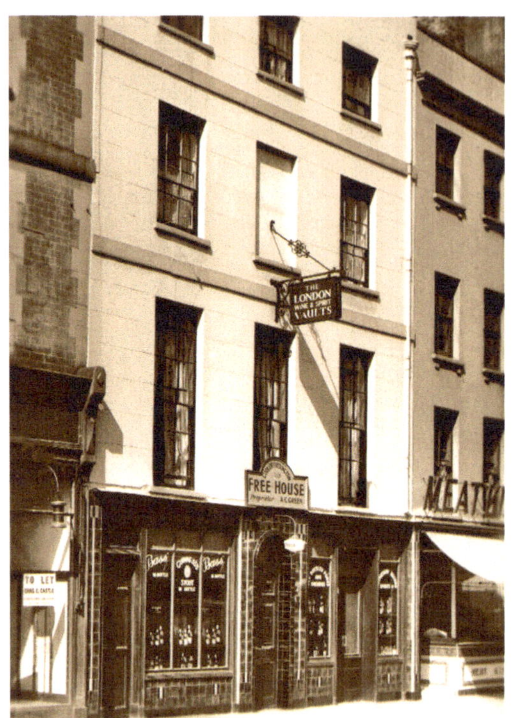

London Wine and Spirit Vaults, High Street

The London Wine and Spirit Vaults was located where McDonald's restaurant now stands. It was a wine and spirit merchant's, also known as Cook & Witherington. A contemporary description of 1870 details 'John Cook. Wholesale and retail wine and spirit merchants. Bass's and Allsopps Pale Ales. Guinness Extra Stout and Alloa Scotch Ales. Established upwards of 50 years'. Confusingly there was also a London Wine and Spirit Stores and a London Ale and Porter Stores in the High Street.

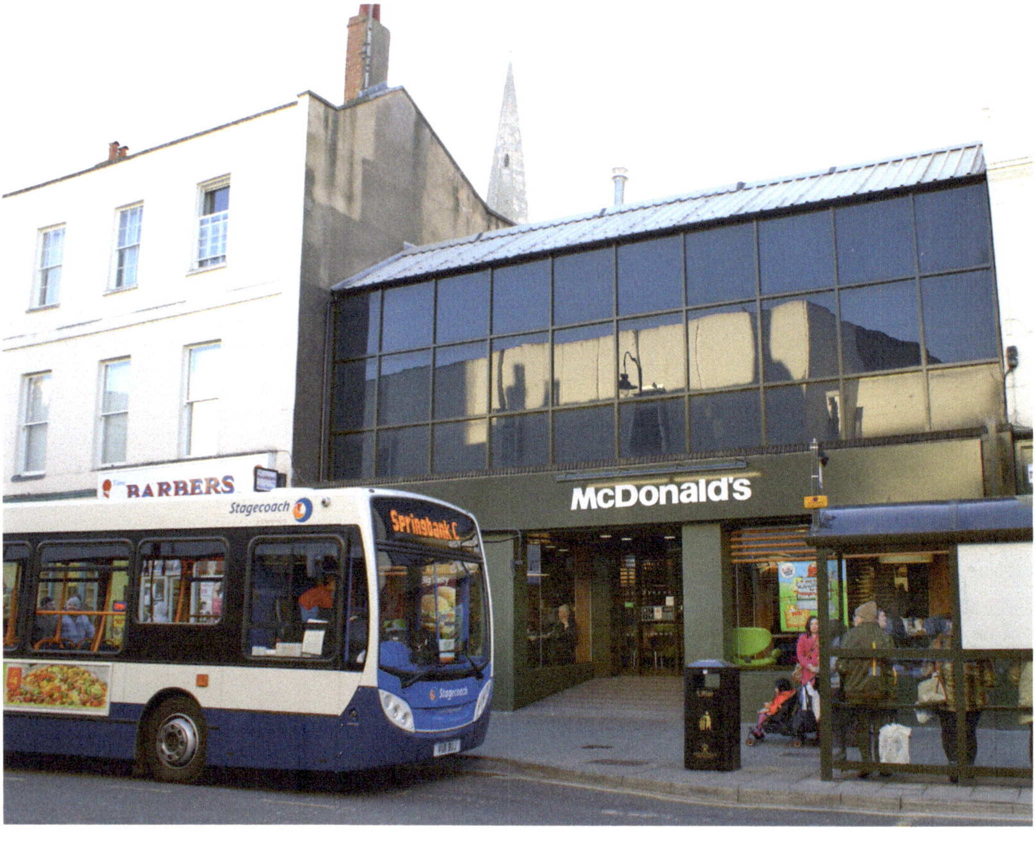

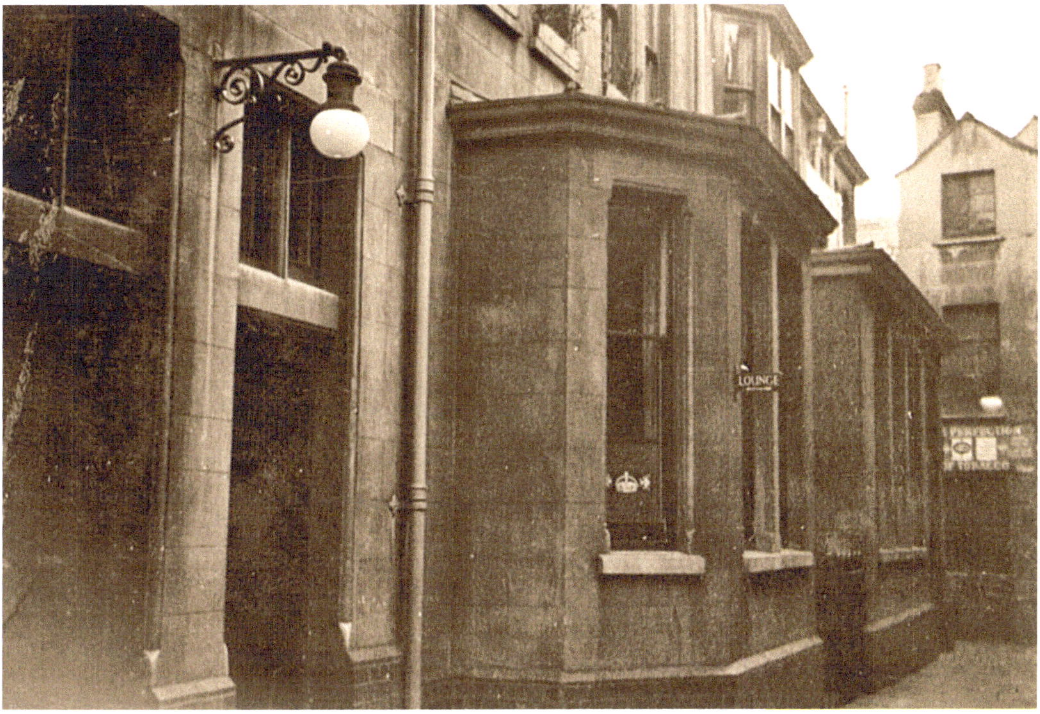

Crown, High Street

Situated in an alley leading from the High Street to Albion Street, the Crown is now a nightclub called Lace. In the early 1970s the Crown had two bars: the Captain's Cabin and a 'psuedo thatched' Stable Bar fronting Albion Street (the old Crown Tap). Renamed the Dirty Duck, the old pub later became Time nightclub, and more recently Moda. In the 1980s the old tap briefly traded as the George & Pilgrim.

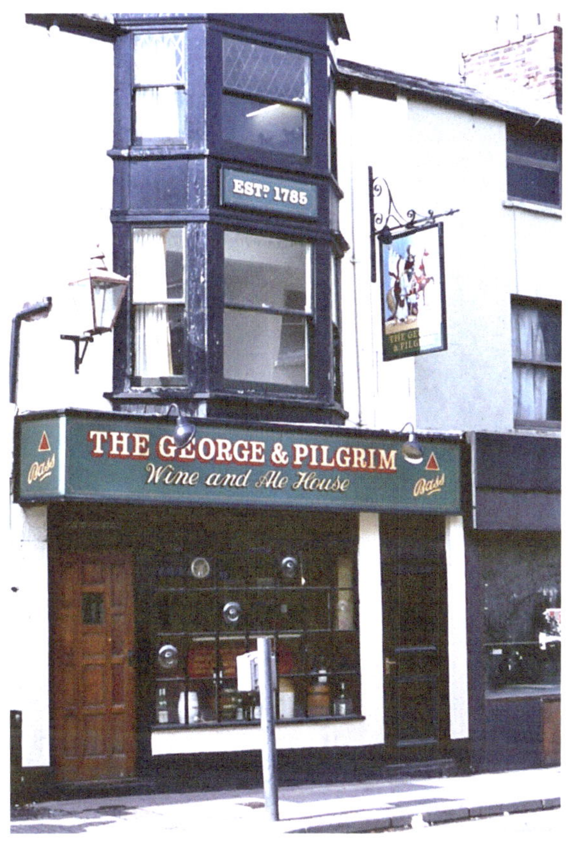

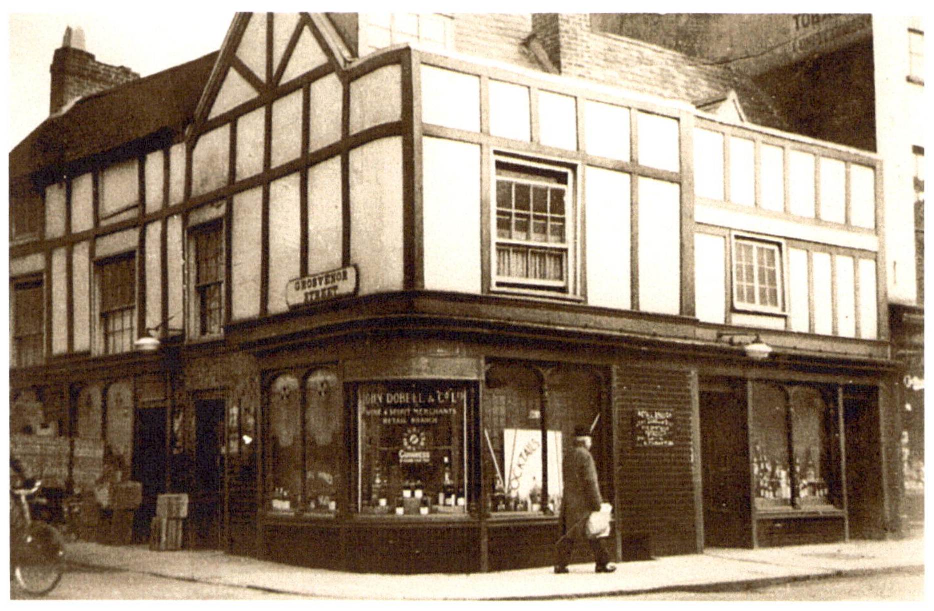

Restoration Inn, High Street

The fifteenth-century Restoration Inn, located on the eastern side of the junction of Grosvenor Street, is probably Cheltenham's oldest pub. In the second half of the nineteenth century the wine and spirit business of John Dobell & Co. acquired the Restoration Inn. After a spell as an Ind Coope pub the Restoration passed into the ownership of Barracuda Inns who converted it to a student bar called Varsity in 2007, but it has since reverted back to a more traditional real ale pub.

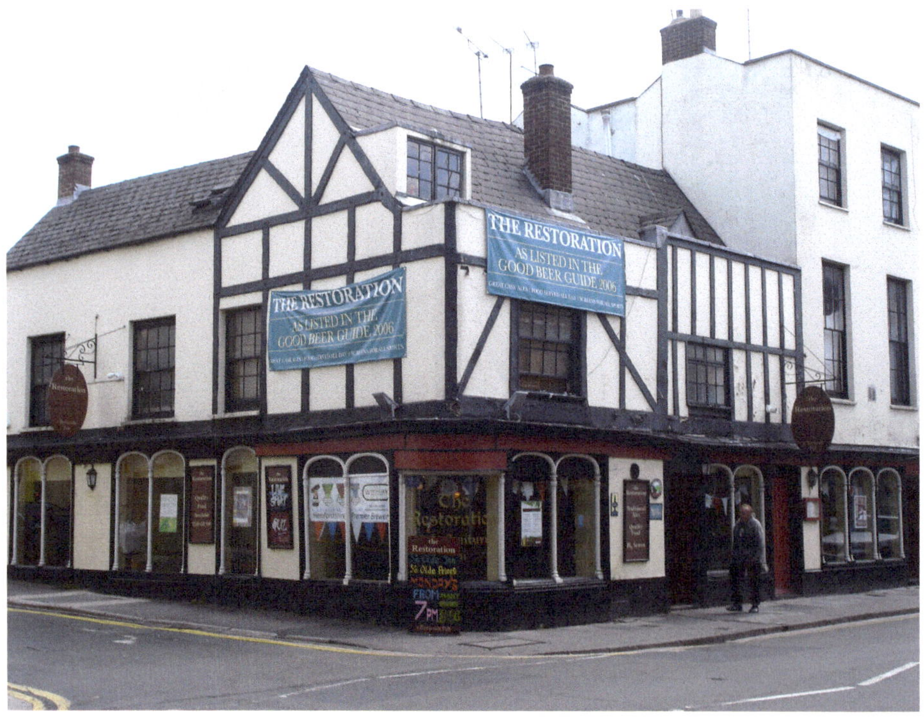

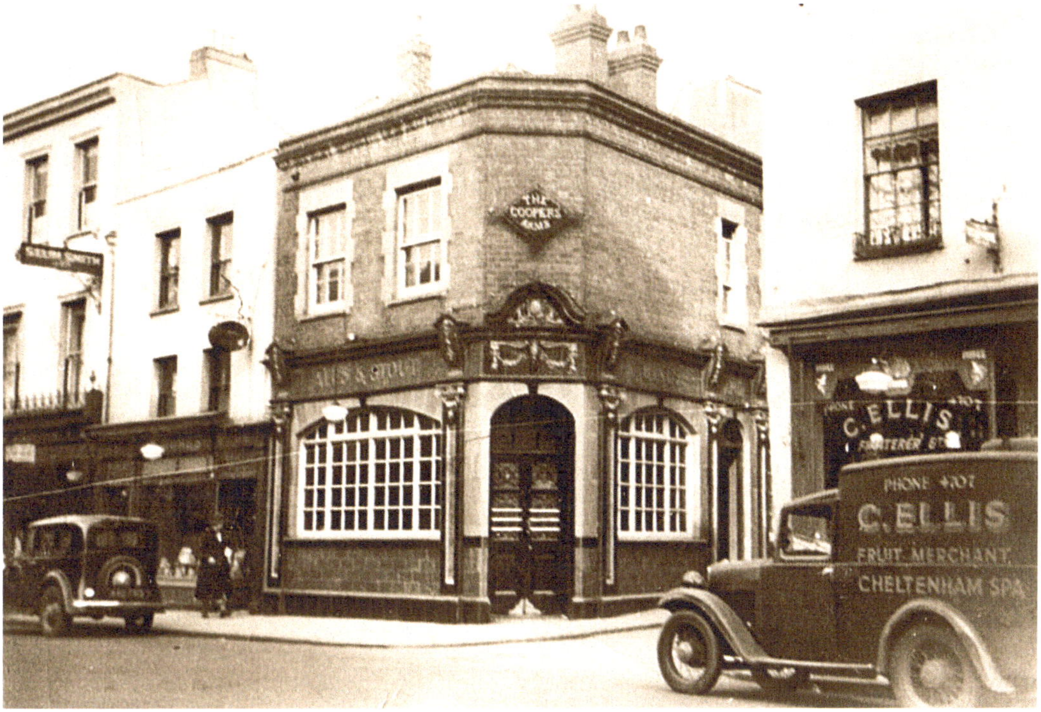

Coopers Arms, High Street

The Coopers Arms was completely destroyed by a fire on 26 March 1909 and rebuilt on the same site by the Cheltenham Original Brewery. The replacement building was, and still is, an architectural gem – resplendent with green glazed tiles with raised lettering. In the late 1980s the pub was simply known as Coopers. Following another refurbishment the premises became known as Cactus Jacks. It is now trading as the Vine.

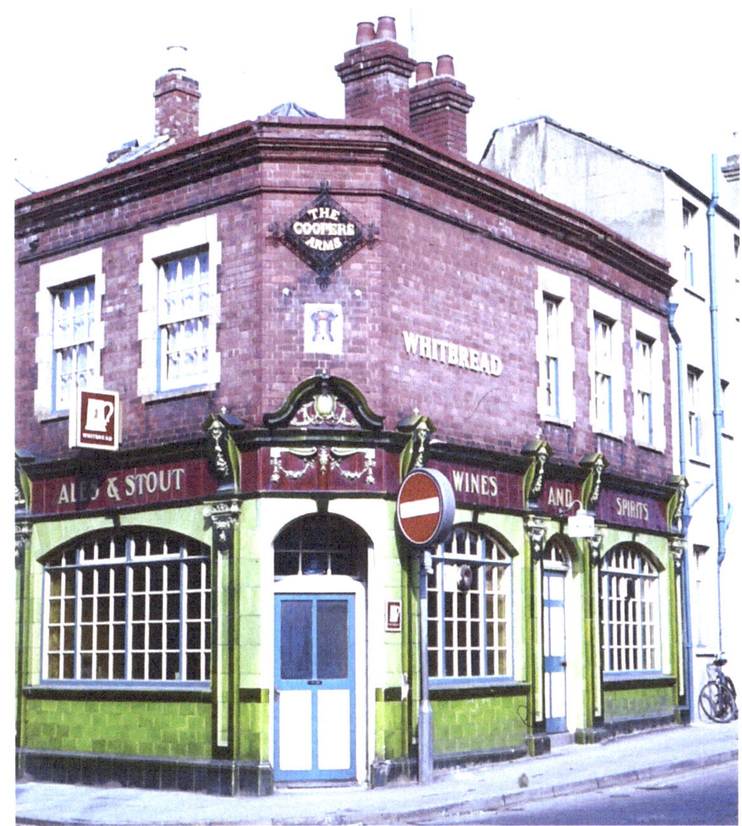

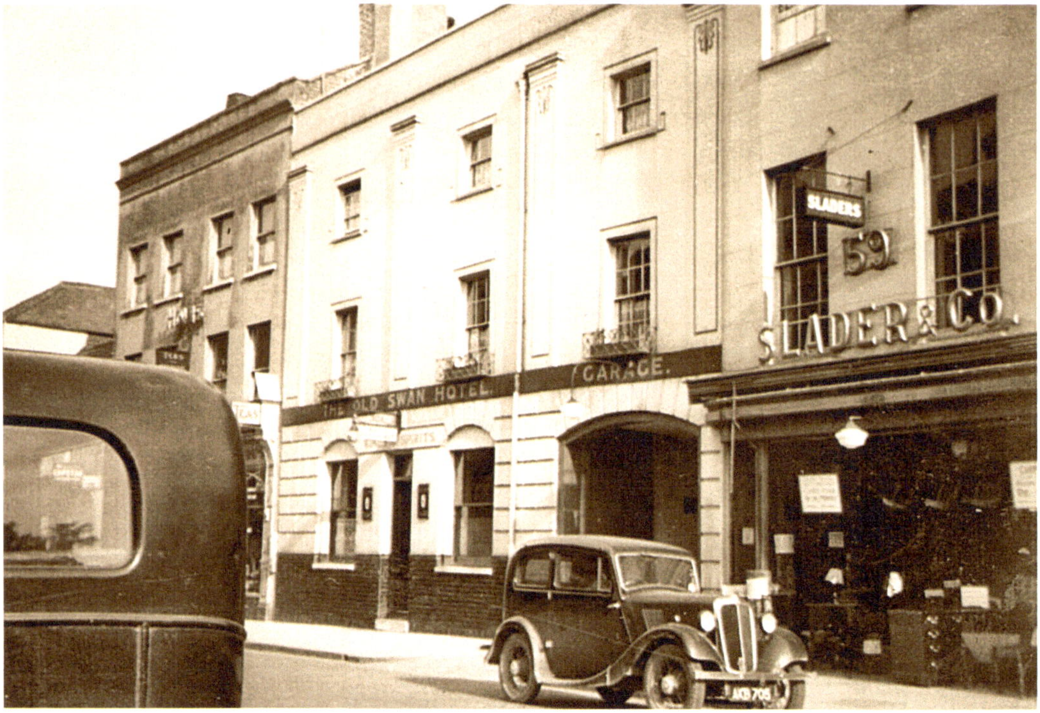

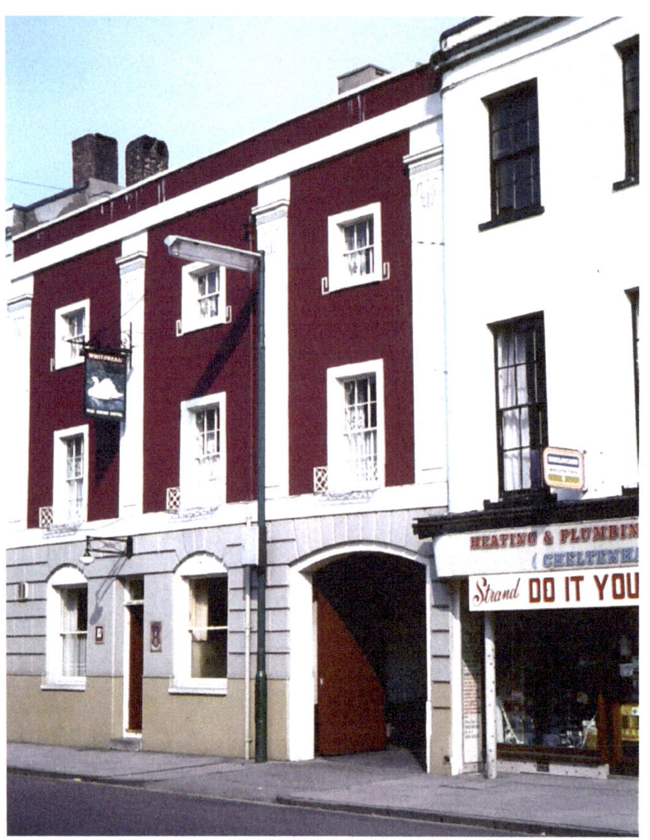

Old Swan, High Street

Whitbread pub planners, in their wisdom, ripped out the authentic multi-roomed Victorian interior of the Old Swan in the early 1980s only to replace the décor with an ersatz 'olde worlde' theme! At the same time a microbrewery was installed in the premises. Unfortunately, both the refurbished pub and quality of the beer were disappointing and brewing soon ceased. In 1995 the pub became an Irish-themed pub called O'Hagan's, reverting back to the Swan in May 2003.

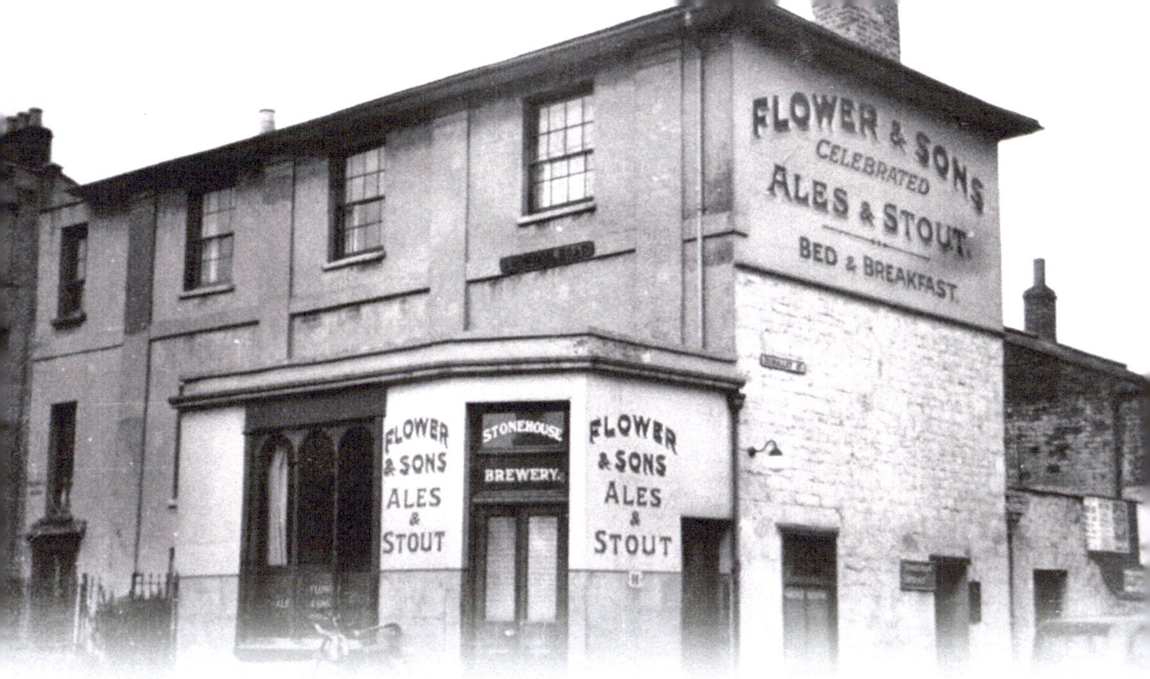

CHAPTER 2

St Paul's & Tewkesbury Road

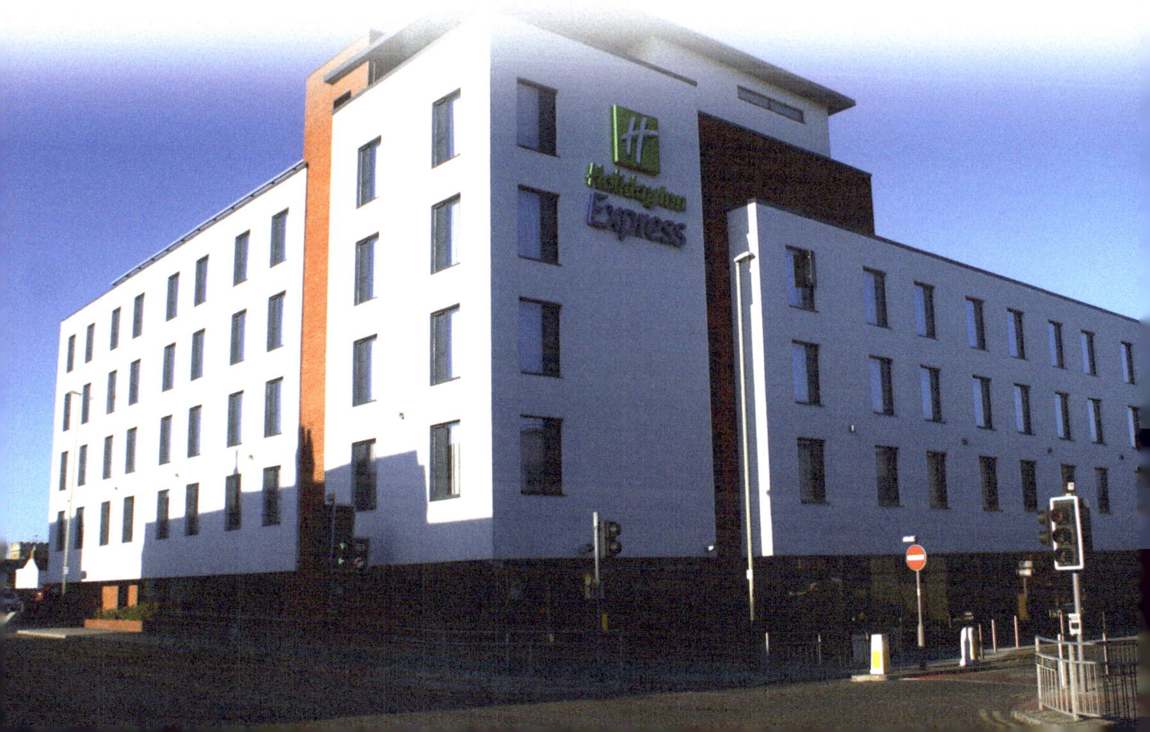

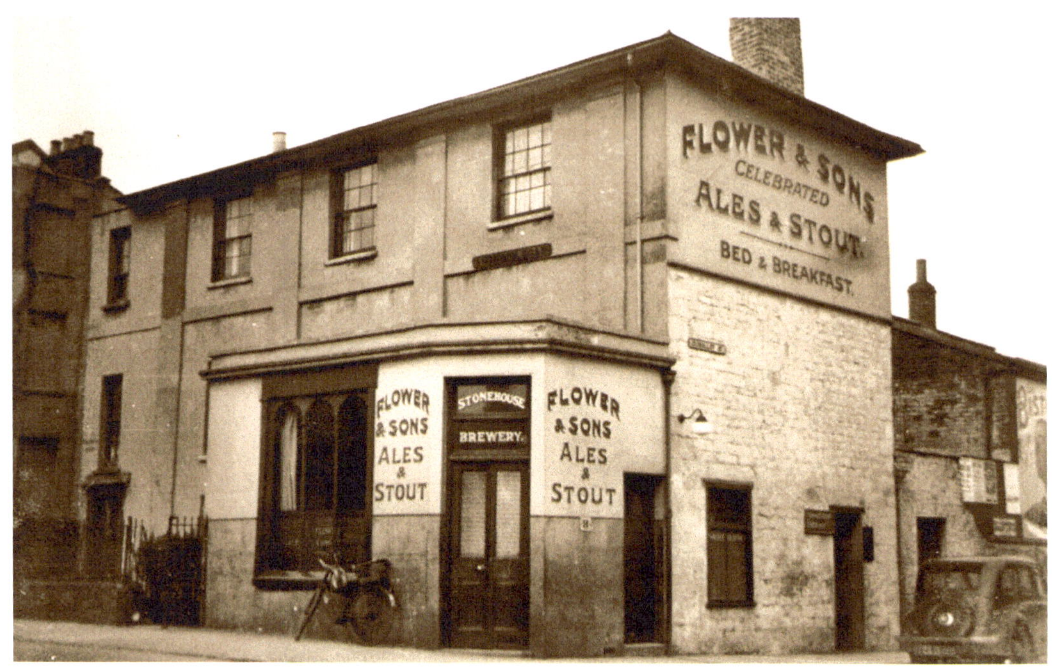

Stonehouse Inn, Swindon Road

The Stonehouse Inn, directly opposite the Cheltenham brewery, once brewed its own beer before being acquired by Flowers & Sons of Stratford-upon-Avon, thus avoiding selling beer from 'across the road' until the 1960s when it passed into the ownership of West Country Breweries. After closure in the early 1980s the building was demolished and the site stood empty until being developed as a Holiday Inn Express – a six-storey, 132-bedroom, £7.5 million development which opened in 2008.

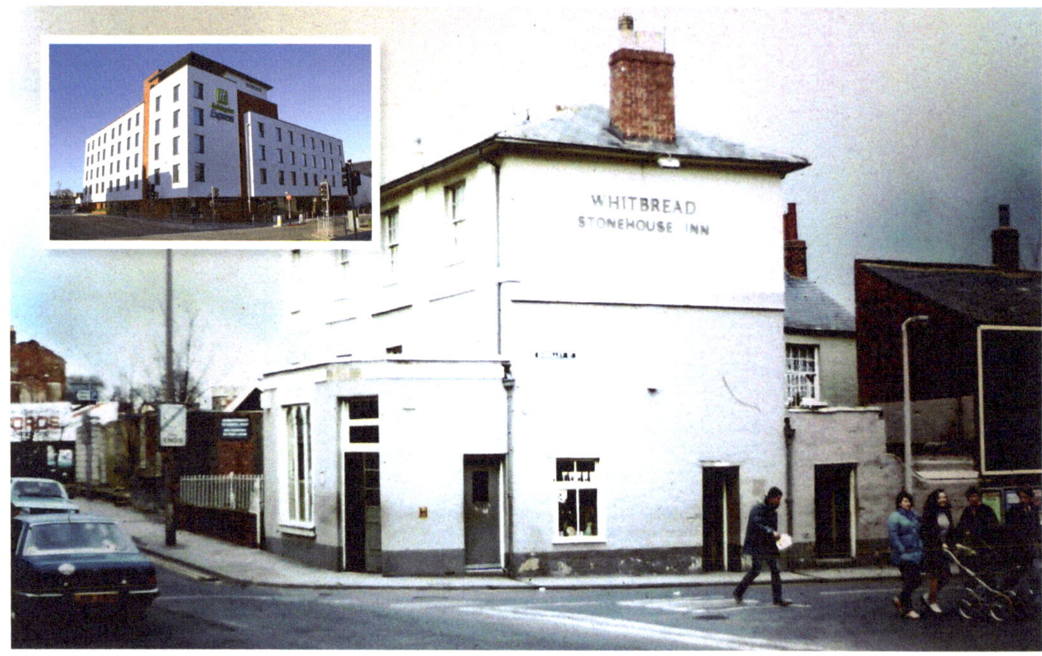

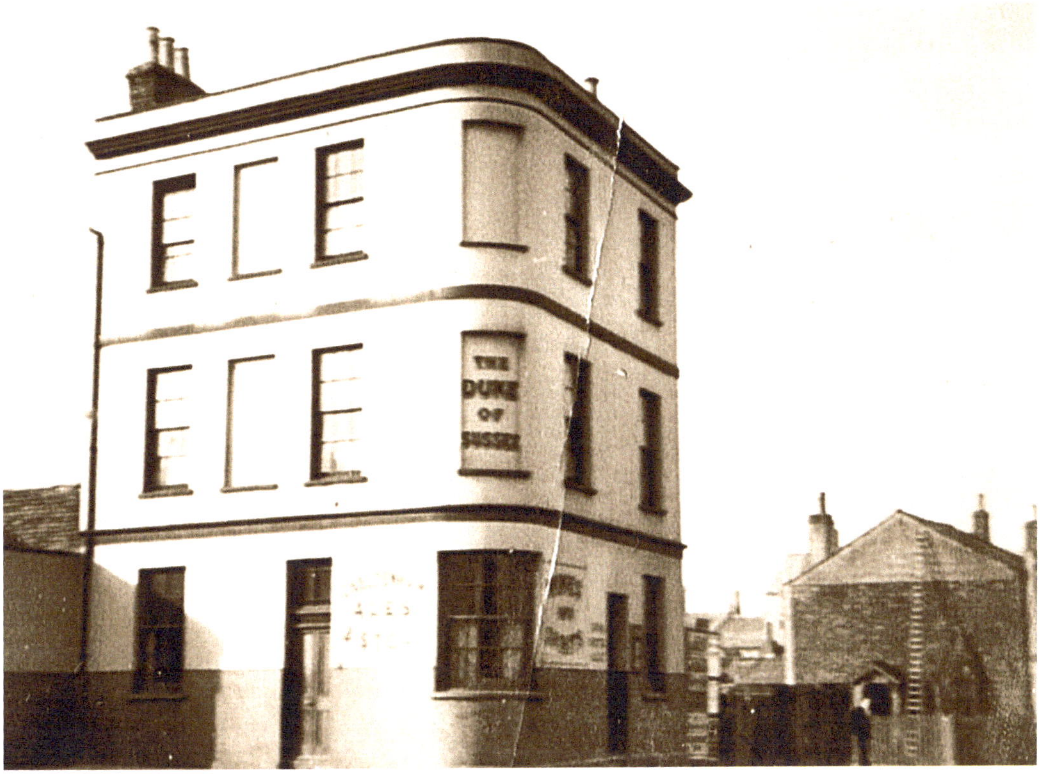

Duke of Sussex, Swindon Road

The Duke of Sussex was bought by Mr Cassidy in the 1980s and for a decade traded as Cassidy's Bar. Arkell's of Swindon acquired the pub in 1999. During June 2000 it was refurbished as the Pickled Duke. In May 2001 the pub was reborn as Bar Cuba, aimed at students from the nearby university. The venture failed and by July 2002 it was on the market. The premises were converted to residential flats (Trinity Gate) in the summer of 2004.

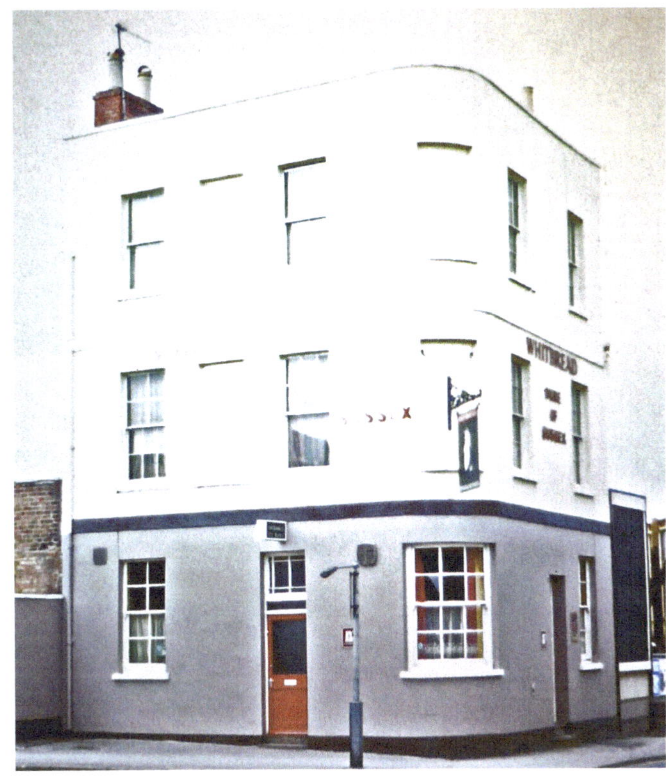

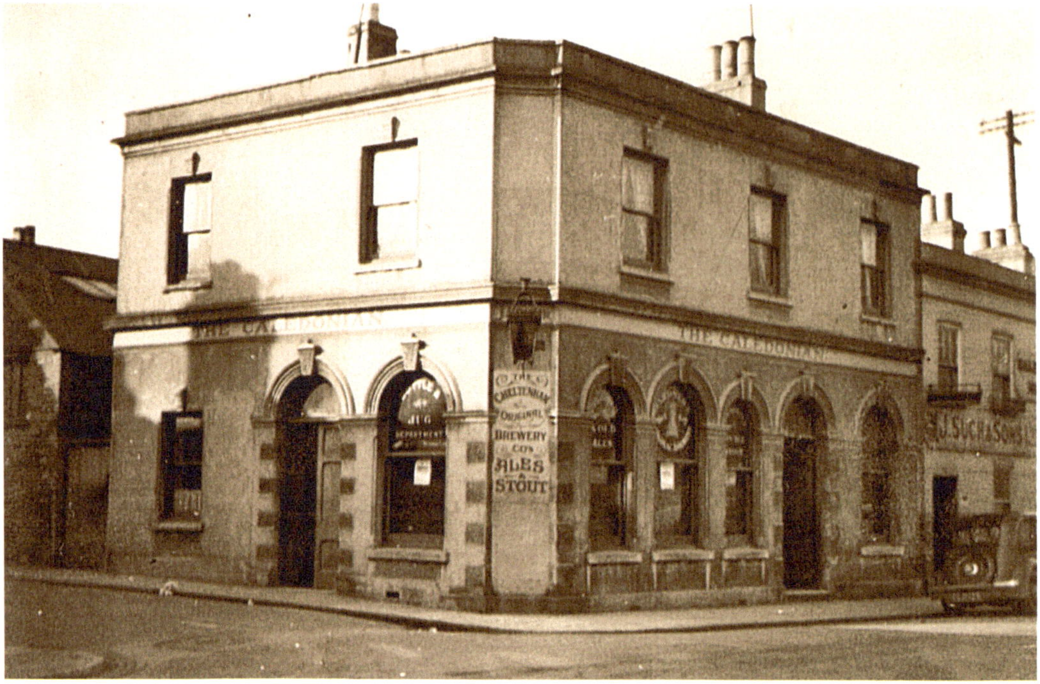

Caledonian Inn, Swindon Road

The Caledonian Inn, on the corner of Swindon Road and King Street, was once a home-brewed ale pub. There are references to a brewery at the premises in 1870 and 1883. The Caledonian Inn last traded in about 1982, by that time a tired Whitbread pub. The derelict building was given a lick of paint in 2007 and a tree was removed from the roof! Despite all odds, it still survives.

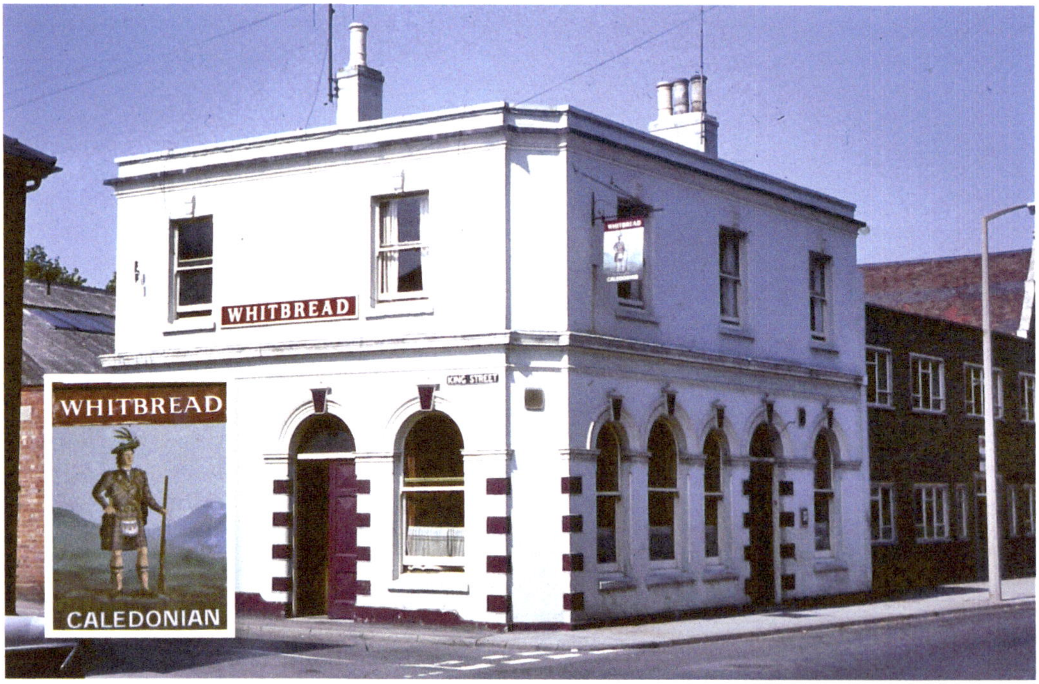

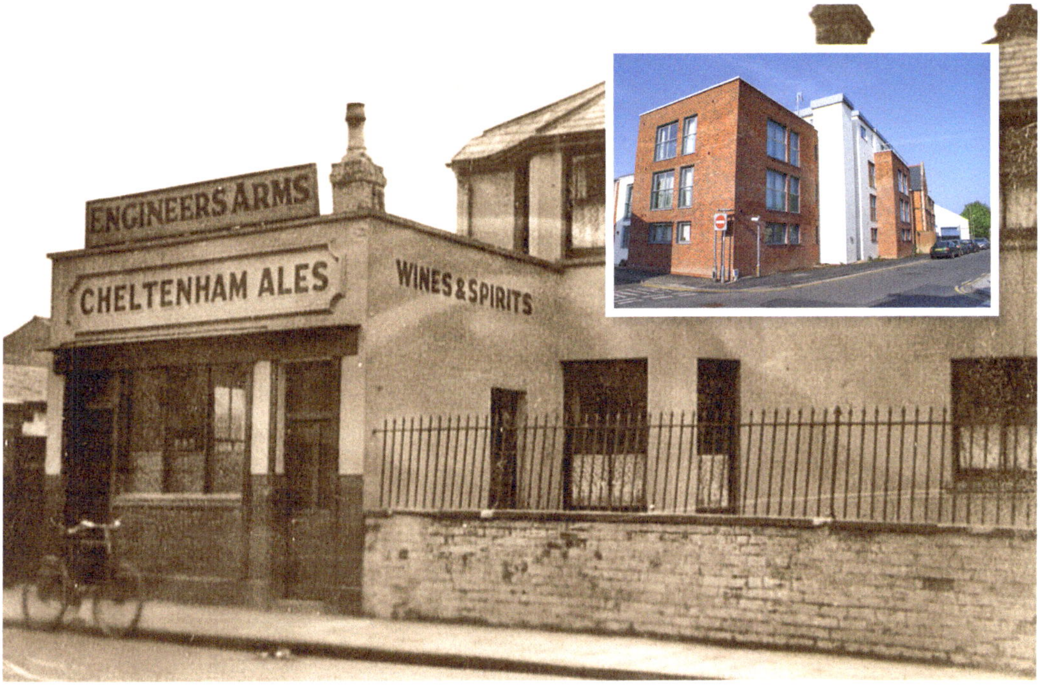

Engineers Arms, St Paul's Road

The Engineers Arms stood almost opposite the Duke of Brunswick, just two of many bygone St Paul's pubs. Entrance was made through a small extension fronting St Paul's Road through which access was gained to larger rooms behind. The Engineers Arms traded briefly as the New Engineers and then as the New Ale House. It closed down in 2002 and was demolished in 2004. The construction of the block of flats which occupy the site was very protracted.

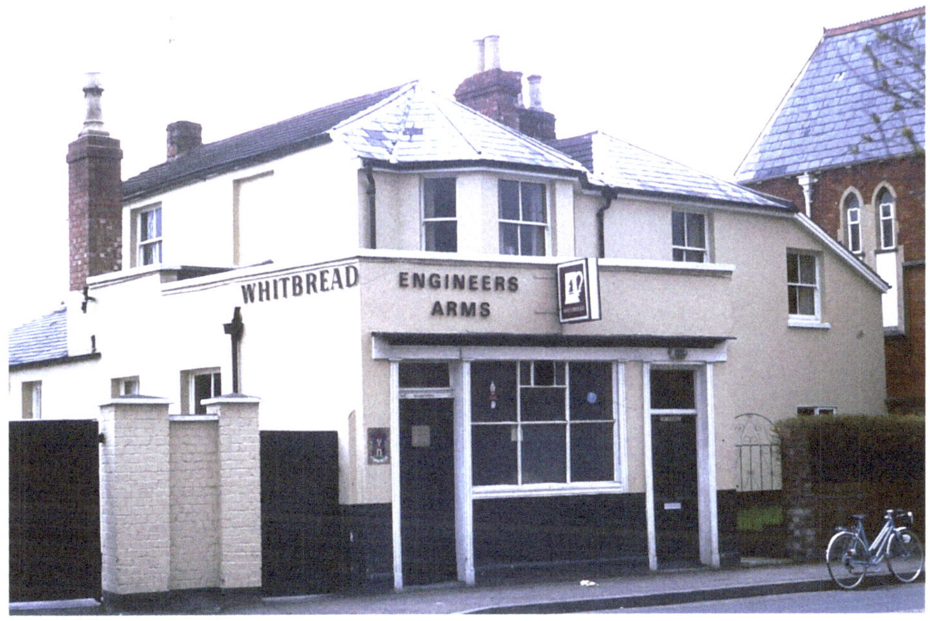

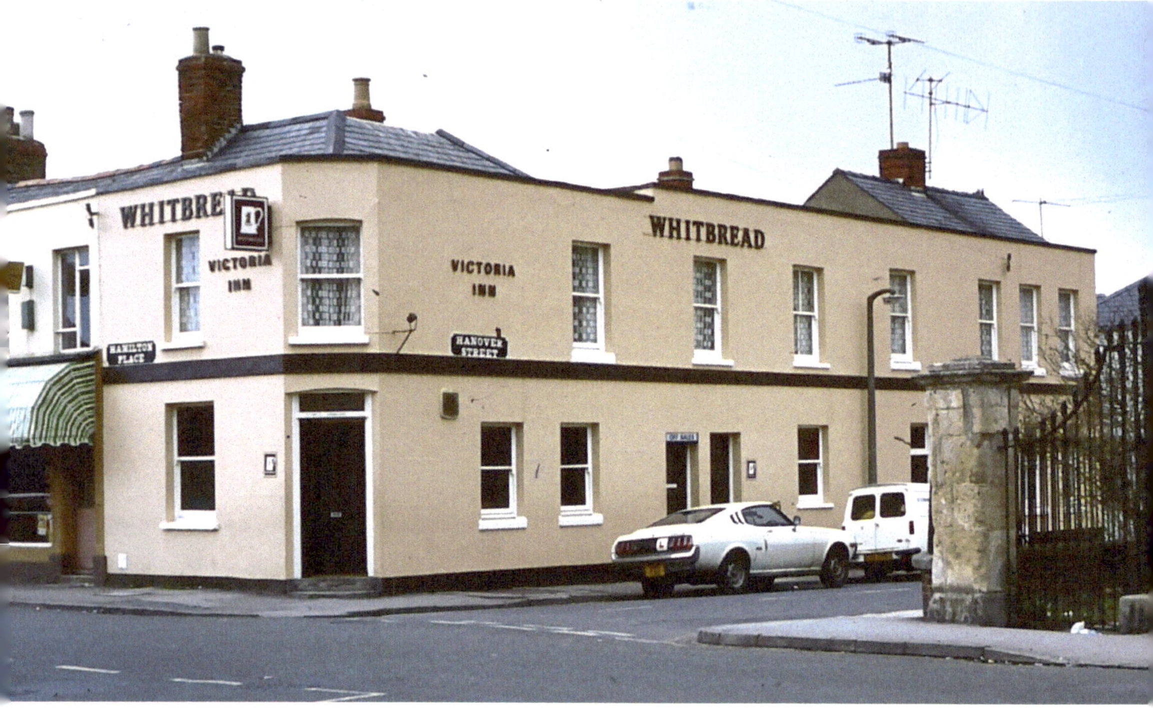

Victoria Inn, St Paul's Road

Located on the corner of St Paul's Road and Hanover Street. George Meek was brewing beer at the Victoria Brewery in 1883. It was acquired from Whitbread in 1991 by Banks' Brewery of Wolverhampton only to be sold again a decade later. A pictorial pub sign of Queen Victoria flashing her bloomers caused some controversy. In 2005 it was renamed the Spa Tavern, and now trades as the St Paul's Tavern.

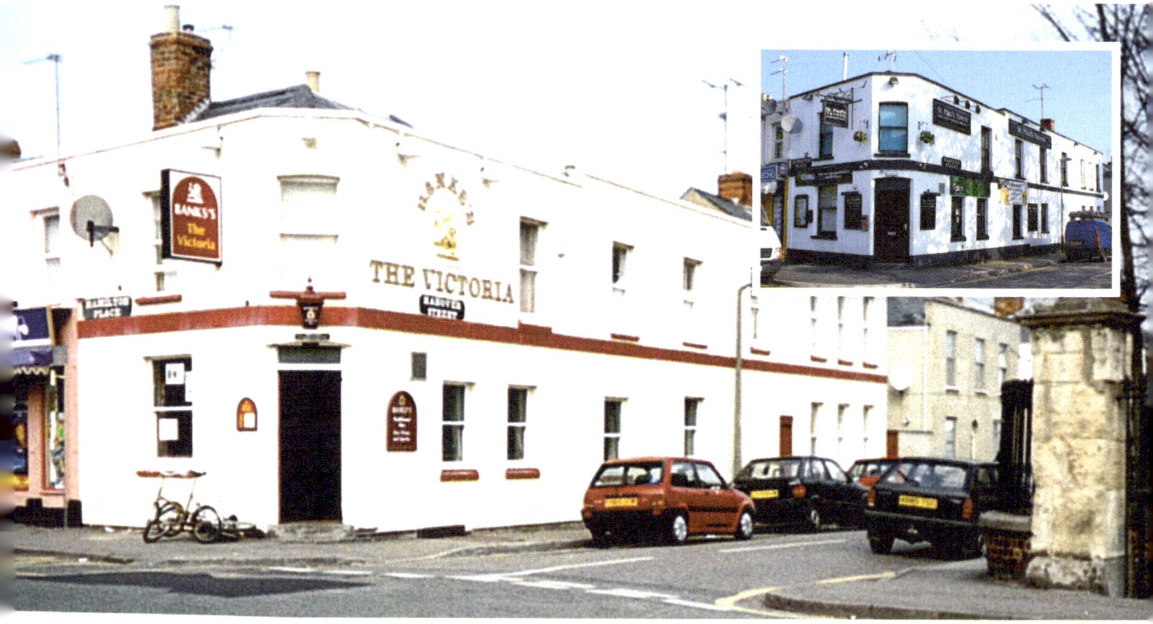

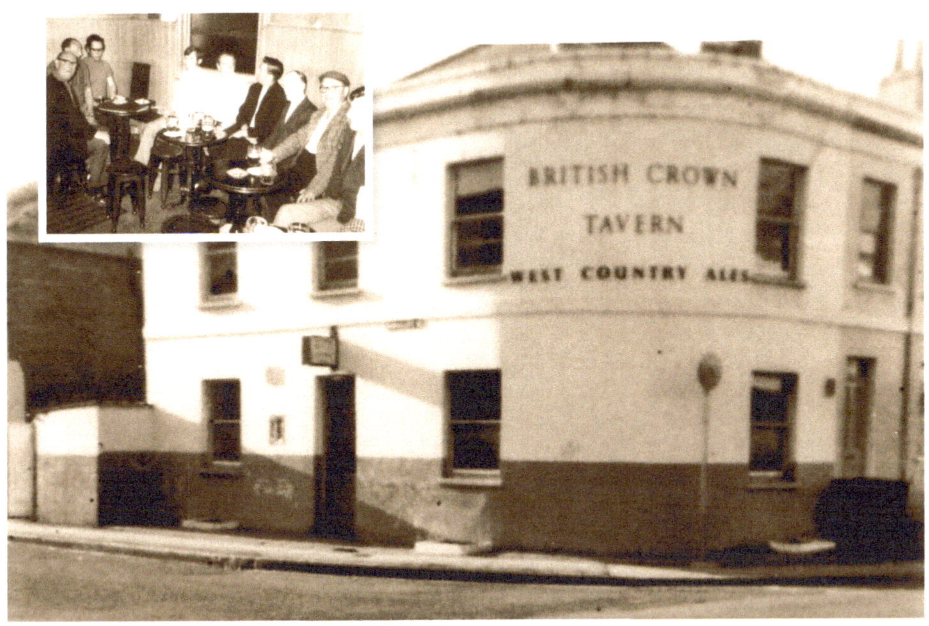

British Crown, Dunalley Street

The British Crown was on the corner of St Paul's Road and Dunalley Street. The building is now residential. In 2003 Mrs Joan Bromage, then aged eighty-one, wrote to the *Gloucestershire Echo* recalling her time at the pub from around 1943 to 1972 when her parents, Fred and Emily Eakets, ran the pub: 'We had coal fires in the bar and we used to have jolly sing songs to the piano. My late husband and I used to make buttered cheese rolls and sell them for sixpence.'

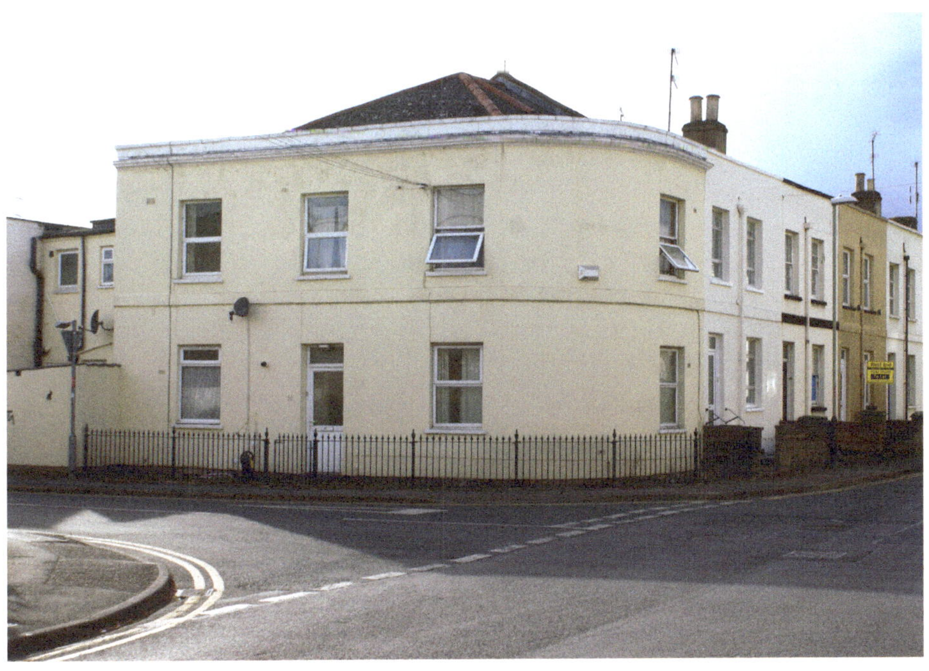

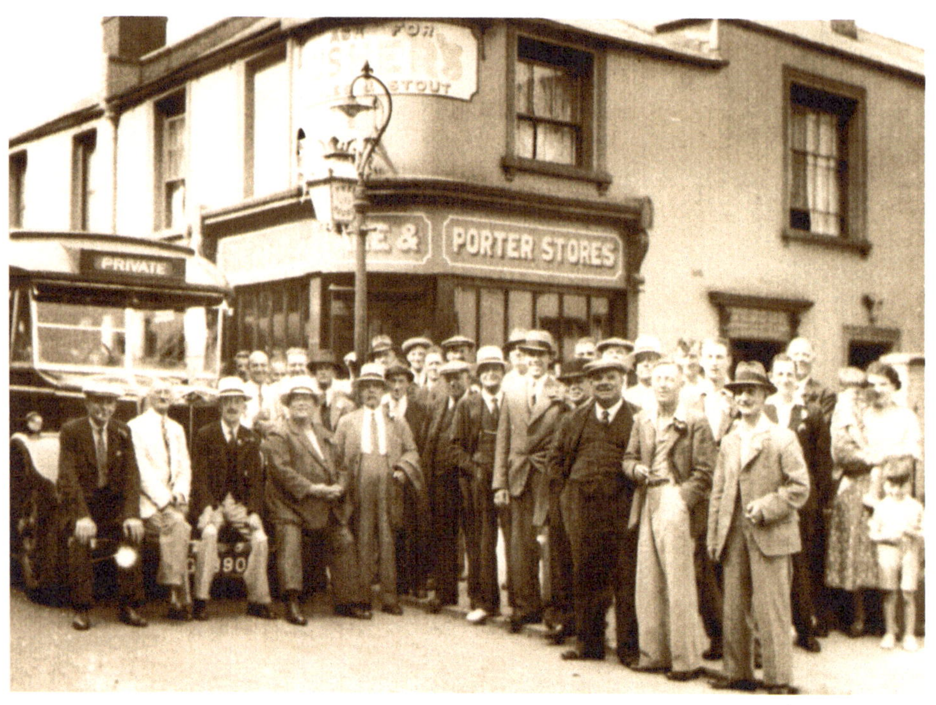

North Place Ale & Porter Stores, North Place

The North Place Ale & Porter Stores was on the western side of North Place between St Margaret's Road and Clarence Road. Note the 'Ask for Ushers Ales & Stout' sign. Ushers Brewery was in Trowbridge, Wiltshire. The site of the old pub is now a car park but was previously occupied by the Black & White coach station. The coach station closed in 1986 but enthusiasts organised a bus rally on the site in 2011. (Image courtesy Jane Taylor)

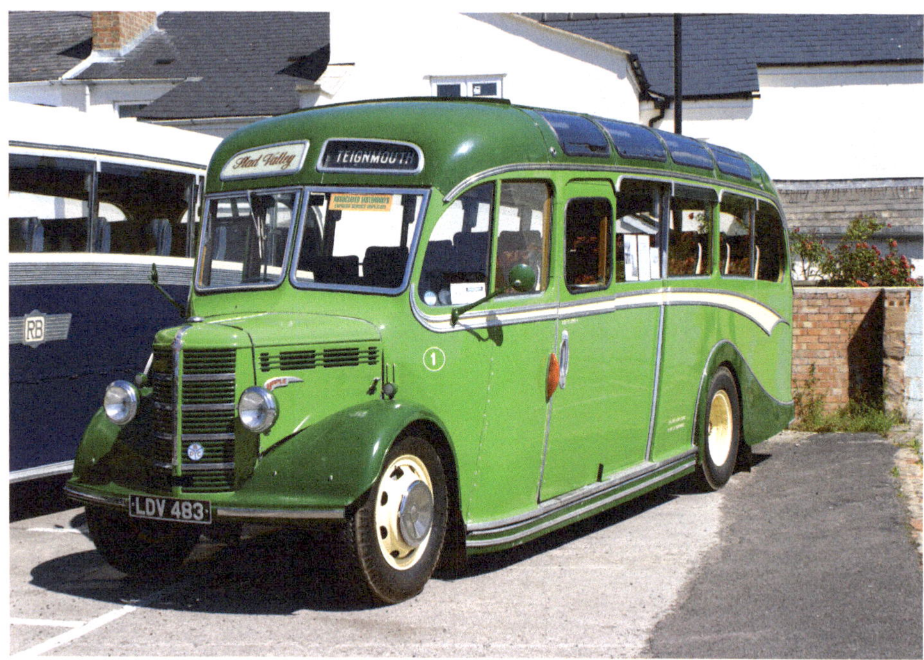

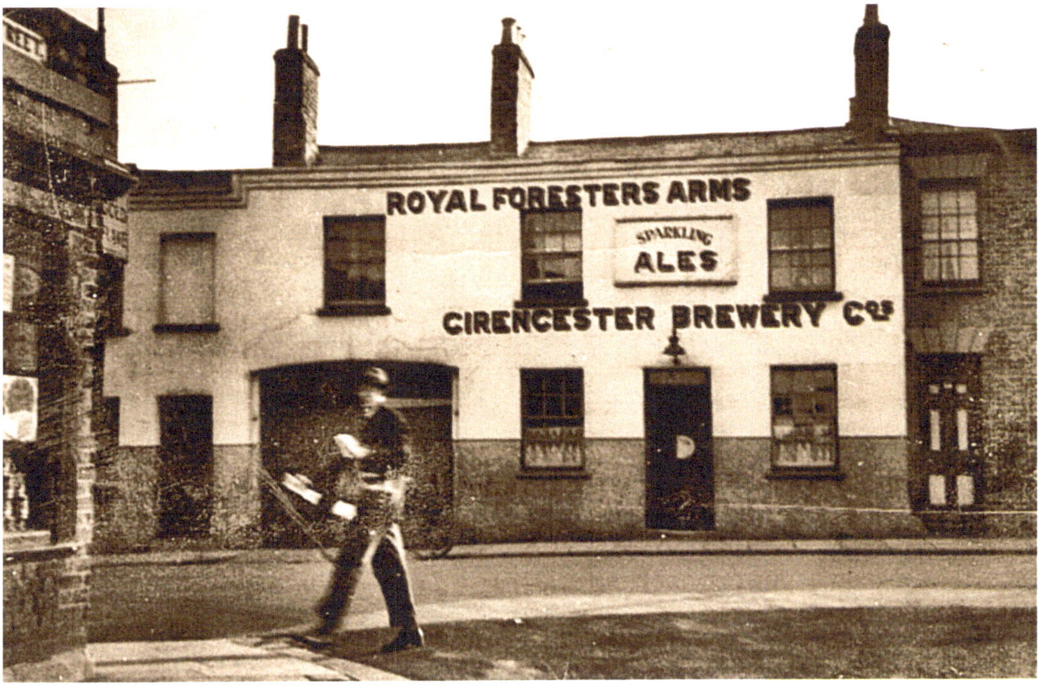

Royal Foresters Arms, Townsend Street

The Royal Foresters Inn was once tied to the Cirencester Brewery, with ownership subsequently passing to the Simonds Brewery of Reading and, eventually, Courage Brewery. The pub backed onto the old Great Western Cheltenham to Stratford Railway line. In the 1990s, under the ownership of Ushers Brewery, the name changed to the Horse & Jockey. The pub closed in 2009 and is now in residential use, but unusually it retains its hanging pub sign.

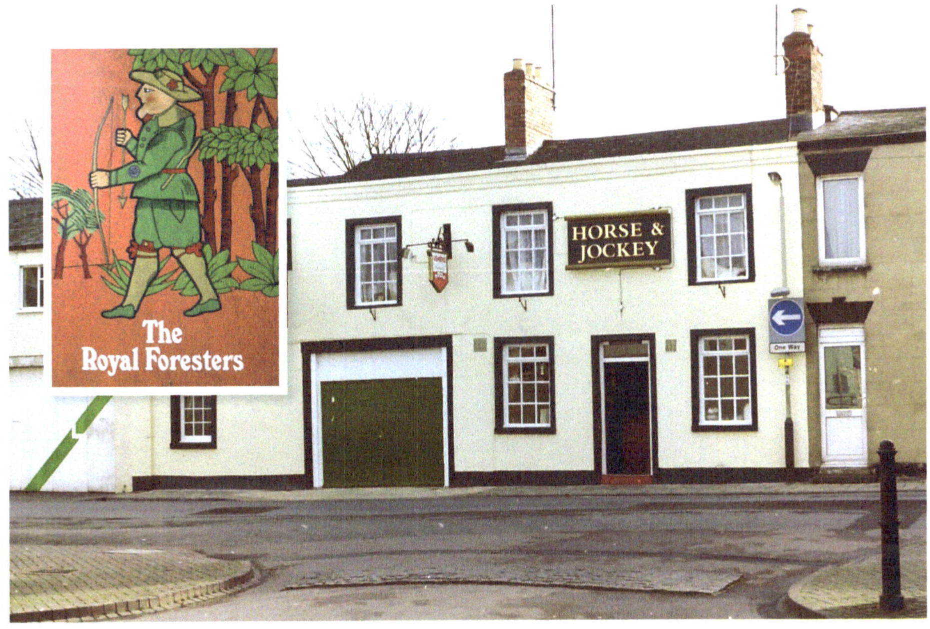

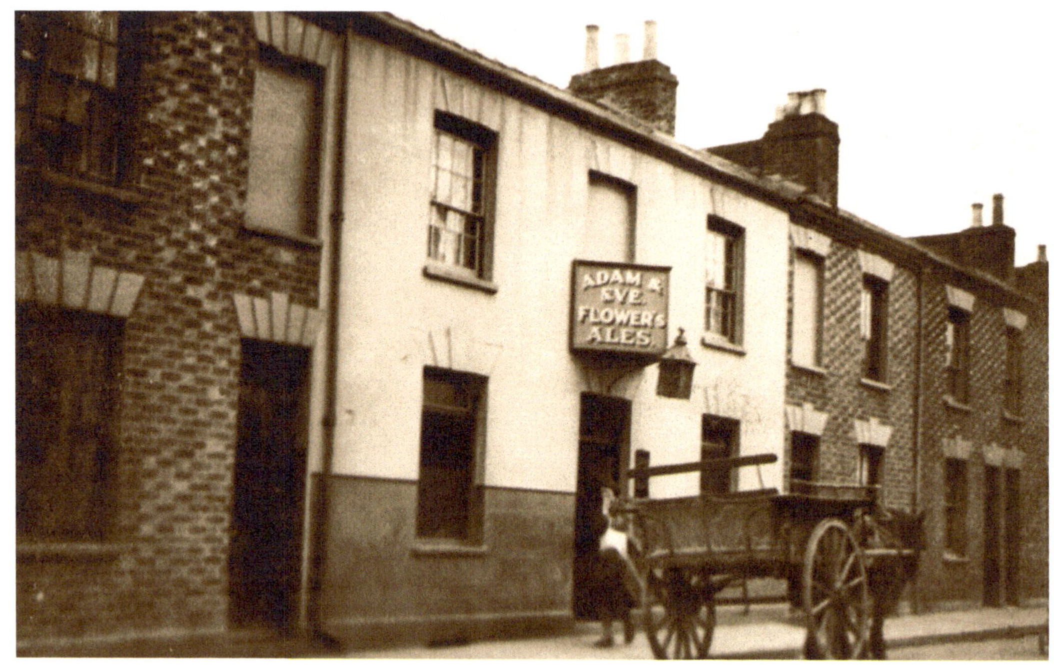

Adam & Eve, Townsend Street

Flowers & Sons of Stratford-upon-Avon bought the Adam & Eve for £800 in August 1920. It later passed into the ownership of West Country Breweries and Whitbread. Brian and 'Dot' Gasson moved into the Adam & Eve in 1978. The quality of the Whitbread PA was superb due to Brian's skills in the cellar. Arkell's of Swindon bought the pub in 1991, and thirty-four years later Brian and Dot are still serving excellent beer in this unspoilt, traditional terraced pub.

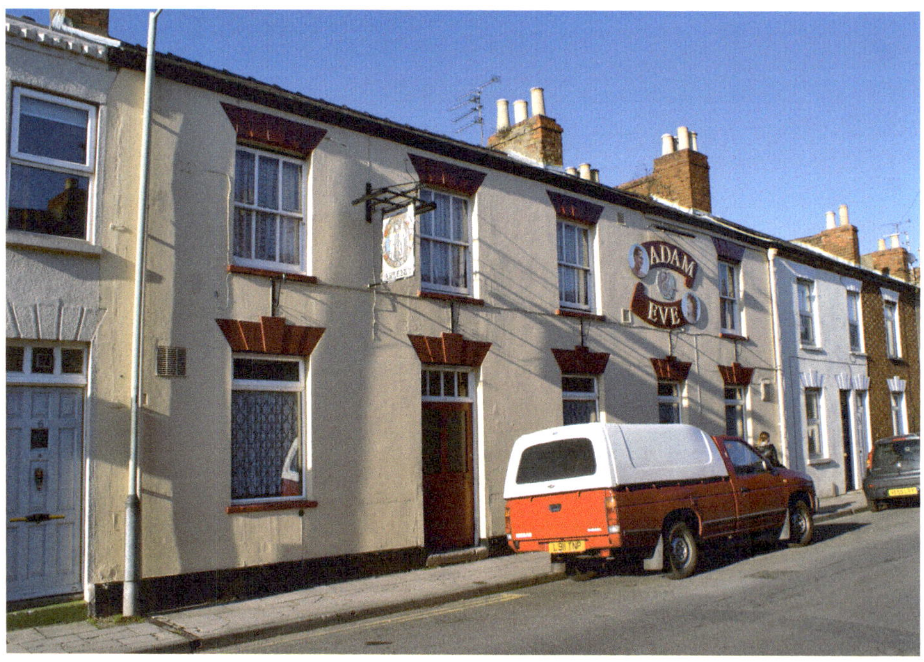

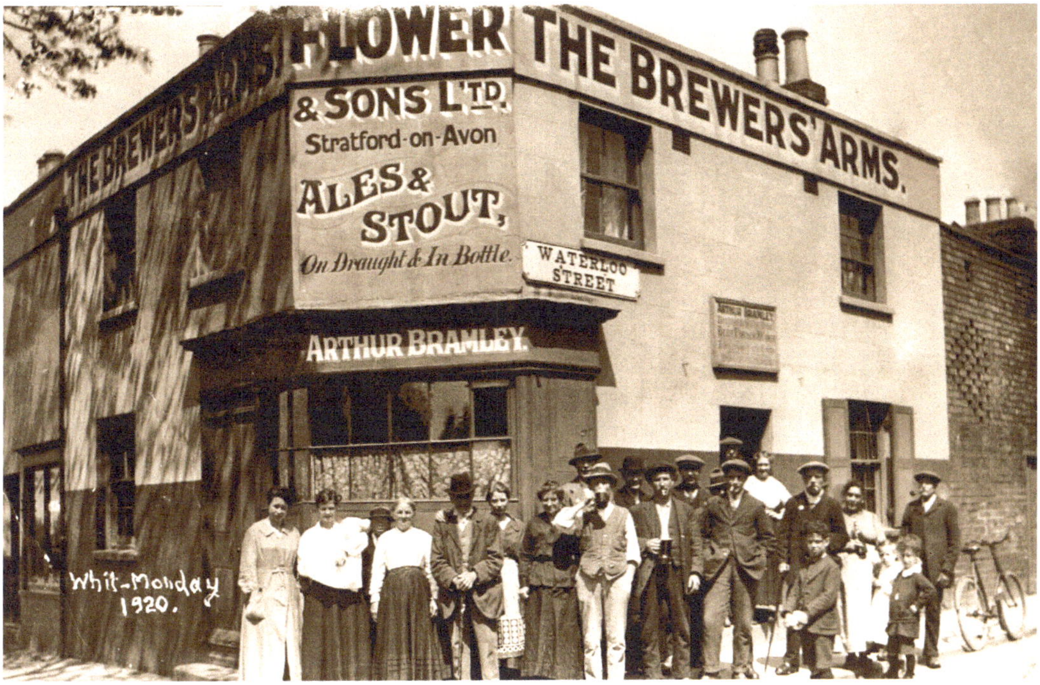

Brewers Arms, Tewkesbury Road

In the late 1950s and early 1960s a pub crawl along Tewkesbury Road involved drinking in eight pubs, a notable achievement but paling into insignificance when compared to the task of drinkers in the 1920s who had to negotiate the Golden Cross, Cross Keys, Cleveland Arms, White Horse, Queens Head, Old Anchor, Barley Mow, Elephant & Castle, Brewers Arms, Worcester Arms, Railway Inn, Vauxhall Arms and the Bridge Inn. The Brewers Arms, on the corner of Waterloo Street, closed *c.* 1930. (Image courtesy of June Webb)

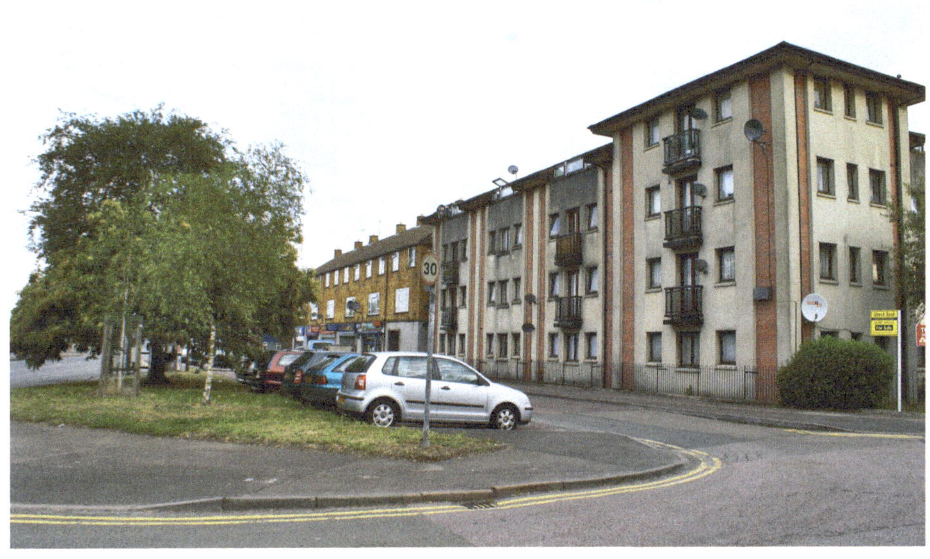

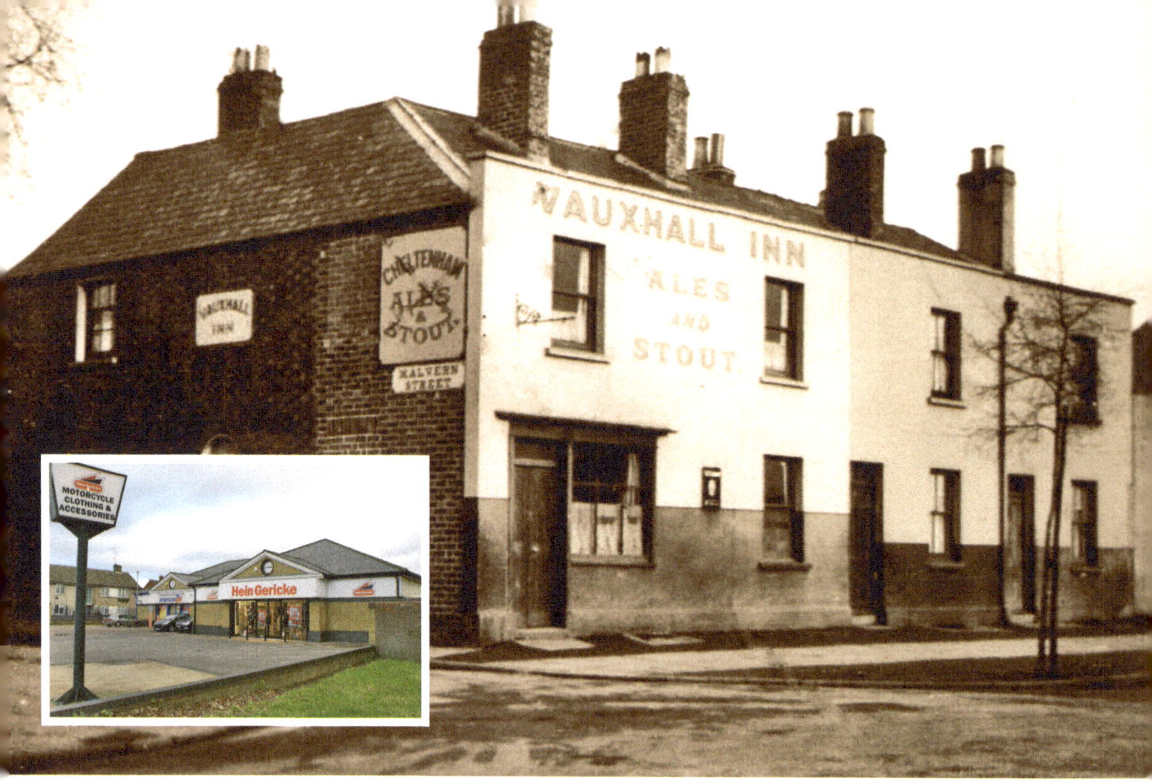

Vauxhall Inn, Tewkesbury Road

The 1960s reconstruction of Tewkesbury Road into an urban dual carriageway, and the associated housing and retail development, involved the demolition of several pubs between the Gloucester Road junction and the railway bridge. The Vauxhall Inn, on the corner of Malvern Street, was demolished and rebuilt. It became the only pub in Tewkesbury Road and in the 1980s was called the Last Drop before finally trading as the Sportsman. Retail premises now occupy the site. (Bottom image courtesy of Mike Williams)

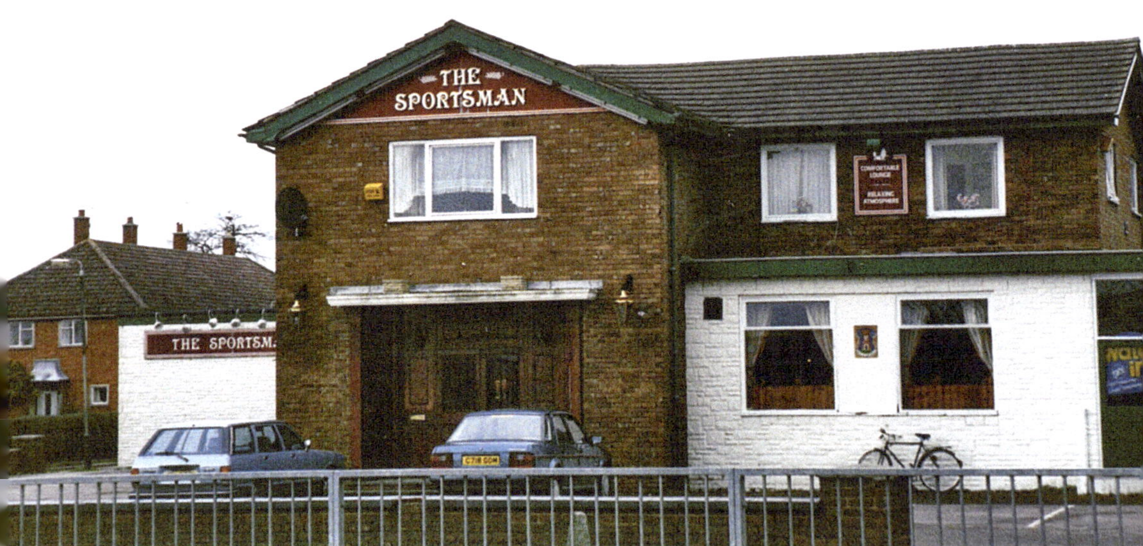

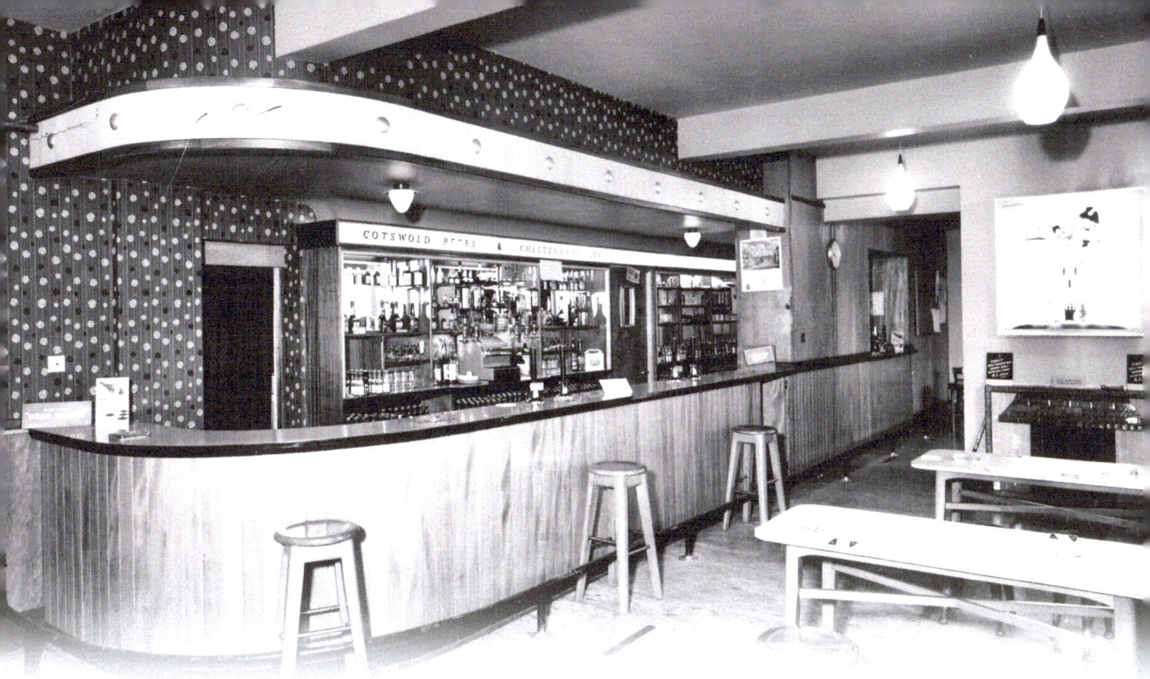

CHAPTER 3

Gloucester Road, Hatherley & Hesters Way

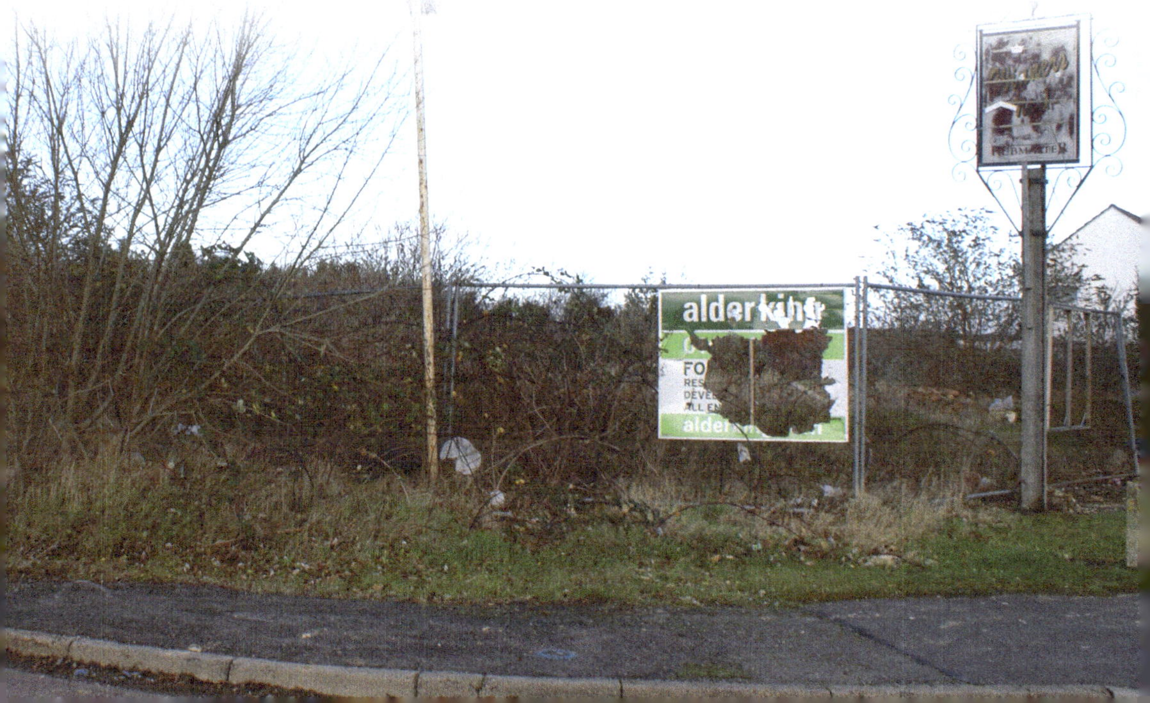

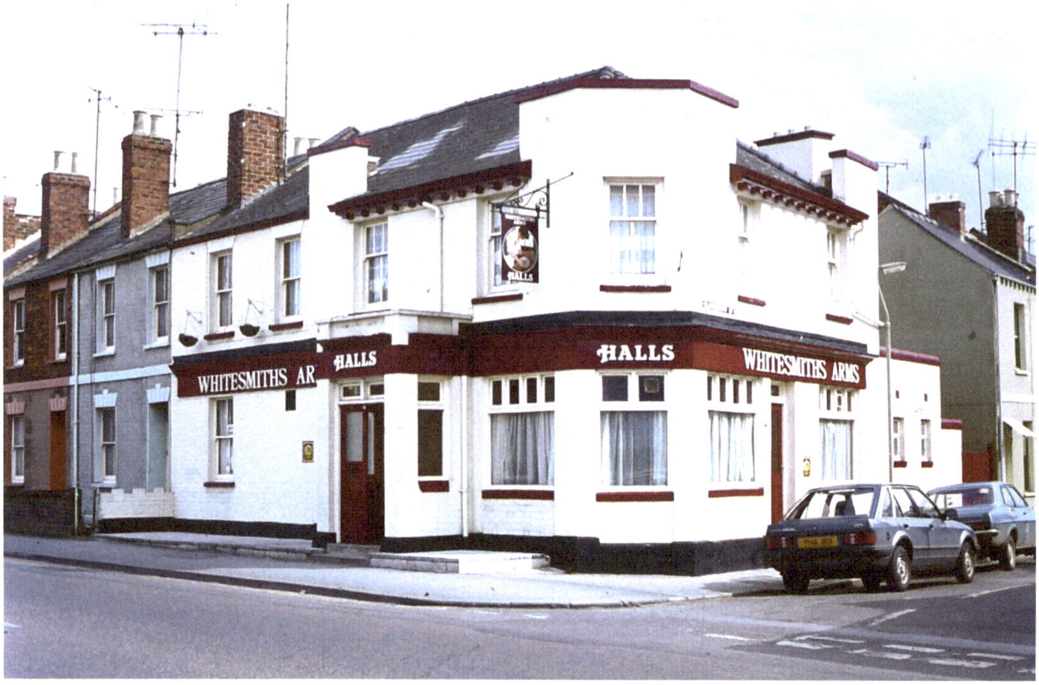

Whitesmiths Arms, Gloucester Road

In the 1960s to 1970s the Whitesmiths Arms was an Ind Coope pub and was converted in the early 1980s to a Halls Oxford & West Brewery pub. This was little more than marketing strategy as the beers were still brewed in Burton upon Trent. During this refurbishment an attractive Halls plaque was inlaid into the pub which is still *in situ*. It is now known as the Junction; the renaming is a mystery as there was no railway junction here.

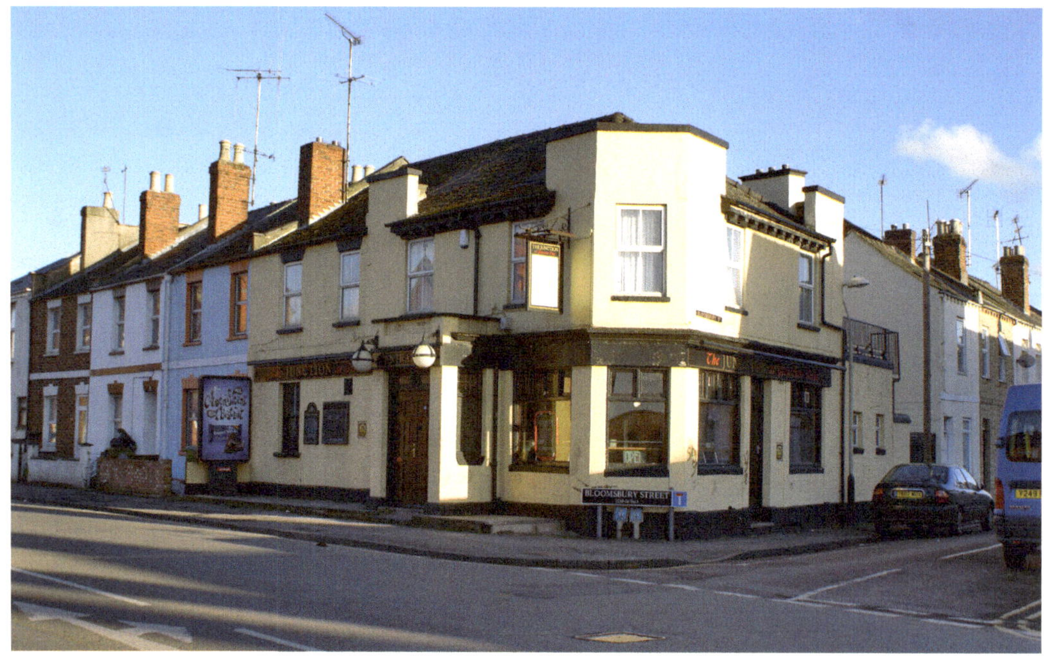

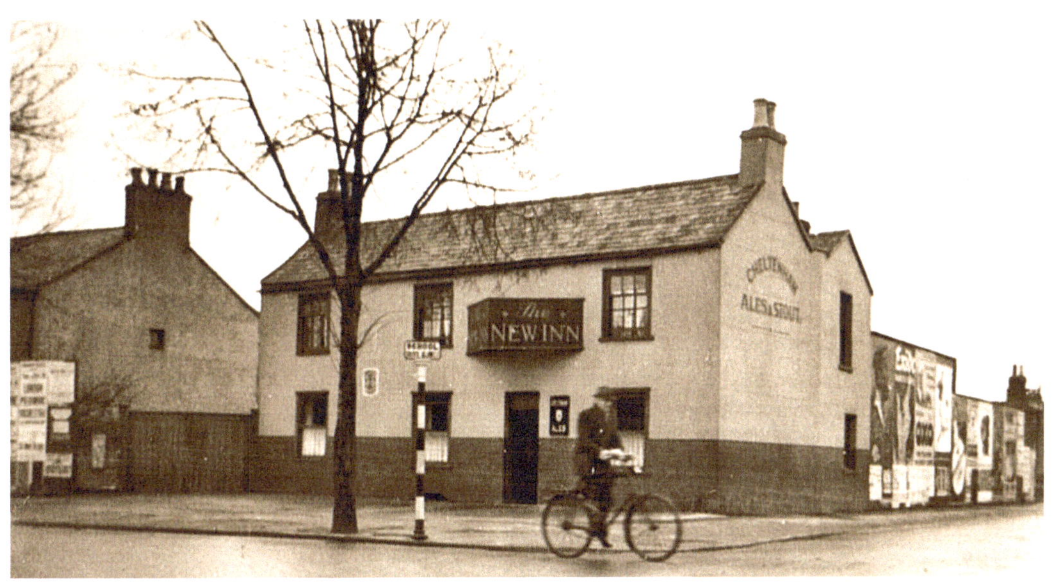

New Inn, Gloucester Road

The New Inn was renamed the New Penny in November 1970 in recognition of the change to decimal currency. The pub closed in June 2006 and was boarded up. In January 2007 vandals set fire to the empty pub causing extensive damage to the ground floor. The New Penny was demolished in the early summer of 2008. It took a surprisingly long time for the demolition work to be completed. Residential flats now occupy the site.

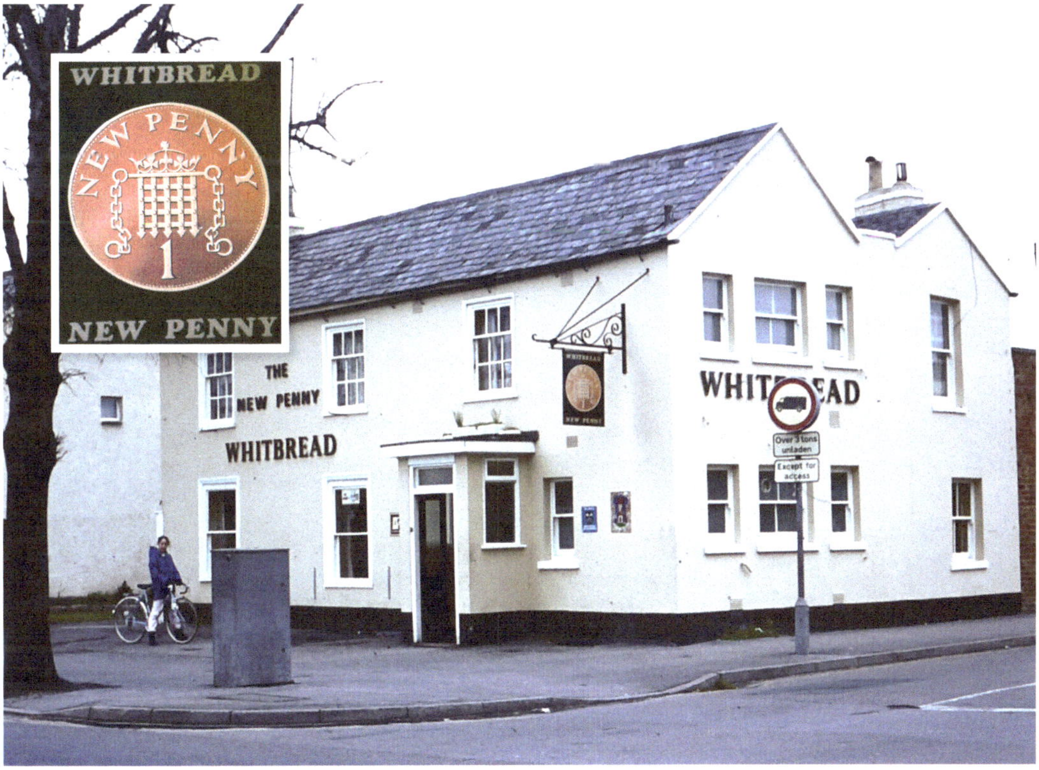

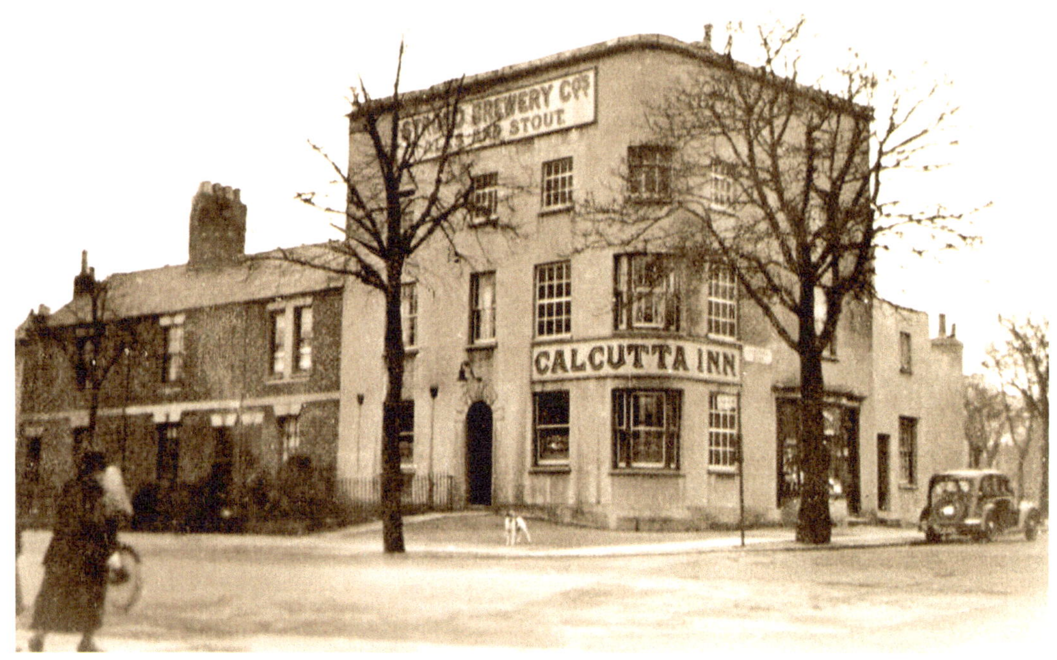

Calcutta Inn, Gloucester Road

The Calcutta Inn, on the junction with Gloucester Road and St George's Road, was a local landmark for many years. The Calcutta Inn closed in summer 1999. A block of twelve one-bedroom apartments, with one two-bedroom penthouse, has been now been built on the site. The new St George's Gate development was described in the letters section of the *Gloucestershire Echo* as 'the mother of all monstrosities, a ludicrously out-of-context edifice'.

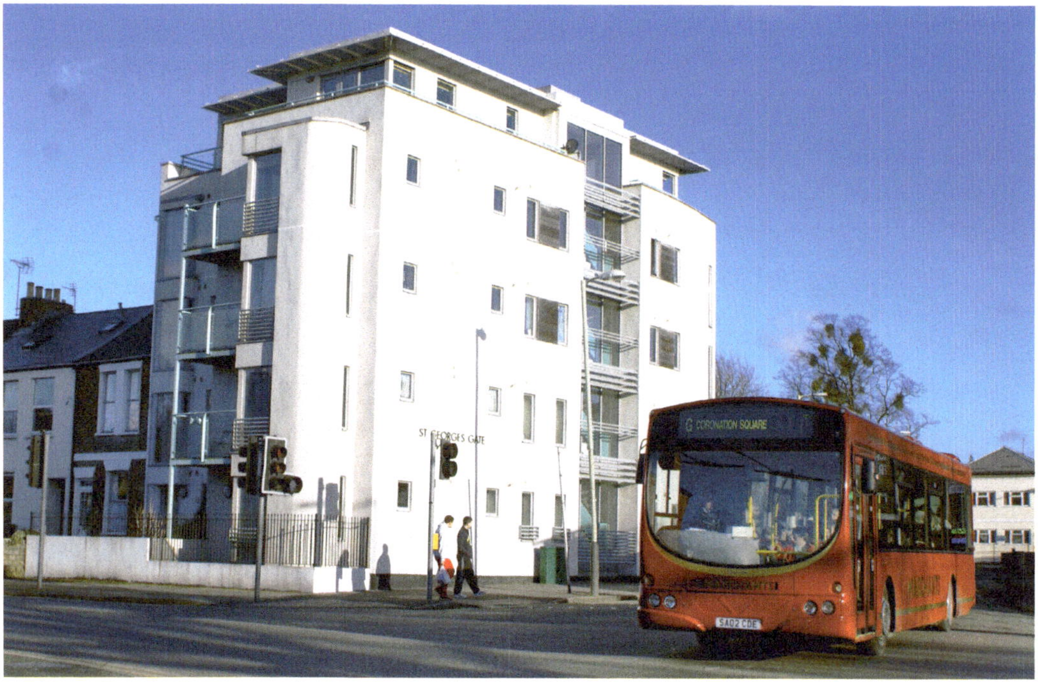

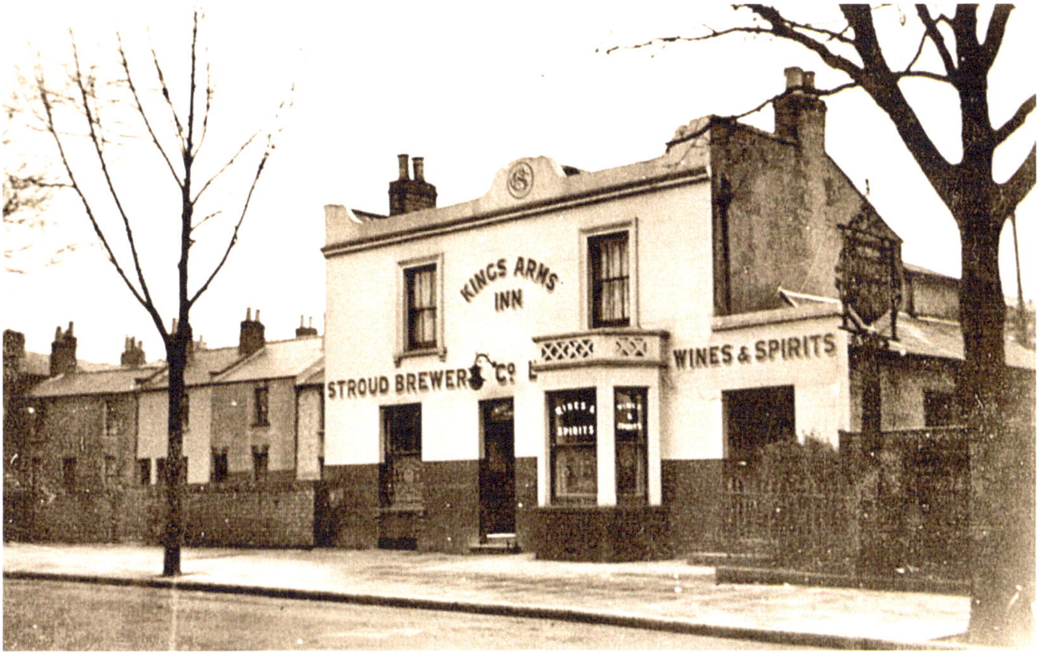

Kings Arms, Gloucester Road

Still trading, the exterior of the Kings Arms has changed very little over the last century. Modern signage has long since replaced the painted lettering which once proclaimed that it sold Stroud Brewery Co.'s Ales, Wines & Spirits. You very rarely see buildings graced with the skilled work of sign-writers these days, which seems a shame – no doubt a case of restrictive planning regulations stifling artistic creativity.

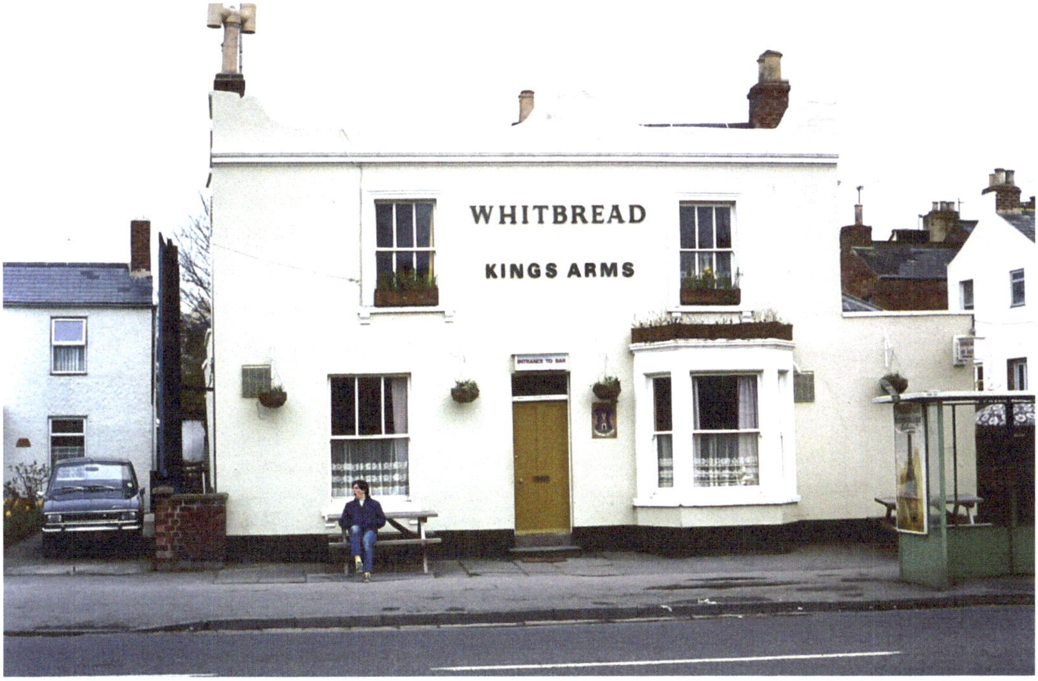

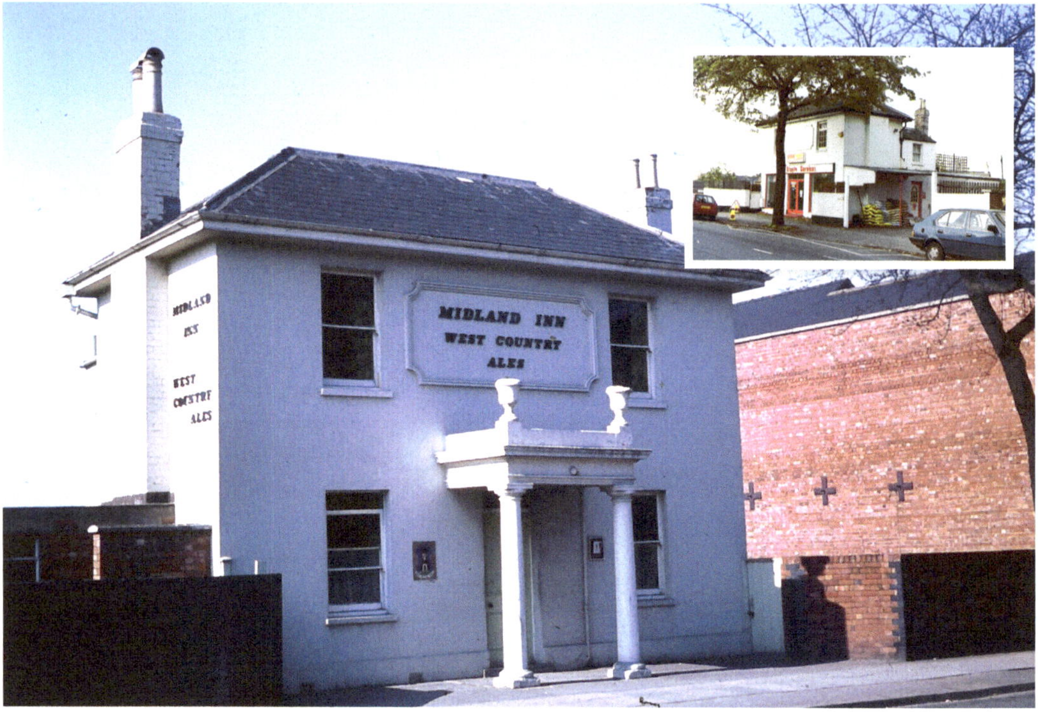

Midland Inn, Gloucester Road

The Midland Inn was situated to the north of the Midland Hotel. Because of its lesser status it was often dubbed the 'Little Midland'. The back yard of the pub overlooked the Midland Railway. The 'Little Midland' closed in the early 1970s. For many years the converted building was the premises of John Stayte Services. The old pub was eventually demolished soon after Christmas 2004. A block of flats called Queensgate now occupies the site.

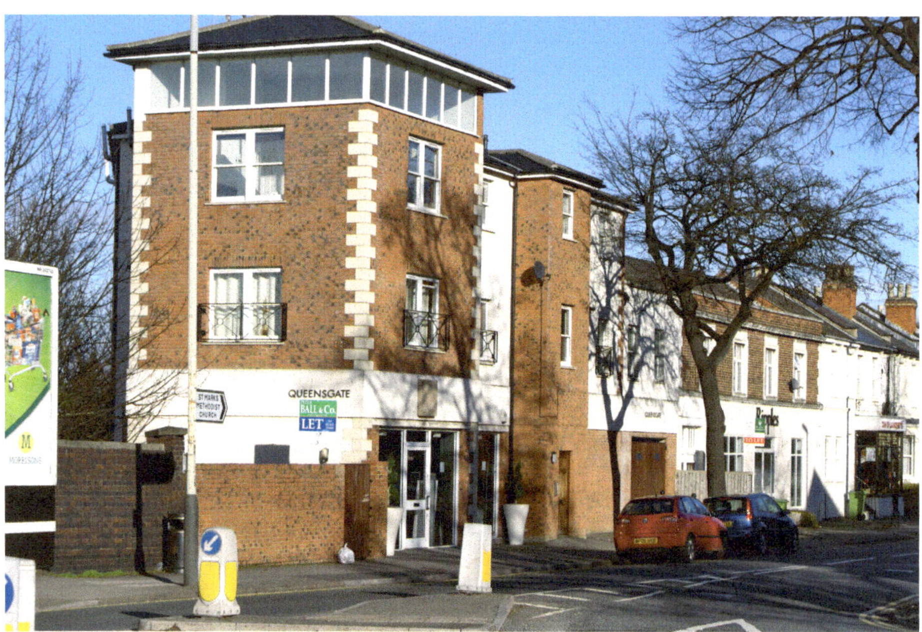

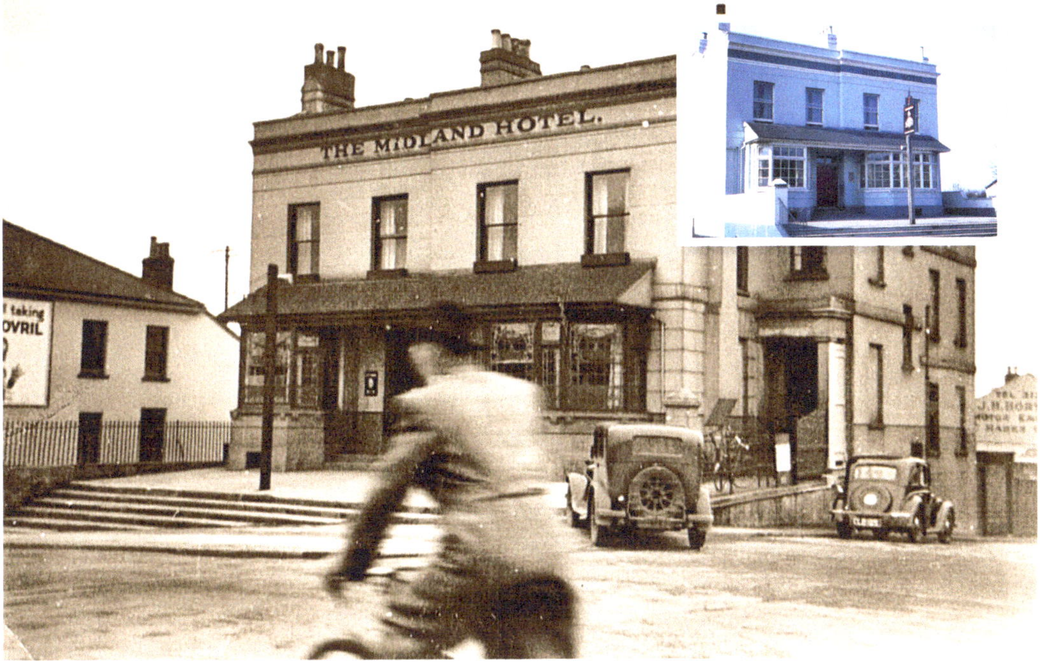

Midland Hotel, Gloucester Road

Situated directly opposite Cheltenham Spa railway station, the Midland Hotel has been offering hospitality for train travellers for at least 170 years. In its earlier days it was known as the Midland Railway Hotel (1885) and the Midland Family & Commercial Hotel (1903). The pub does a roaring trade during the Cheltenham Festival in March when thousands of race-goers arrive and depart from the station.

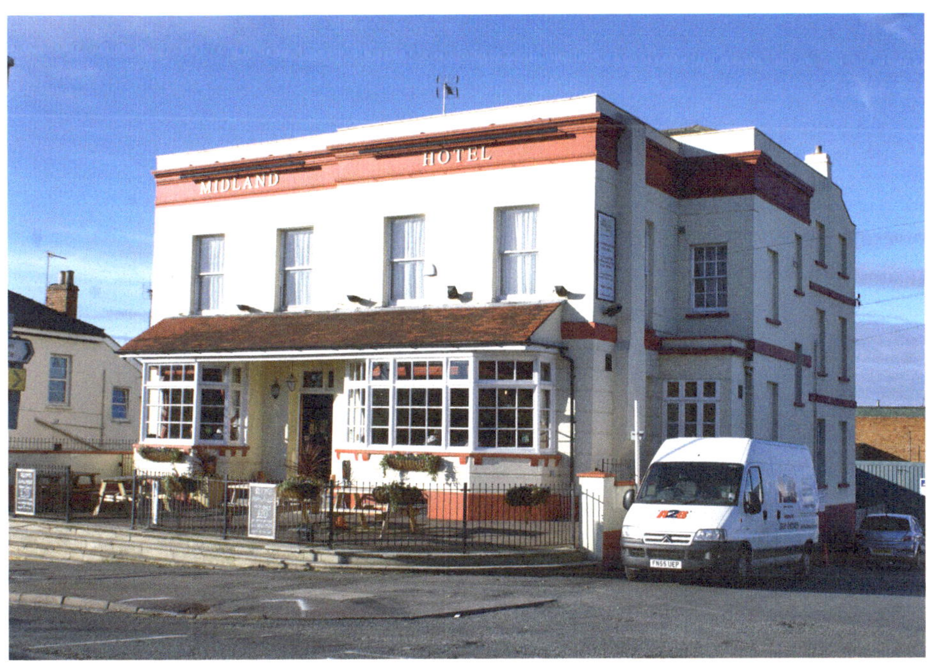

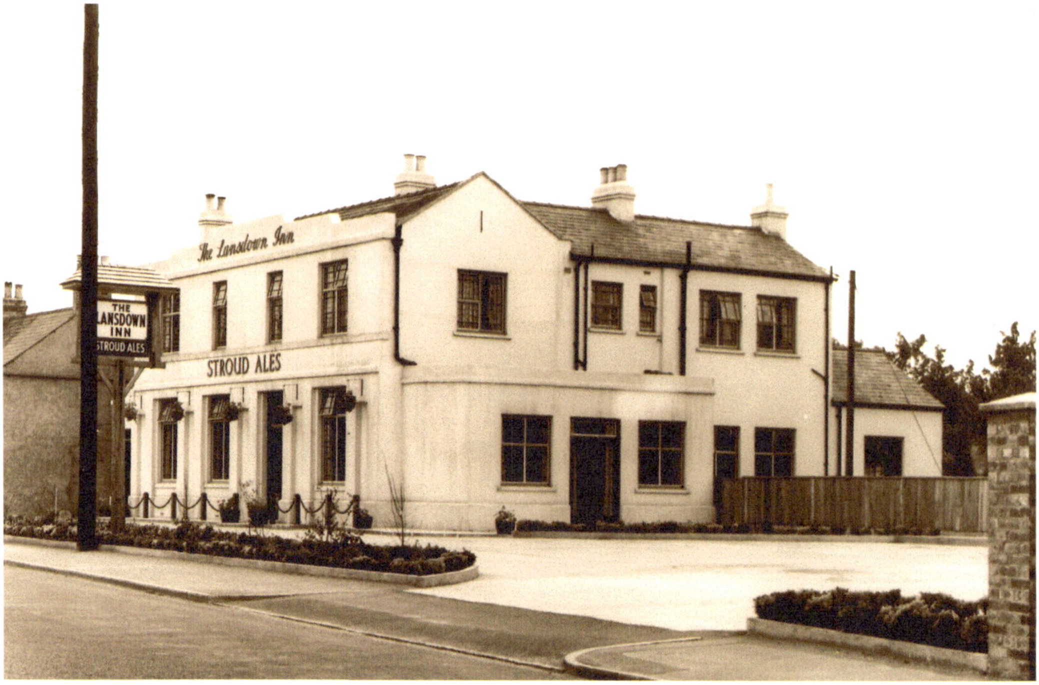

Lansdown Inn, Gloucester Road

The Lansdown Inn was a fine regency pub. The *Stroud Brewery Courier* reported in December 1948 that 'The bar is proving very popular, a feature of which is the attractive mural paintings on the walls executed by Mr Cedric J. Kennedy of Cheltenham illustrating the Amberley Inn and the Prince Albert Inn at Rodborough'. The Lansdown Inn was demolished in the mid-1980s and TGI Friday now occupies the site. (Image courtesy of Annie Blick)

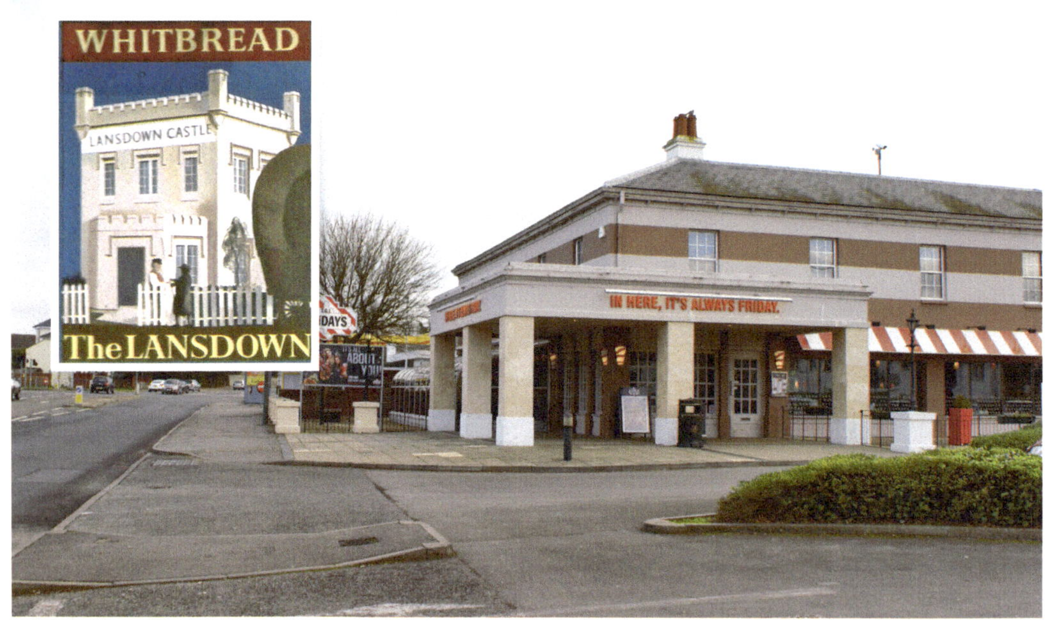

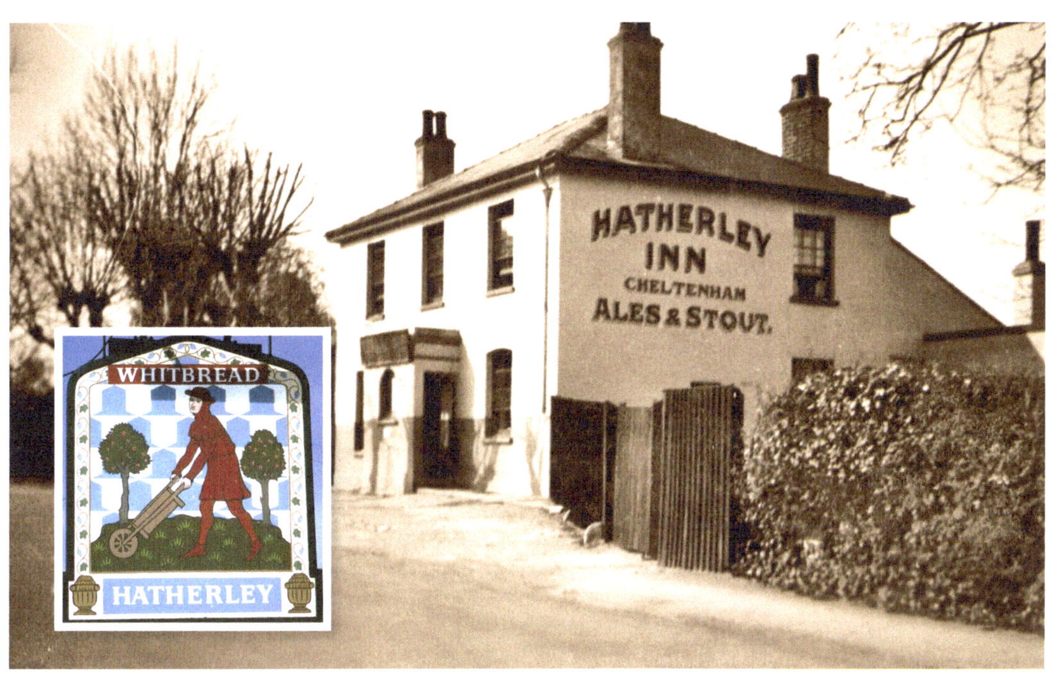

Hatherley Inn, Hatherley Road

The Hatherley Inn was once tied to George Stibbs' Albion Steam Brewery of Albion Street, subsequently passing into the ownership of the Cheltenham Original Brewery. The building has been enlarged and much altered over the years. The name was changed to the Three Crowns in the late 1980s but has since reverted back to the 'Hatherley'. It is now owned by Greene King.

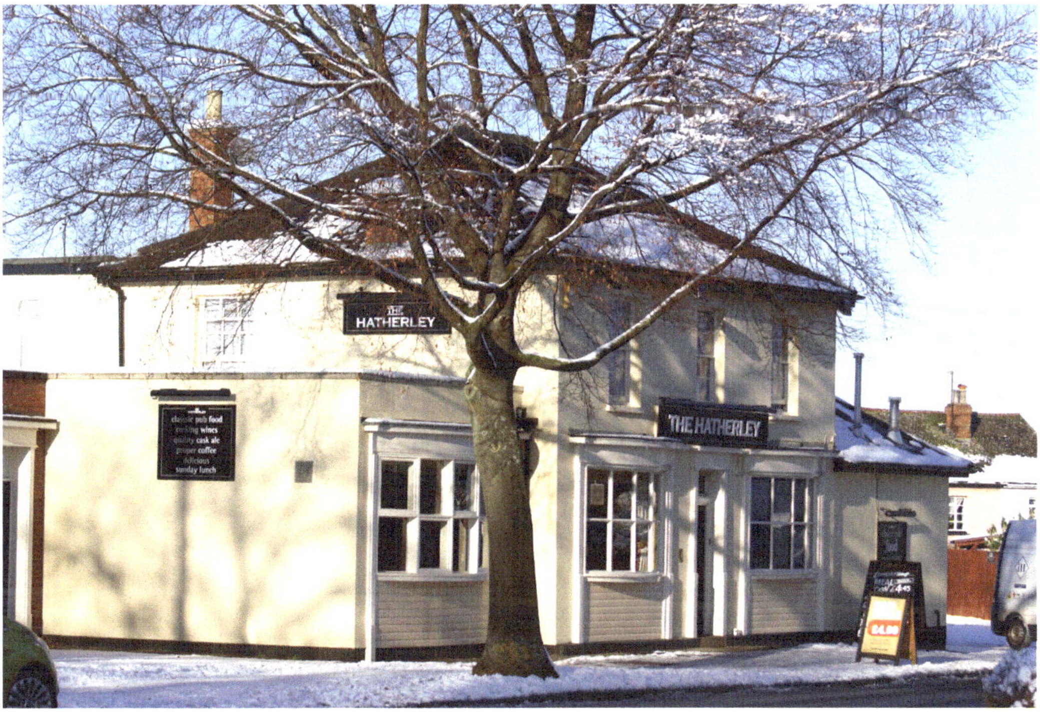

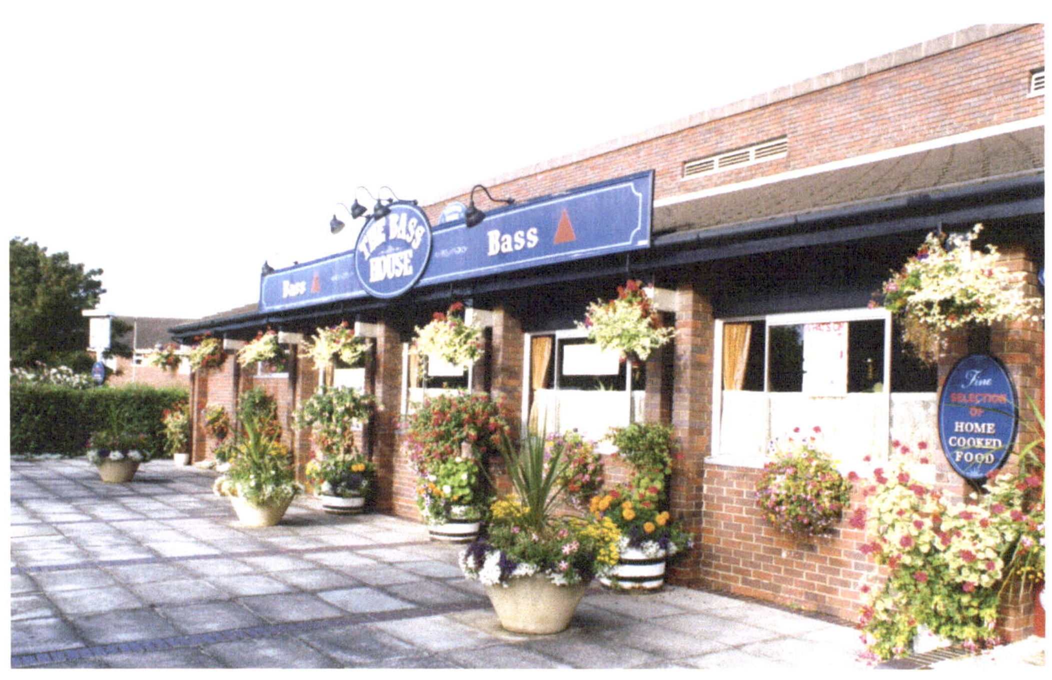

Bass House, Alma Road

The Bass House opened on 16 December 1978 and, as it name implies, it was tied to Bass Brewery of Burton upon Trent. In its heyday the pub frequently won prizes in the 'Cheltenham in Bloom' competition for its wonderful floral displays. In the autumn of 2006 an application was submitted to demolish the pub and replace it with housing. Despite objections, the Bass House called 'last orders' for the final time on 9 March 2007 and was demolished on Thursday 19 April.

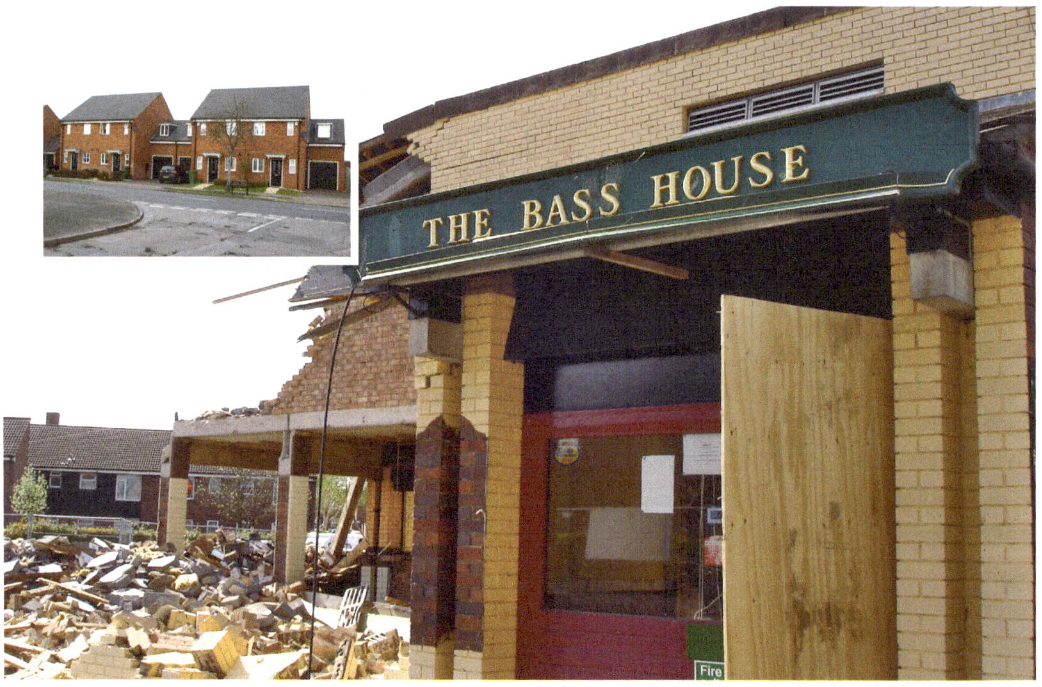

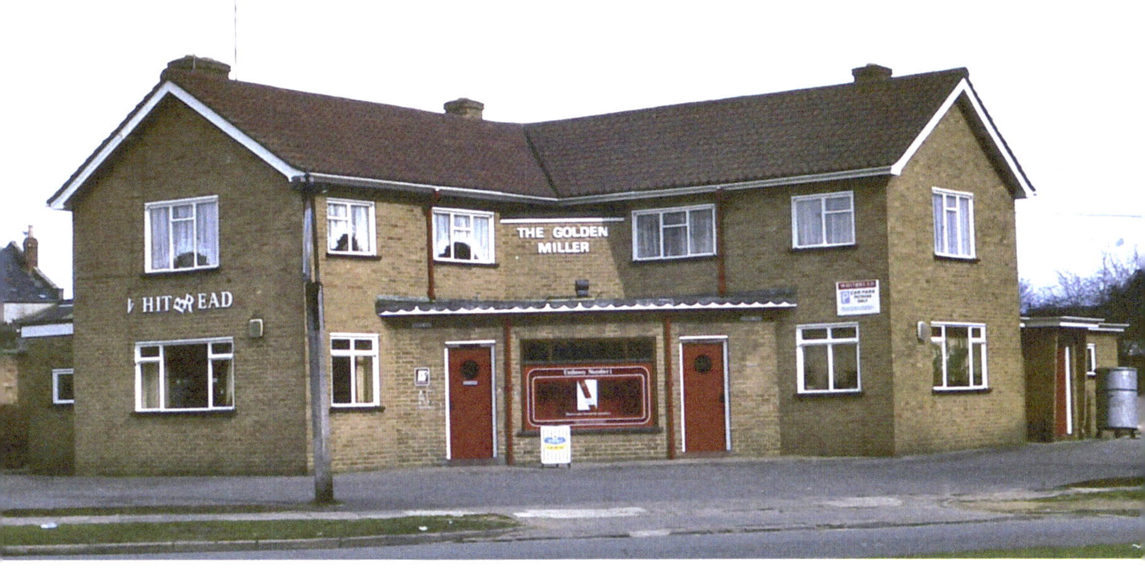

Golden Miller, Rowanfield

The Golden Miller, named after the famous racehorse who won five successive Cheltenham Gold Cups from 1932–36, was built as part of the Rowanfield Estate housing development in the 1950s. In July 2002 the pub was renamed Cotterill's, a tribute to ex-Cheltenham Town football manager Steve Cotterill who guided Cheltenham Town to Division Two of the Nationwide League. The pub was demolished in 2005 and in 2011 a residential block for overseas students opened on the site.

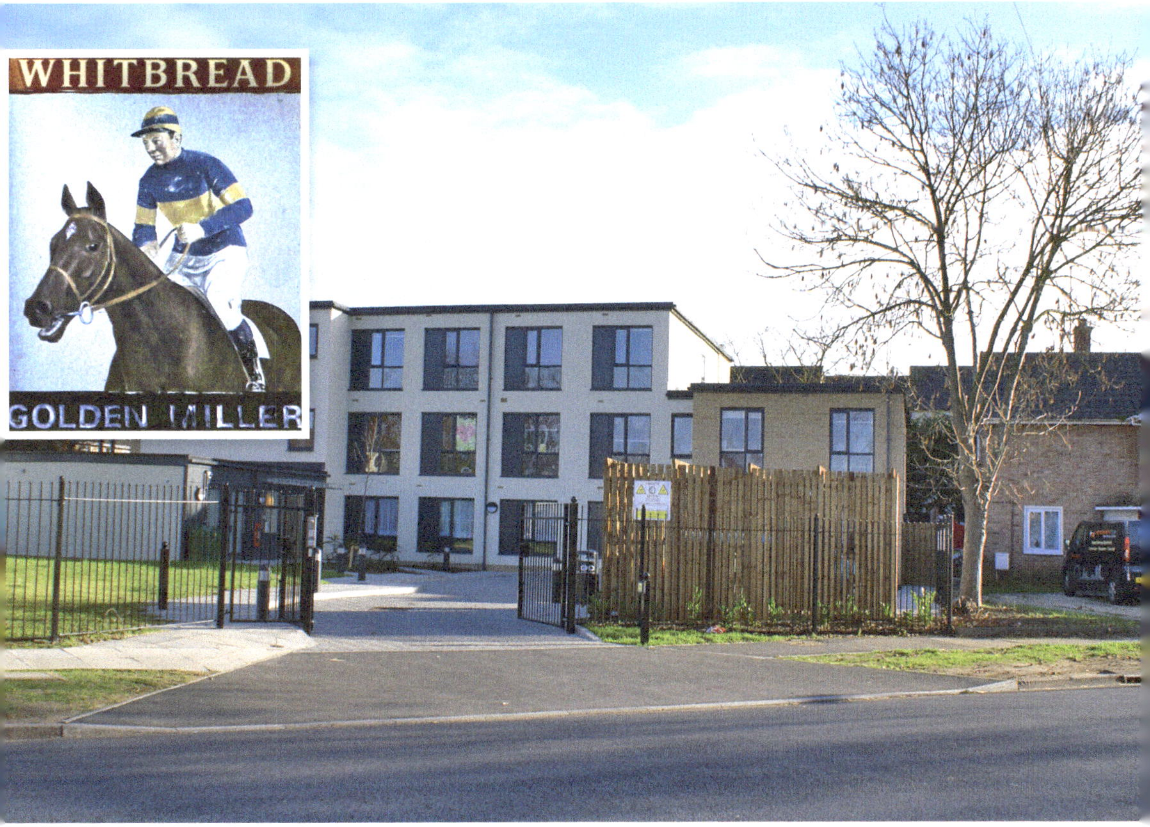

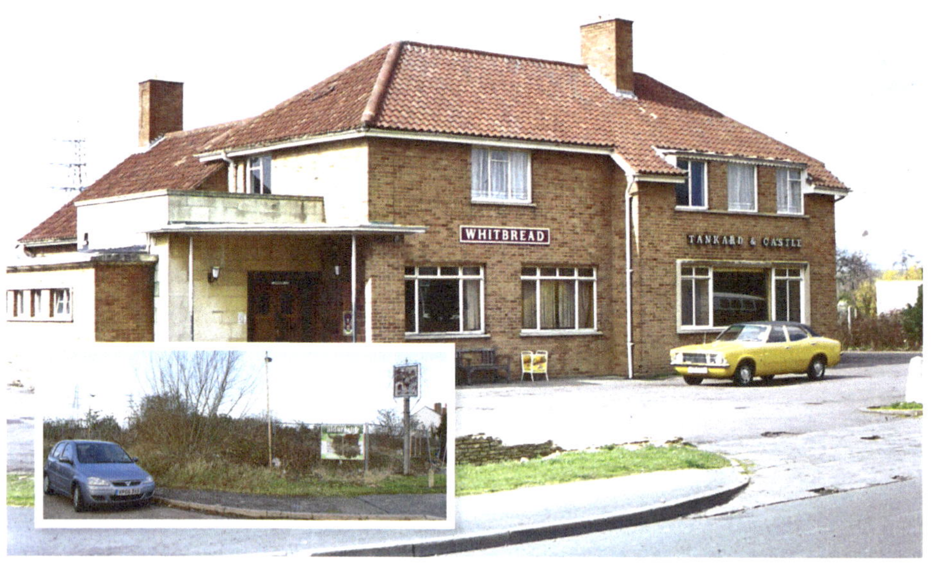

Tankard & Castle, Hesters Way

The Tankard & Castle, built as an estate pub in the 1950s, had a significant name as it represented the Tankard emblem of Stroud Brewery and the Castle emblem of the Cheltenham Brewery. This little bit of history seemed to matter little to the owners in the early 1990s who changed the name to the Goat & Bicycle. In an attempt to give the pub a new lease of life and a better reputation, the name was changed again to Winners No. 1. It closed shortly after a refurbishment in July 1997 and has now been demolished. (Image courtesy of Annie Blick)

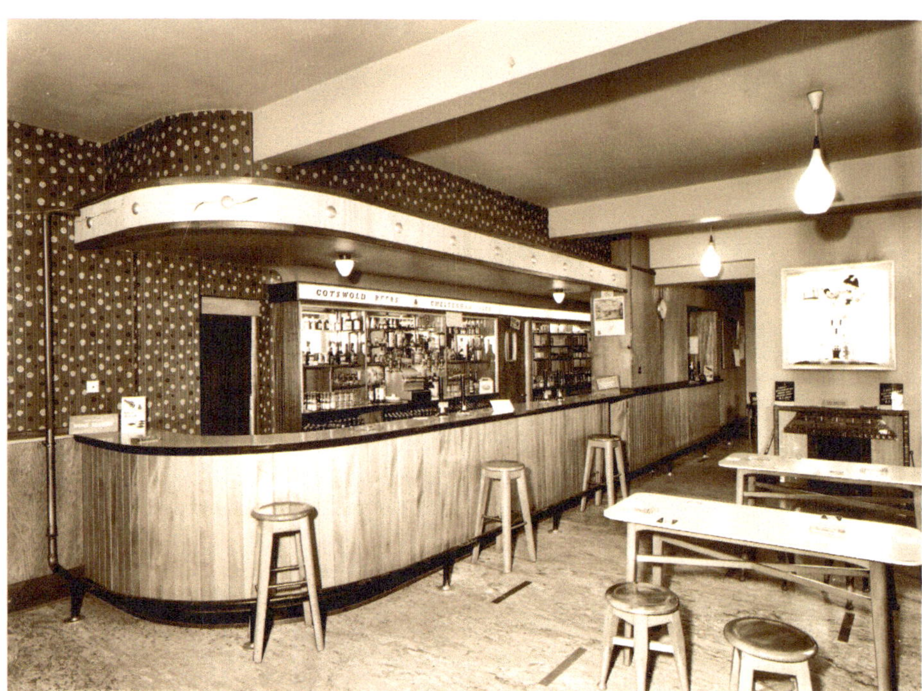

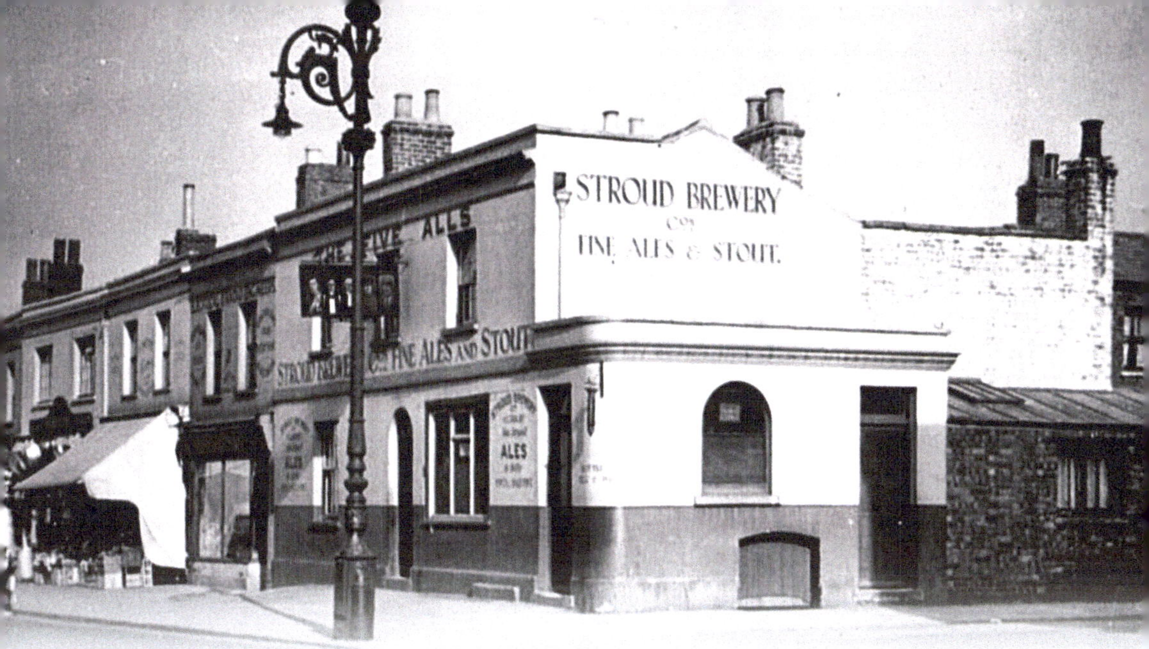

CHAPTER 4

Bath Road & Leckhampton

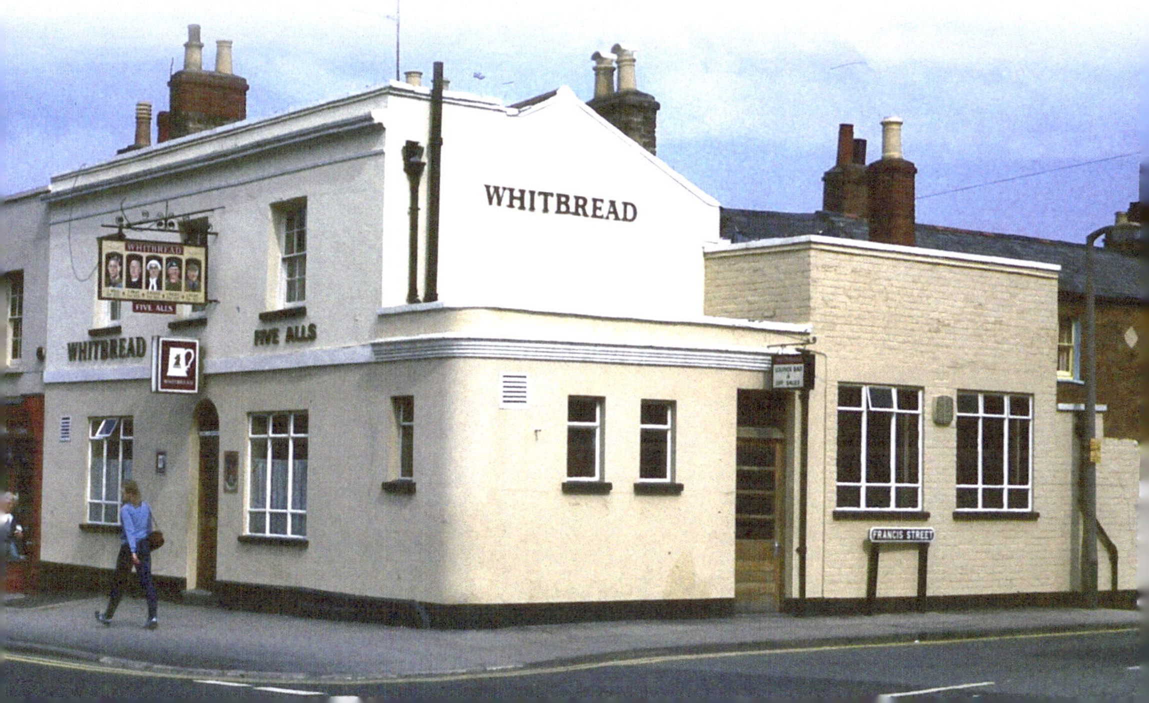

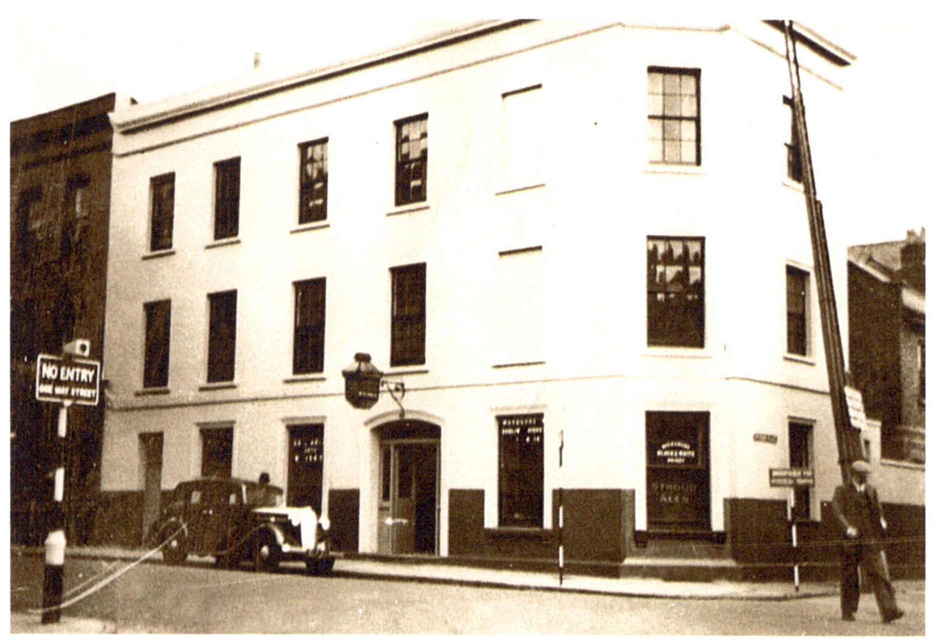

Crown & Cushion, Bath Road

The Crown & Cushion was one of just seven pubs to be tied to William Sadler Hall's Cranham Brewery, based at the Royal William on the Painswick Road. In 1904 the business was sold to Godsell & Sons of Salmon Springs for £13,000. The Crown & Cushion later became a Stroud Brewery pub. It had a legendary juke box in the 1960s and Cheltenham Folk Club was founded here. More recently the pub was trading as the Old Amsterdam. It is now G's Bar.

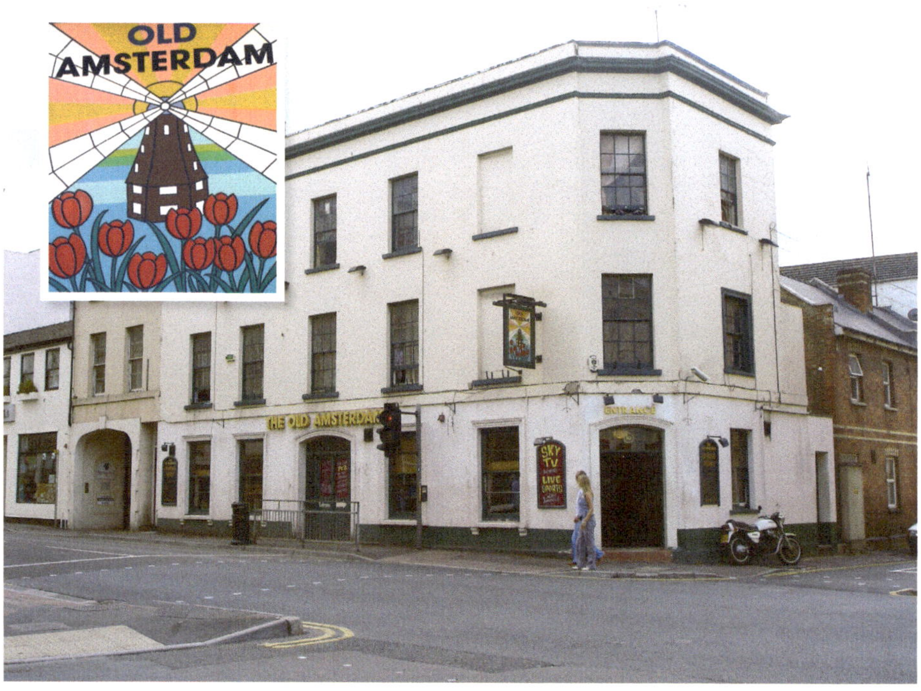

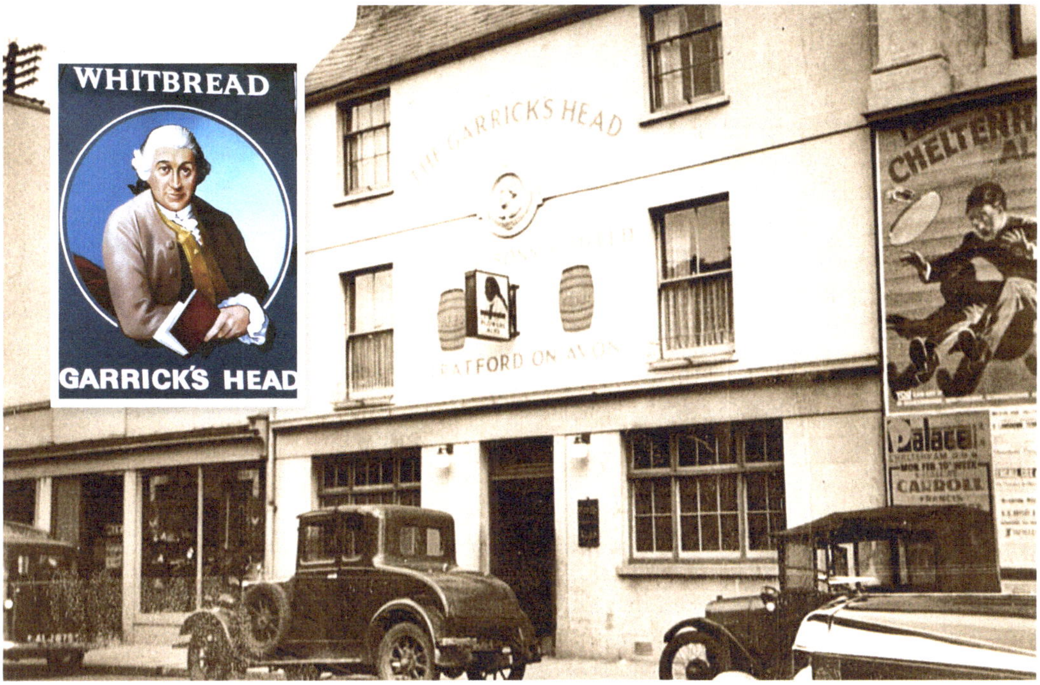

Garrick's Head, Bath Street

The Garrick's Head was once owned by the Flowers Brewery of Stratford-upon-Avon. It was named after David Garrick, the famous actor, who was born in Hereford in 1717. His plasterwork head still graces the exterior of the pub, but he doesn't get a second glace today. In November 1999 the pub reopened as Slak, essentially a young persons' music venue. The exterior colour scheme can only be described as garish.

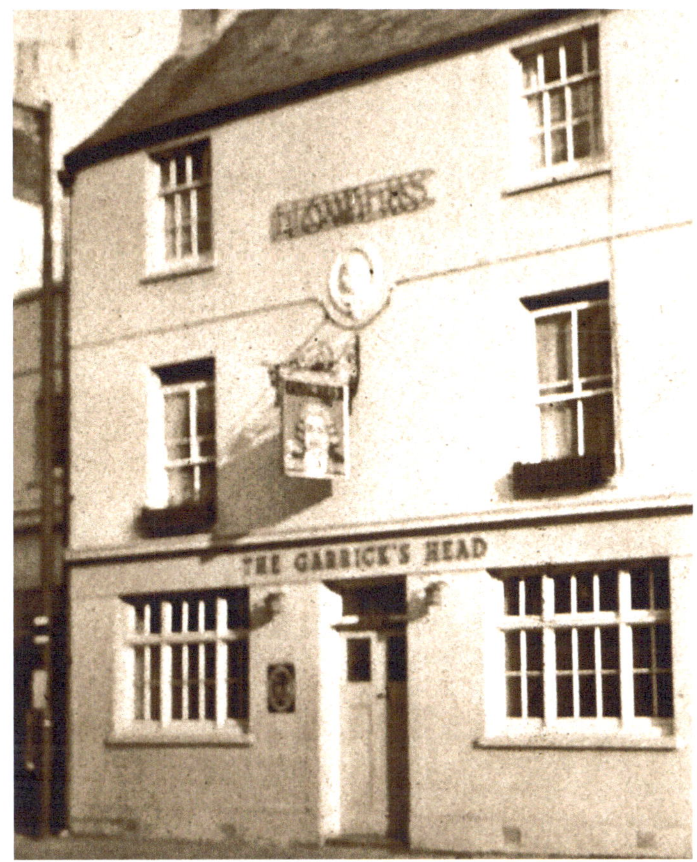

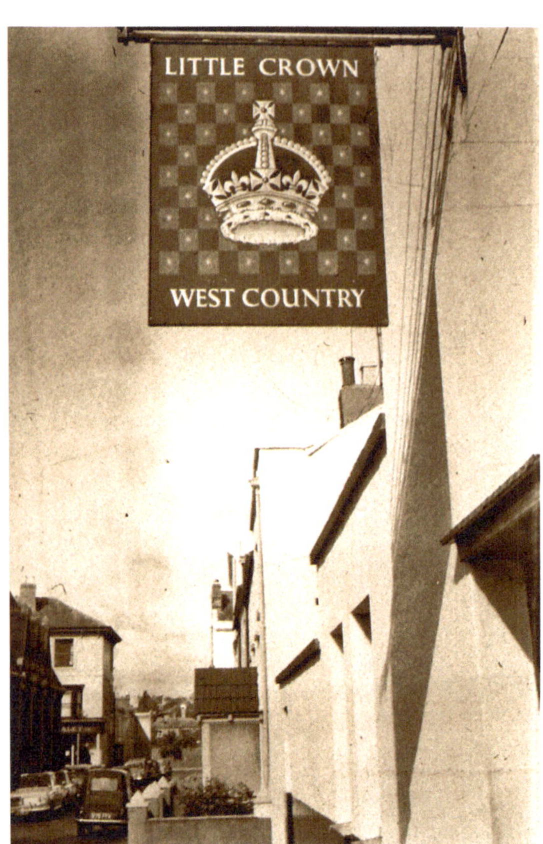

Little Crown Inn, Commercial Street
Once tied to the Nailsworth Brewery, the Little Crown was a small pub on the corner of Bethesda Street and Commercial Street (previously Union Street South). The Little Crown closed down in 1980. It is now a veterinary surgery, which became well known in the 1990s when the BBC filmed *Vets in Practice* there.

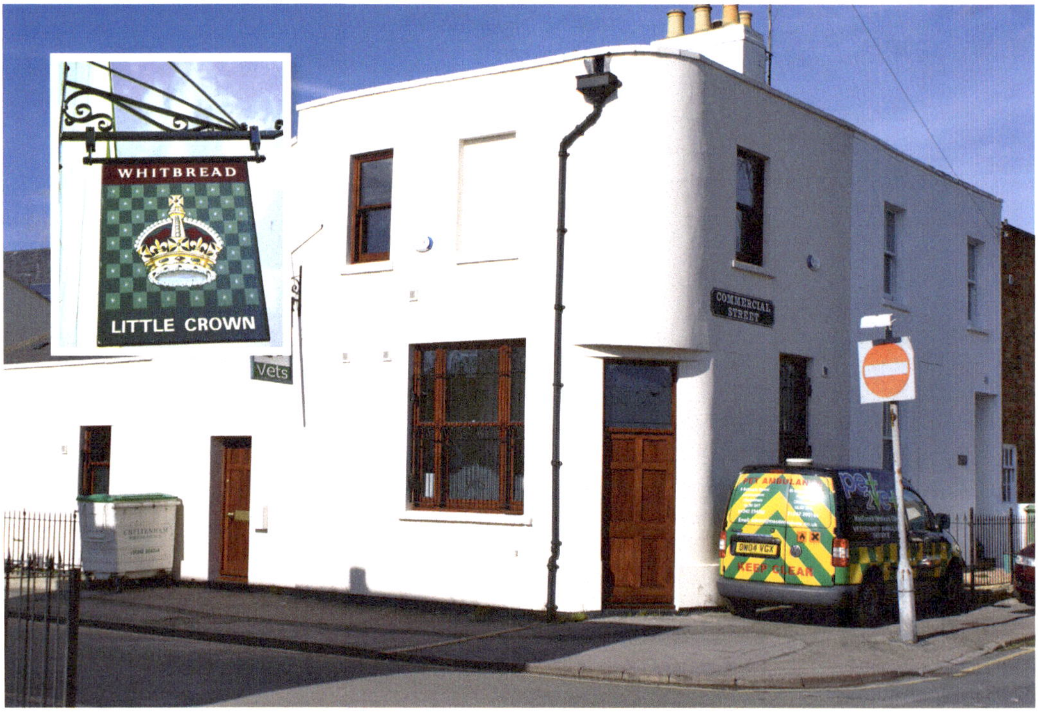

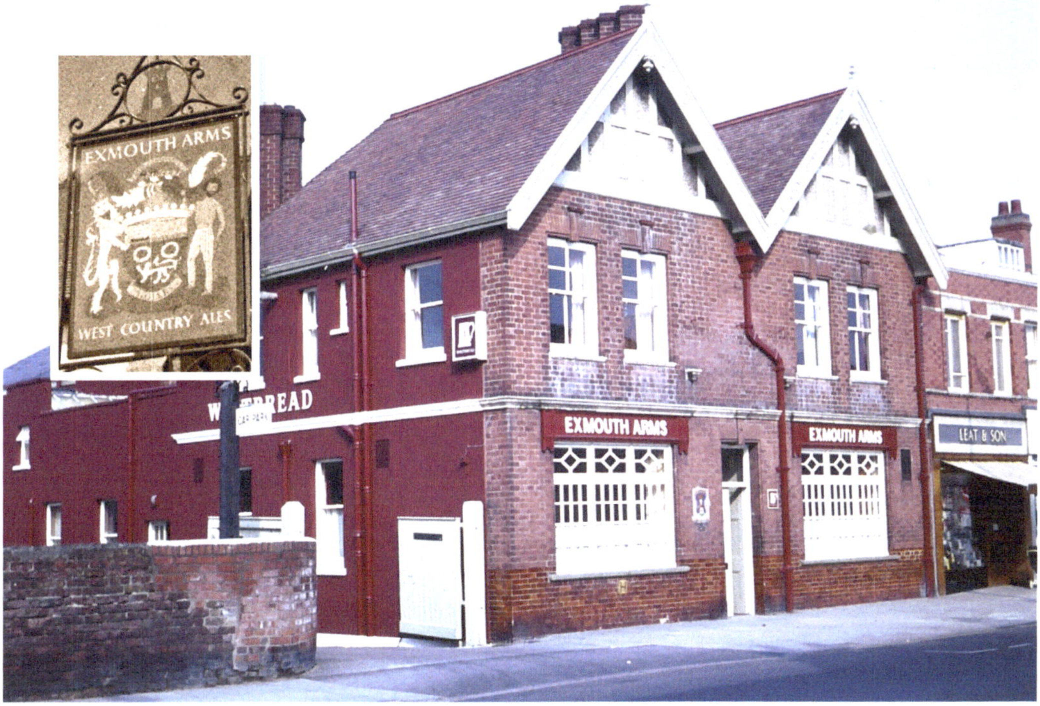

Exmouth Arms, Bath Road

In 1921 James Kitching is listed as a brewer at the Exmouth Arms Brewery. It is possible that the building to the rear of the pub might have once been the brewery. The Cheltenham Original Brewery later acquired the Exmouth Arms and the etched letters 'OB' can still be seen in the front windows. Arkell's of Swindon bought the pub in 1991. A West Country Ales 'Best in the West' plaque is still *in situ*.

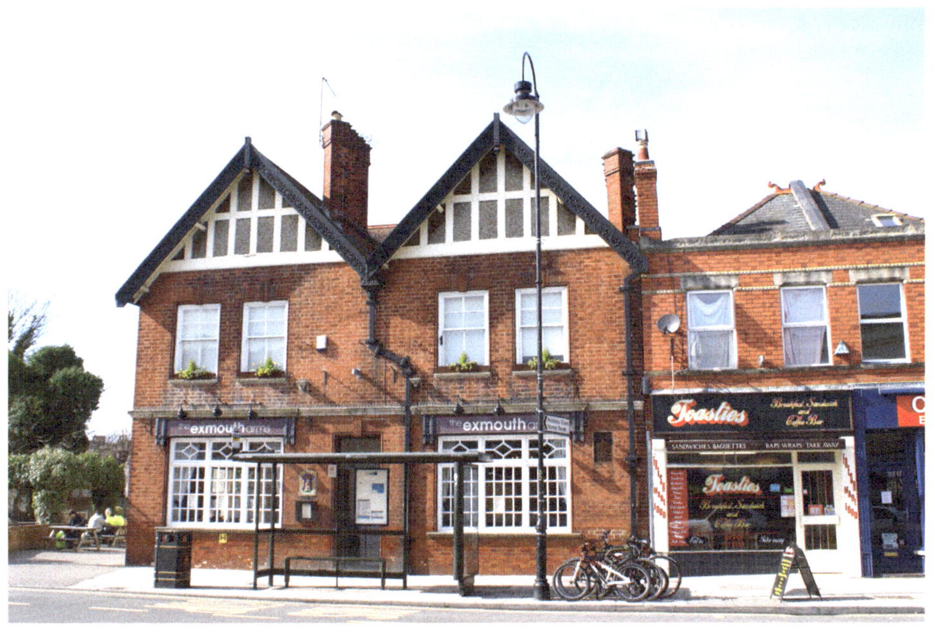

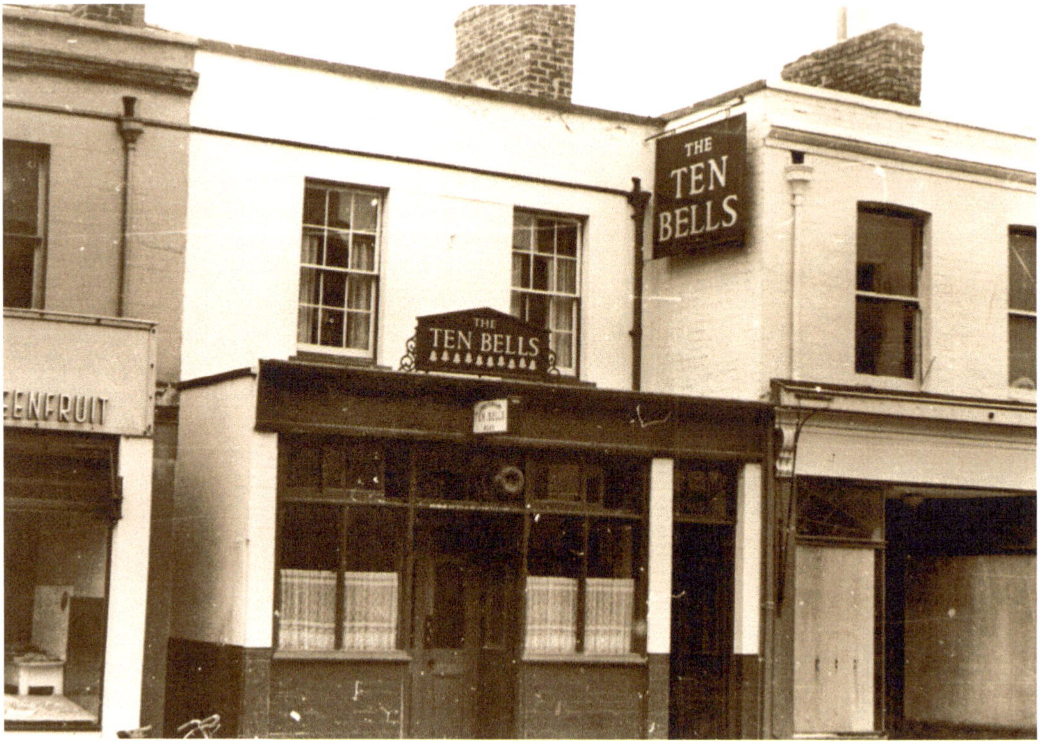

Ten Bells, Bath Road

The Ten Bells was a small terraced pub that called 'last orders' for the final time on 18 April 1964. The premises were then converted into an off-licence. When this closed in recent times the building opened as a coffee bar, but it is now in use as a shoe shop.

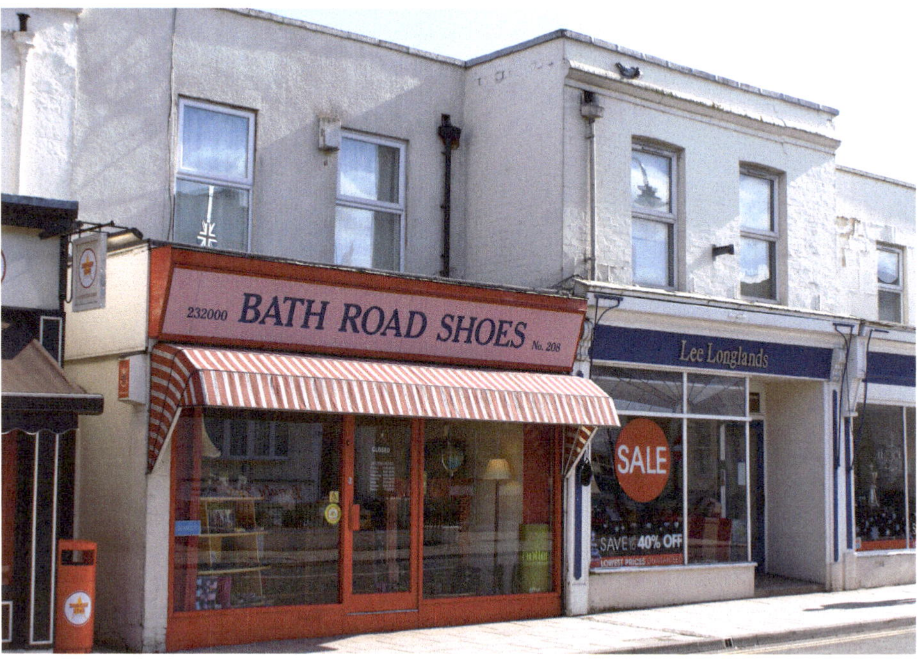

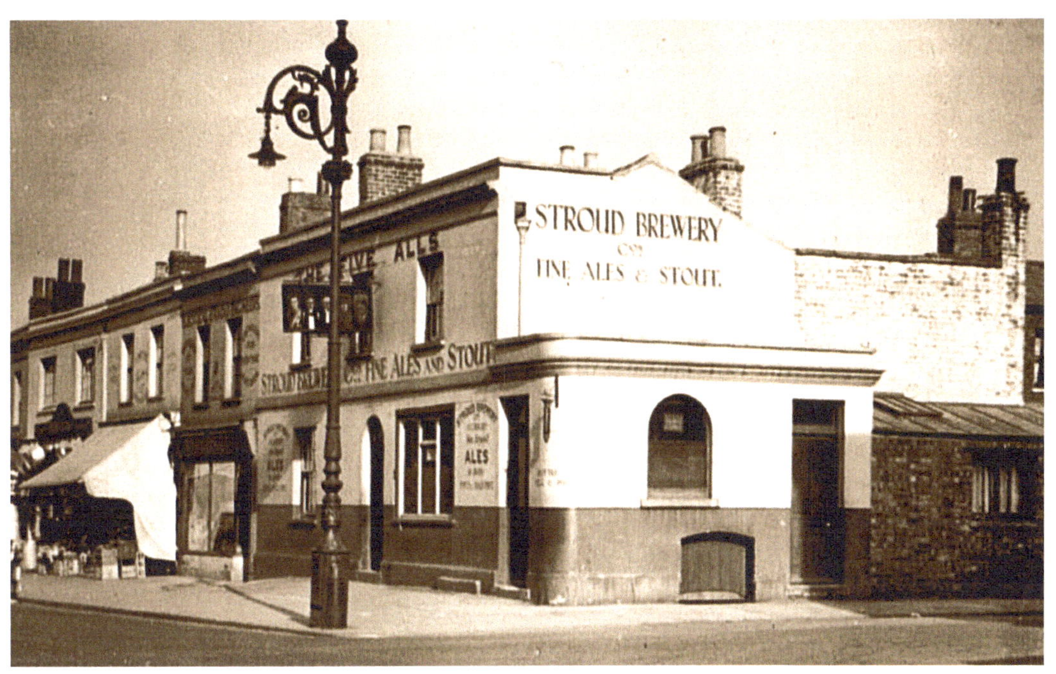

Five Alls, Bath Road

The Five Alls, like the Crown & Cushion, was once a Cranham Brewery pub. Passing through the successive ownership of Godsell & Sons, Stroud Brewery, West Country and Whitbread Breweries, the pub is now owned by a pubco. Sadly, a West Country Breweries 'Best in the West' ceramic plaque inlaid into the wall mysteriously disappeared a couple of years ago.

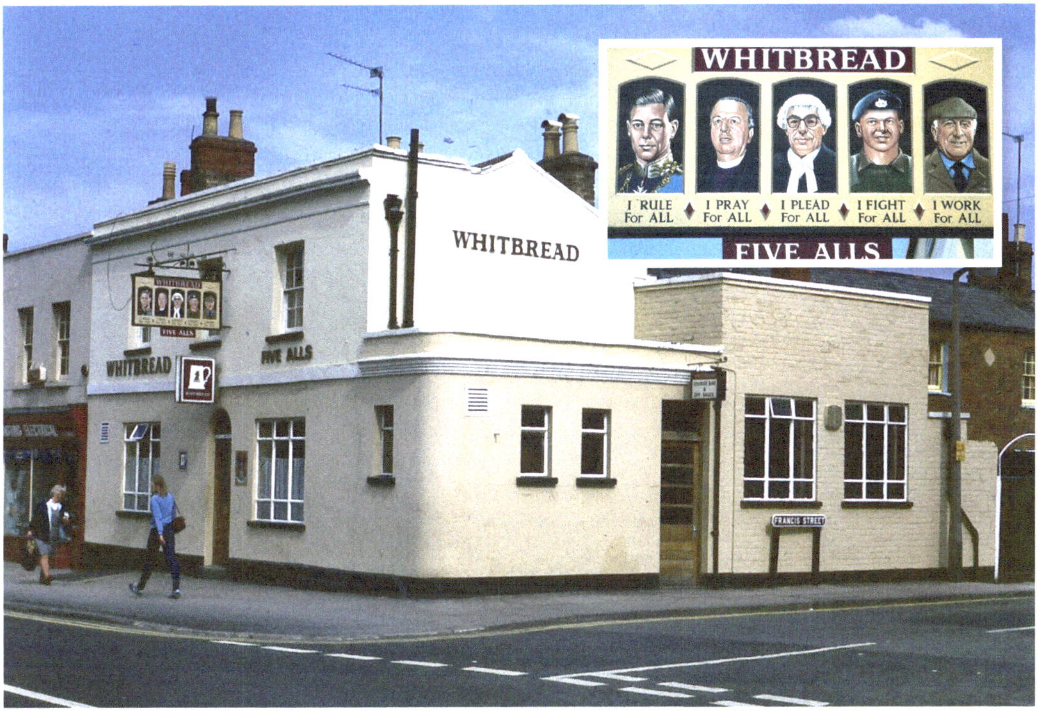

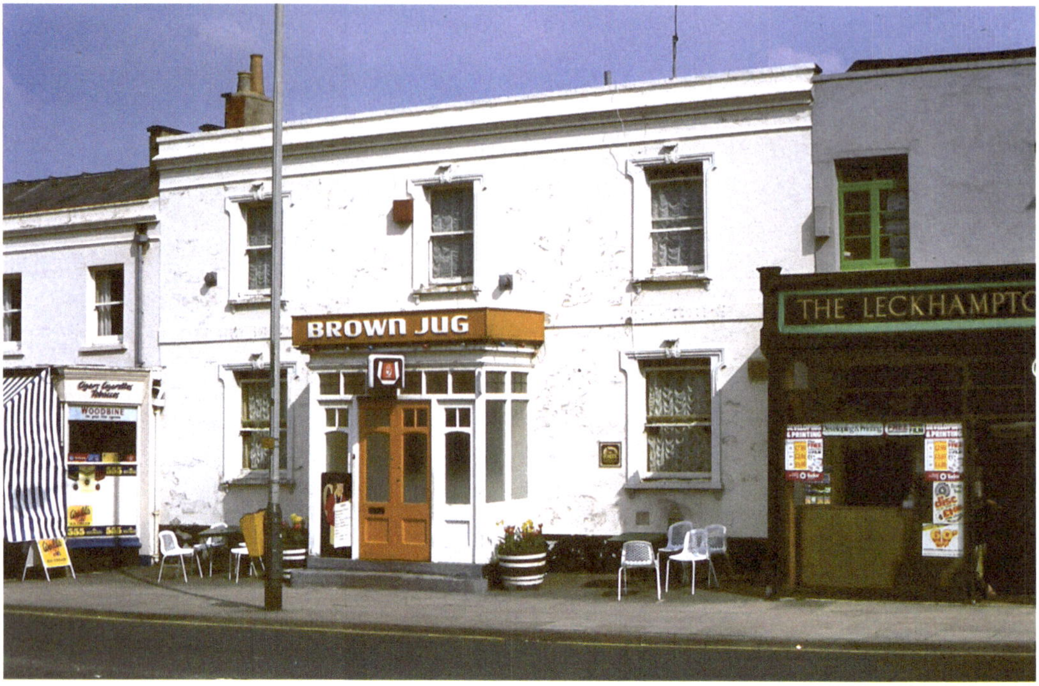

Brown Jug, Bath Road

Adolphus White, with his wife and ten children, is recorded as a brewer at the pub at the end of the nineteenth century. After his death in April 1895 the Brown Jug was briefly supplied with beers from Cripps & Co. Cirencester Brewery. Samuel Allsopp & Sons of Burton upon Trent owned the Brown Jug in the 1920s, and a merger with Ind Coope in 1934 resulted in Burton ales being available at the pub until it was acquired by Wadworth & Co. of Devizes in the 1990s.

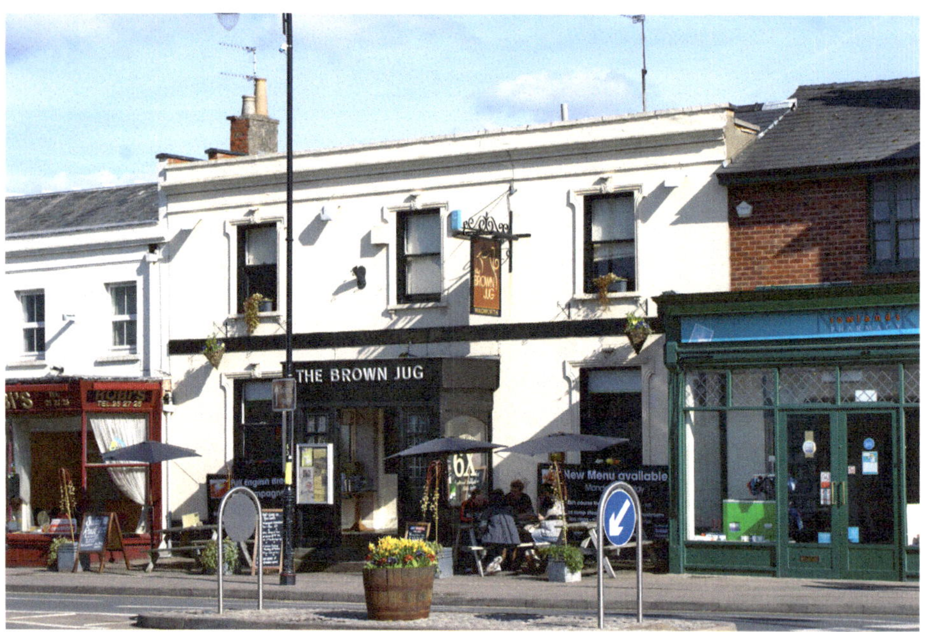

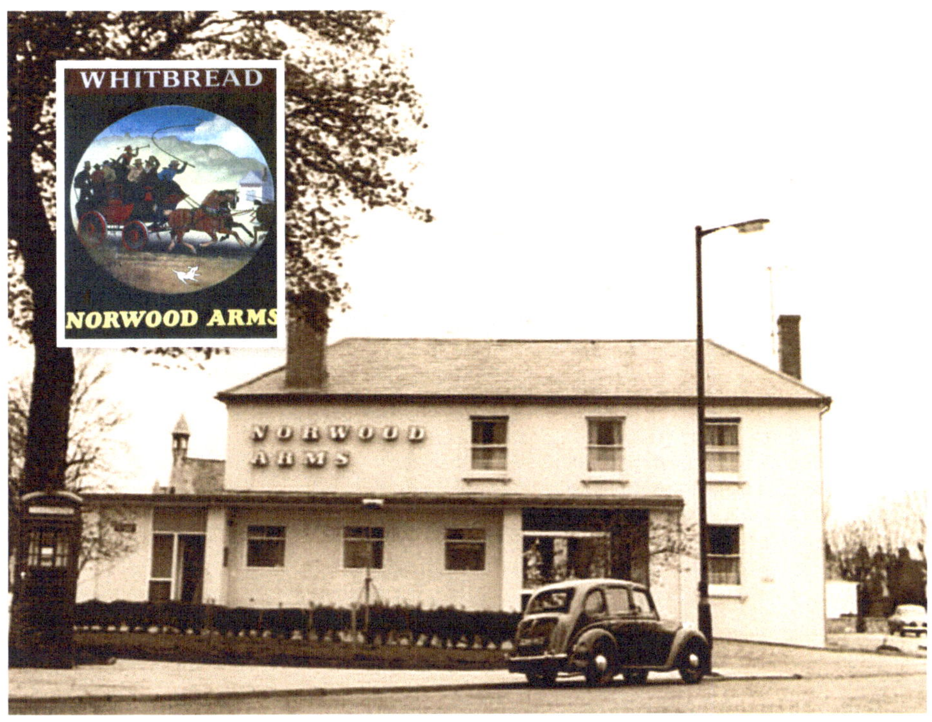

Norwood Arms, Leckhampton Road

The Norwood Arms has been extensively altered and modernised over the years. It is difficult to imagine that over a century ago there was a brewery on the premises. Harry Warner is listed as brewer and landlord at the Norwood Arms in 1903. Cheltenham District Light Railway opened their Leckhampton route in 1905, making it possible to travel to the Norwood by electric tram. The Norwood is now owned by Greene King.

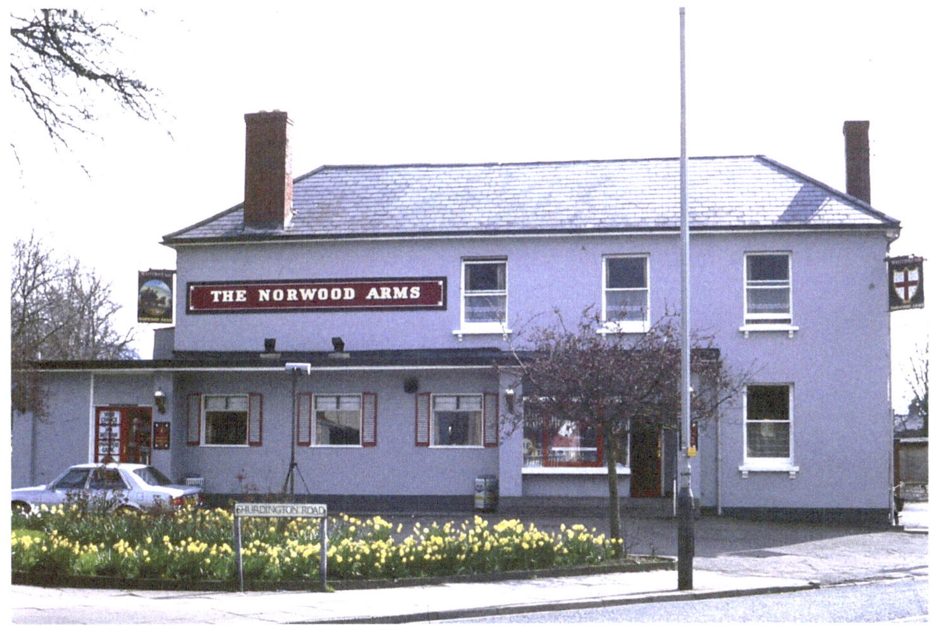

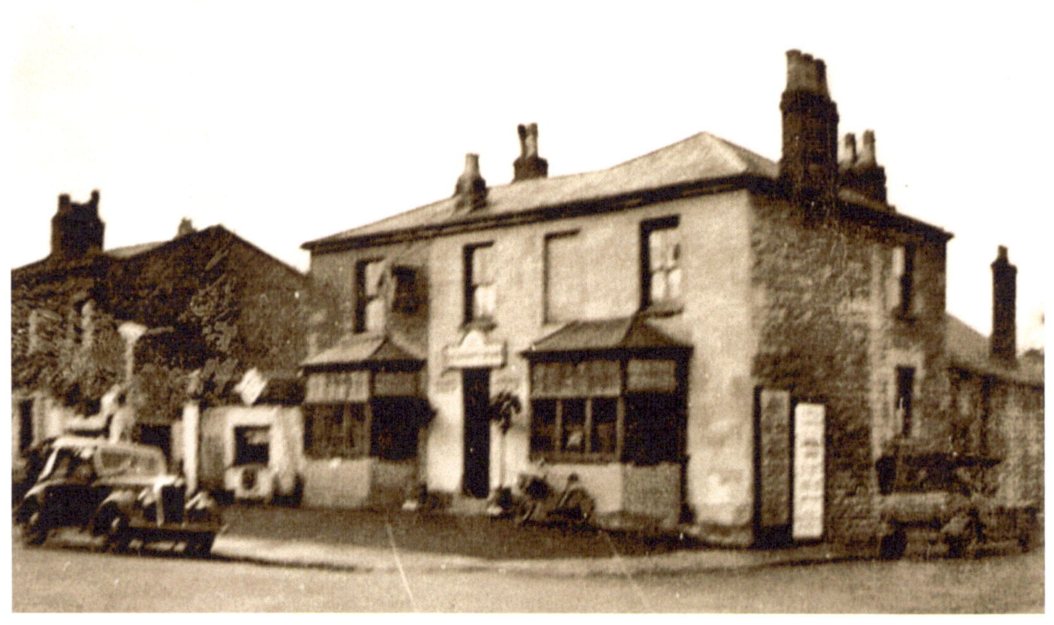

Leckhampton Inn, Shurdington Road

The Leckhampton Inn closed in April 2001. Residential apartments now occupy the site of the pub. In the early 1990s the Leckhampton Inn hosted the Cheltenham Folk Club and some well-known artists performed there including Martin Carthy and Kate Rusby. In May 1998 a dalek on a charity raising mission made a visit. A barman explained, 'We had to take his off wheels off and remove one of our doors to get him in.'

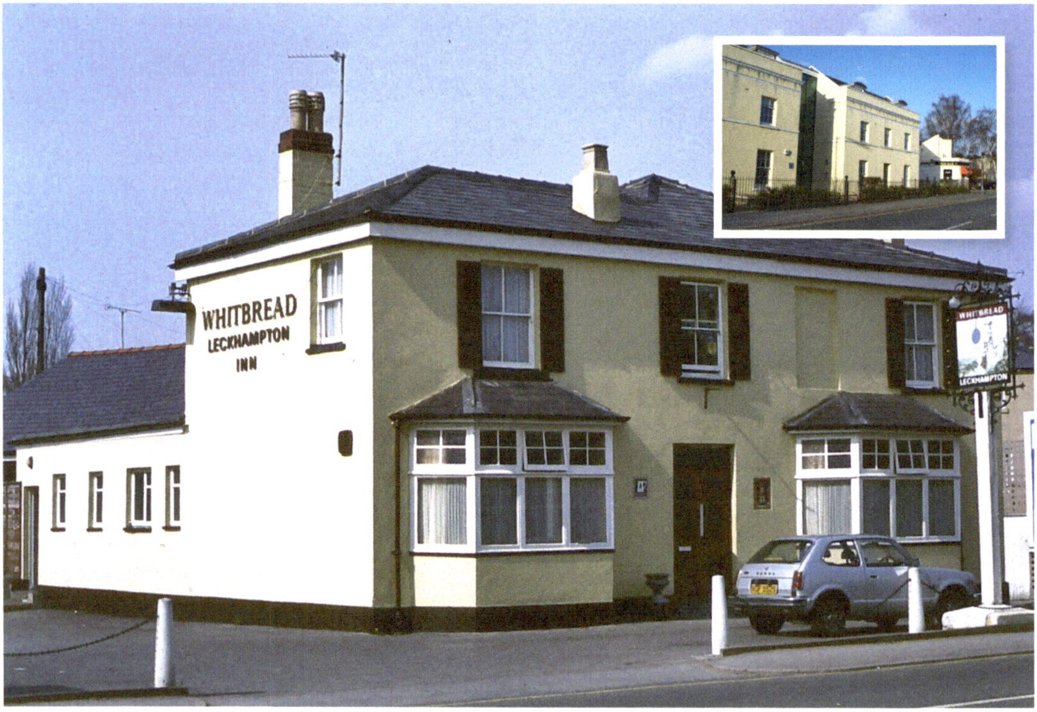

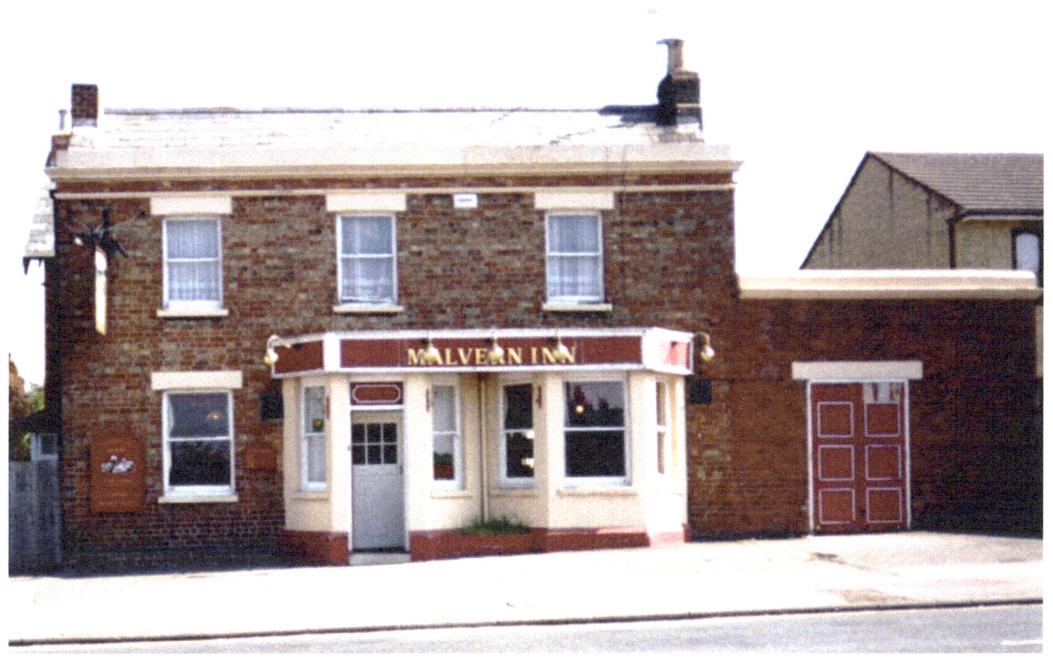

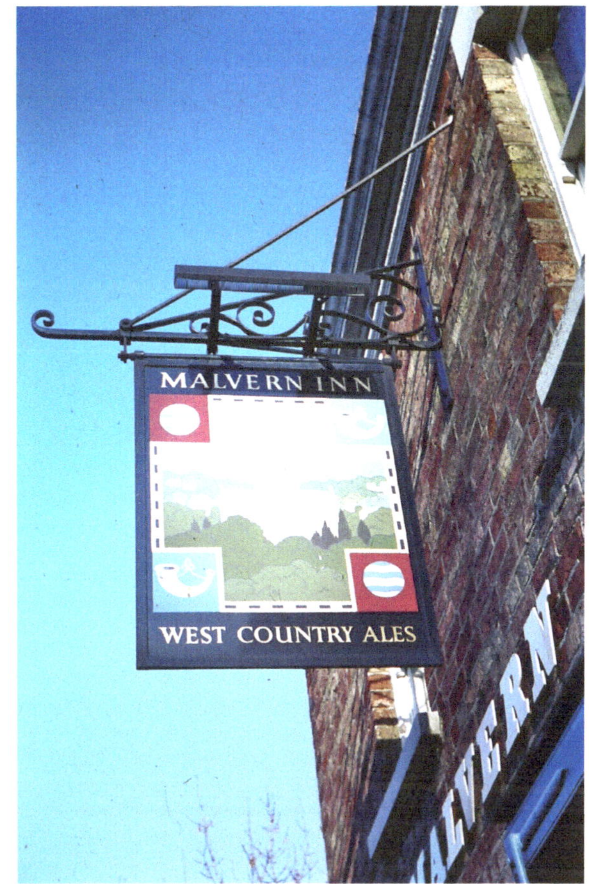

Malvern Inn, Leckhampton Road

Despite a determined campaign to keep the pub open, the Malvern Inn closed in September 1997 and the building is now residential. In March 1902 the Malvern Inn was frequented by local people with a grudge against Henry J. Dale of the Leckhampton Quarry Company. He had fenced off the Common Land on Leckhampton Hill, declaring it out of bounds. Probably fuelled by several pints Cheltenham Ales, the protesters left the pub and joined other protesters where they tore down his hillside residence, Tramway Cottage.

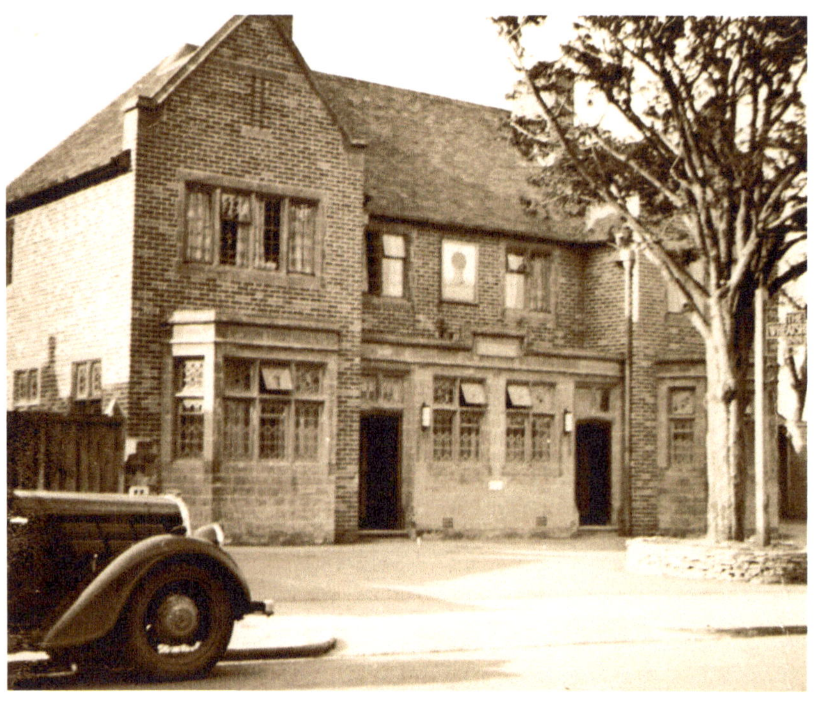

Wheatsheaf Inn, Old Bath Road

The wonderfully named D. J. Crump is listed as a brewer at the Wheatsheaf Inn in 1856. In the 1960s the pub's skittle alley was a popular venue for live music, known as Club 66 and then the Grotto. A regular visitor at Club 66 was Cheltonian Brian Jones, later to become guitarist in the Rolling Stones. The same skittle alley held the World Shove Ha'Penny Championships from 1988 until about 1998. The Wheatsheaf is now owned by Wadworth of Devizes, Wiltshire.

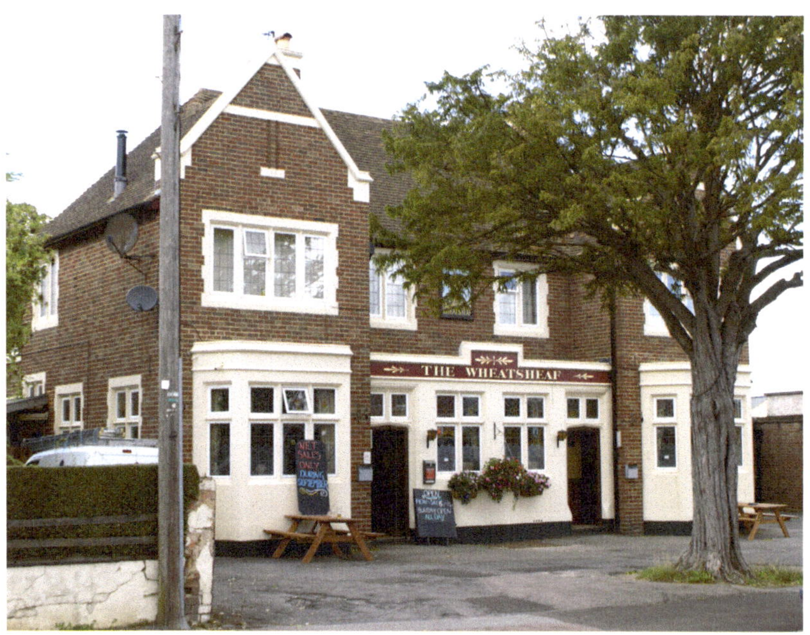

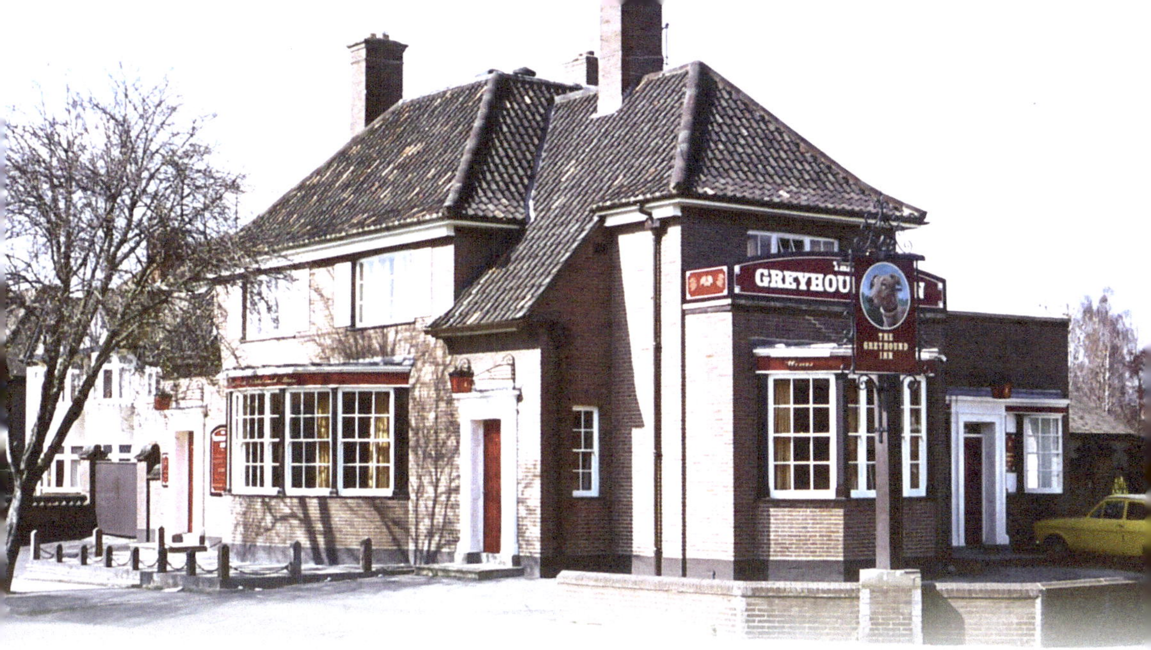

CHAPTER 5

All Saints, Pittville, Prestbury & Whaddon

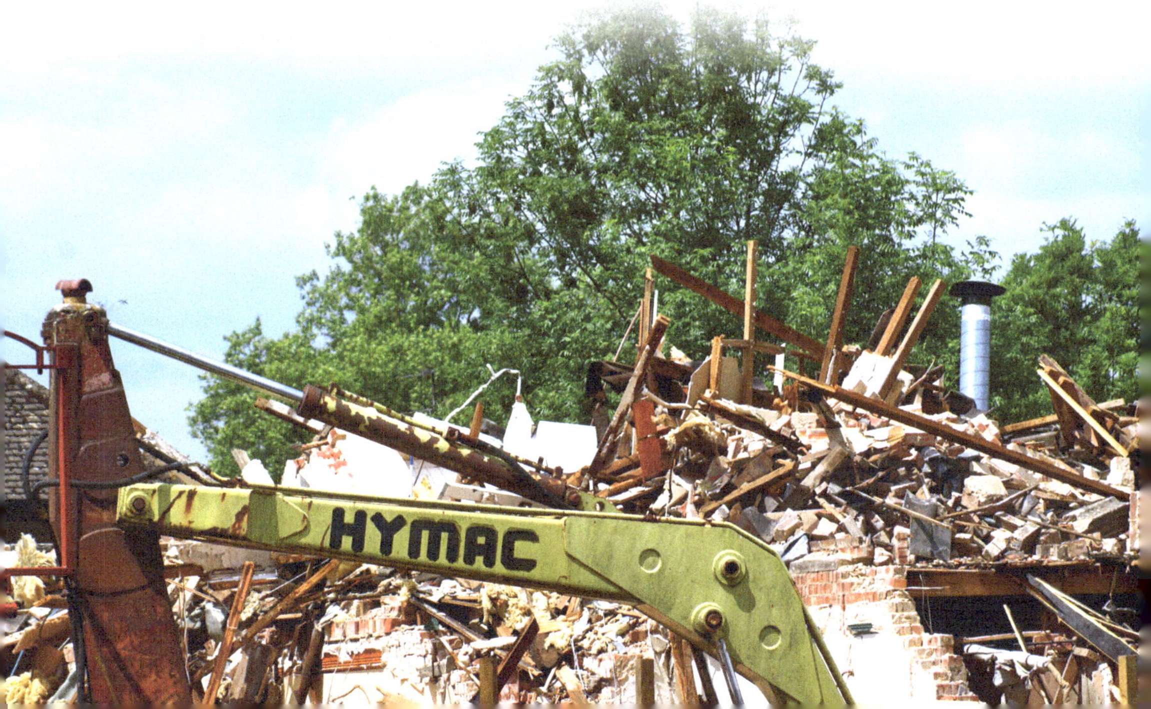

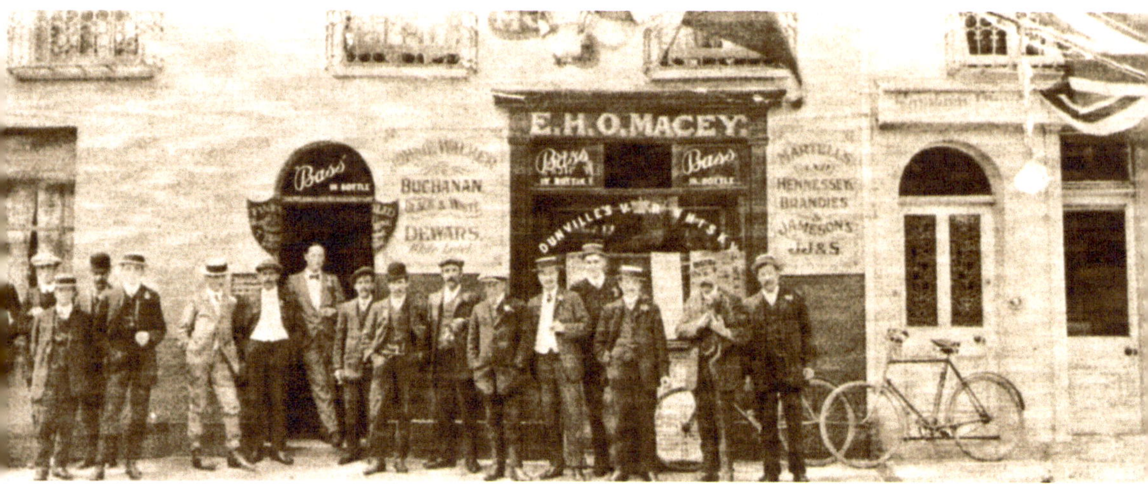

Pittville Hotel, Pittville Street

The Pittville Hotel was demolished in 1968 as part of a clearance scheme on the western side of Portland Street to create space for car parking. However, the most recent date that I can find it trading as a pub is in 1939 when John Wright was landlord. The photograph shows the pub in 1910 decked out for the Coronation of King George V. The immaculately dressed landlord, Mr Macey, is standing in the doorway.

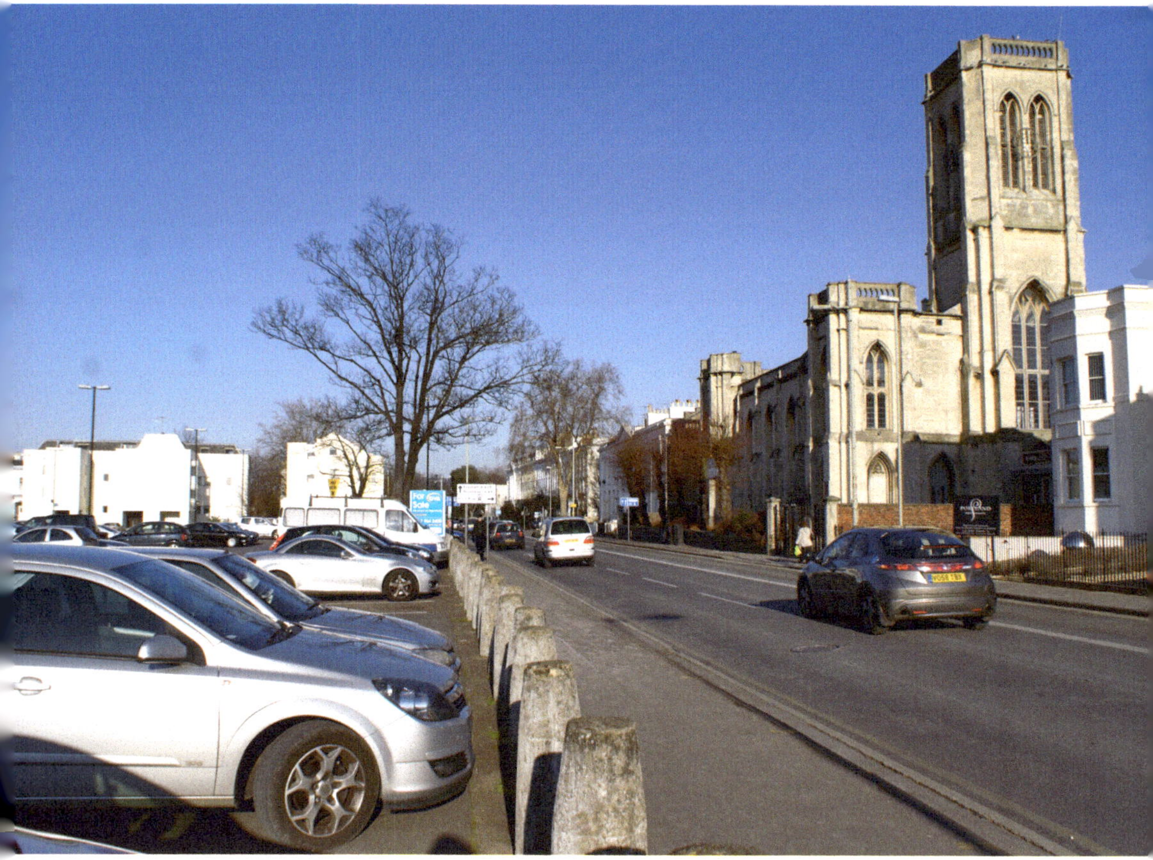

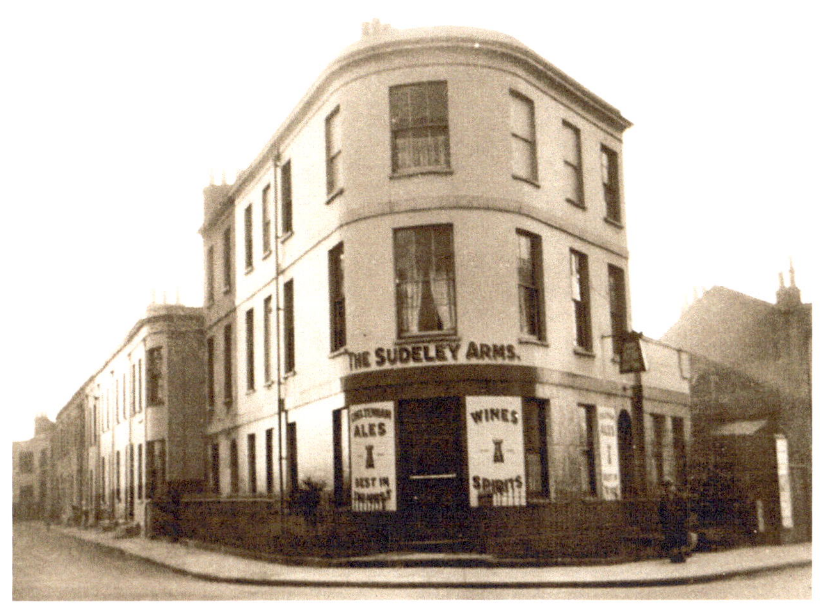

Sudeley Arms, Prestbury Road

The Sudeley Arms, on the corner of Prestbury Road and Portland Square, was tied to the Nailsworth Brewery in Edwardian times. Gustav Holst, composer of The Planets Suite, was born nearby in 1874, I wonder if he ever nipped into the pub for a pint? In 1960 Mrs Matilda Craddock of the Sudeley Arms, then aged ninety-seven, was England's oldest licensee – perhaps she knew Gustav Holst!

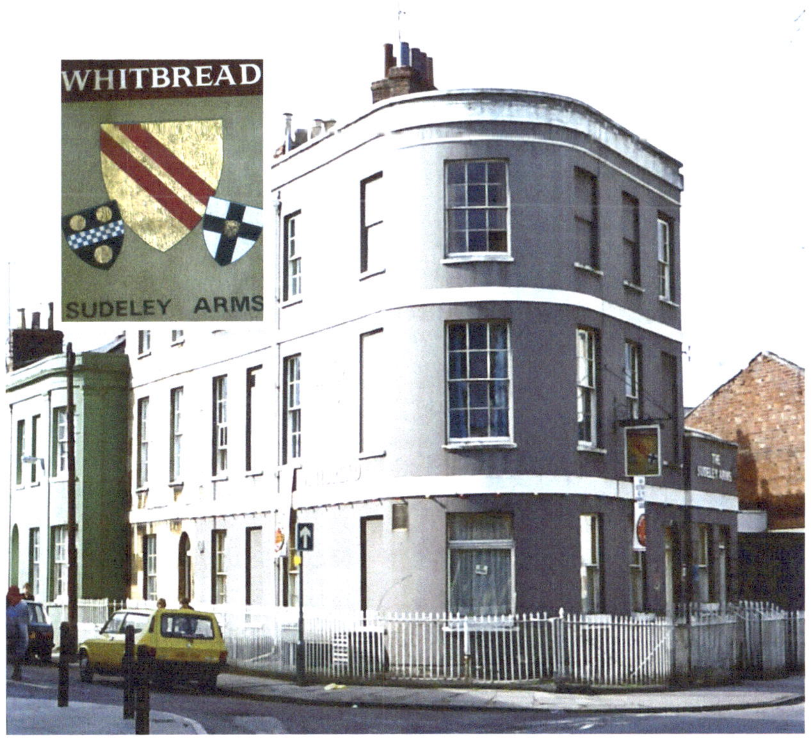

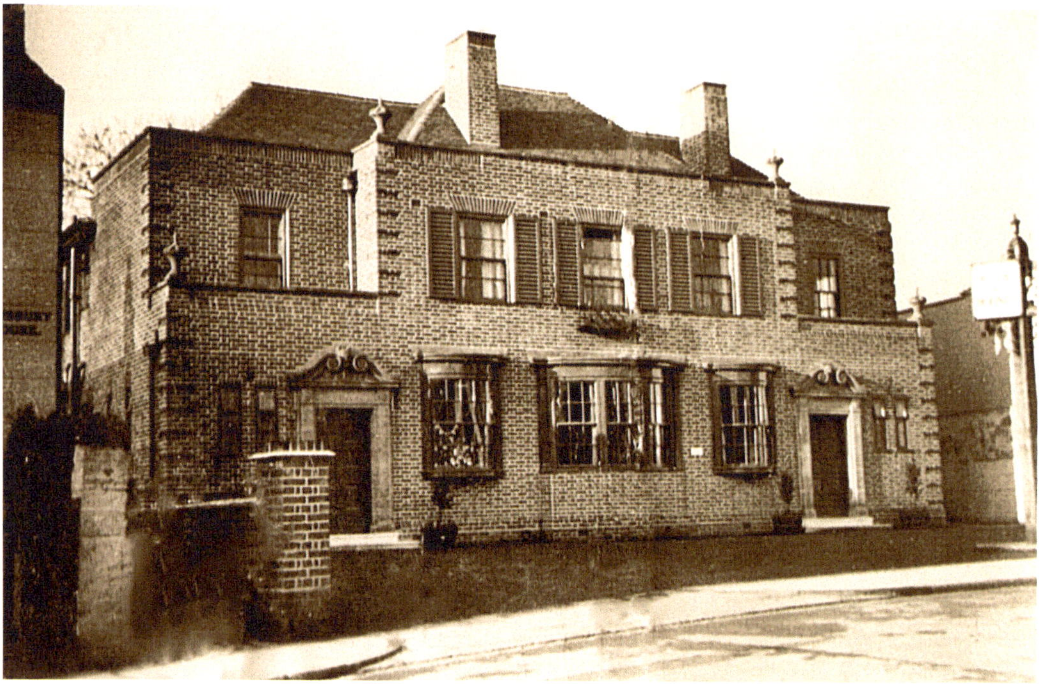

Fox & Hounds, Prestbury Road

The original Fox & Hounds was replaced with a much larger, symmetrically designed, brick-built building commissioned by the Cheltenham Original Brewery in the 1930s. Today it is one of the last surviving 'estate' pubs in the town – the nearby Greyhound and Cat & Fiddle have recently been demolished. A relaxing of the restrictive 'beer tie' imposed by pub companies and an open market rent review would help secure the future of these community pubs.

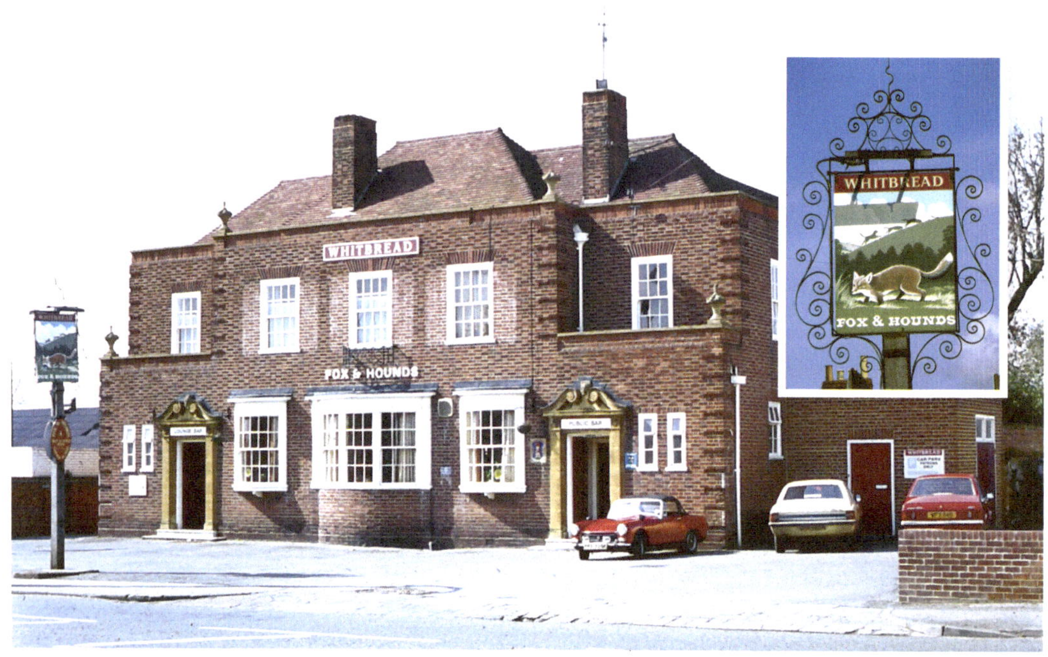

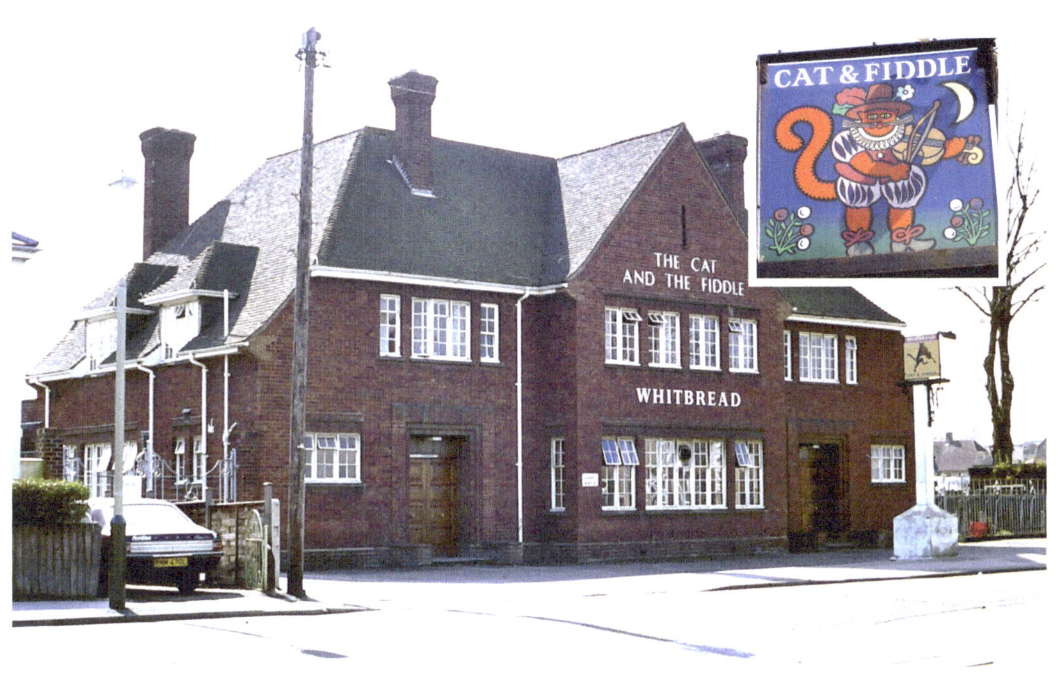

Cat & Fiddle, Whaddon Road

The Cat & Fiddle was demolished in February 2012 to make way for a residential development. The large brick building was built for the Cheltenham & Hereford Brewery to serve the Whaddon Estate. It was acquired by Arkell's Kingsdown Brewery of Swindon in 1999 but, unfortunately, trade failed to pick up, despite being very popular when Cheltenham Town Football Club played across the road at their Whaddon Road ground. Another community pub lost.

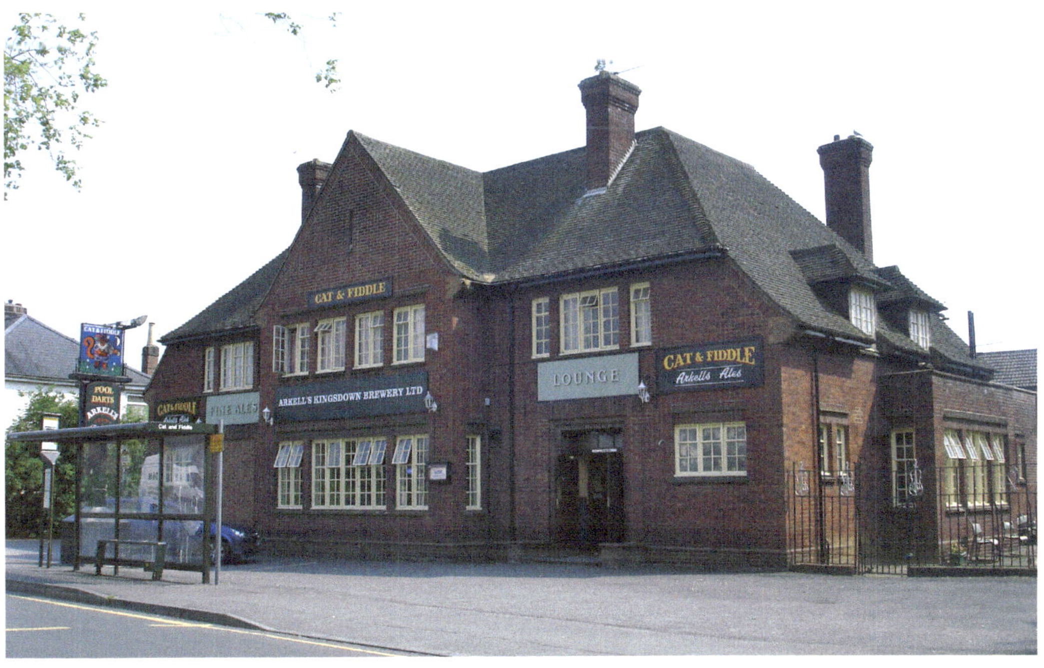

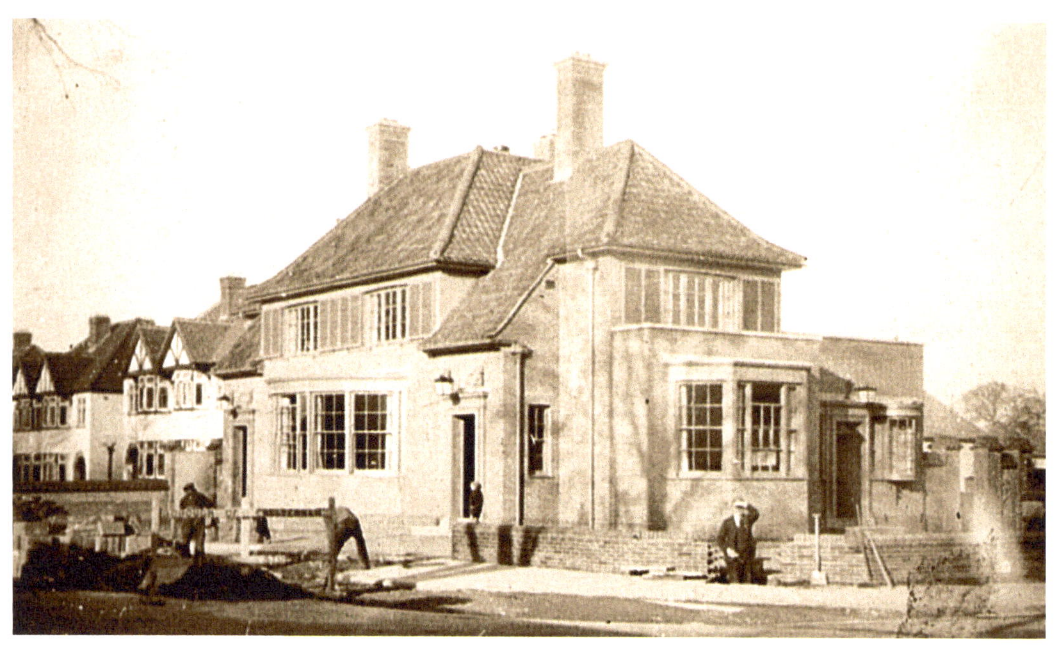

Greyhound Inn, Hewlett Road

In February 2012 the site of the Greyhound Inn was just a pile of rubble. The once-popular Greyhound Inn was acquired by a property developer whose sole intention was to run the pub down so that he could redevelop the site for housing. His plans met with opposition from the Cheltenham MP, CAMRA, local residents and even the Borough Council. When his application was refused he appealed and, somehow, won. Premature demolition followed.

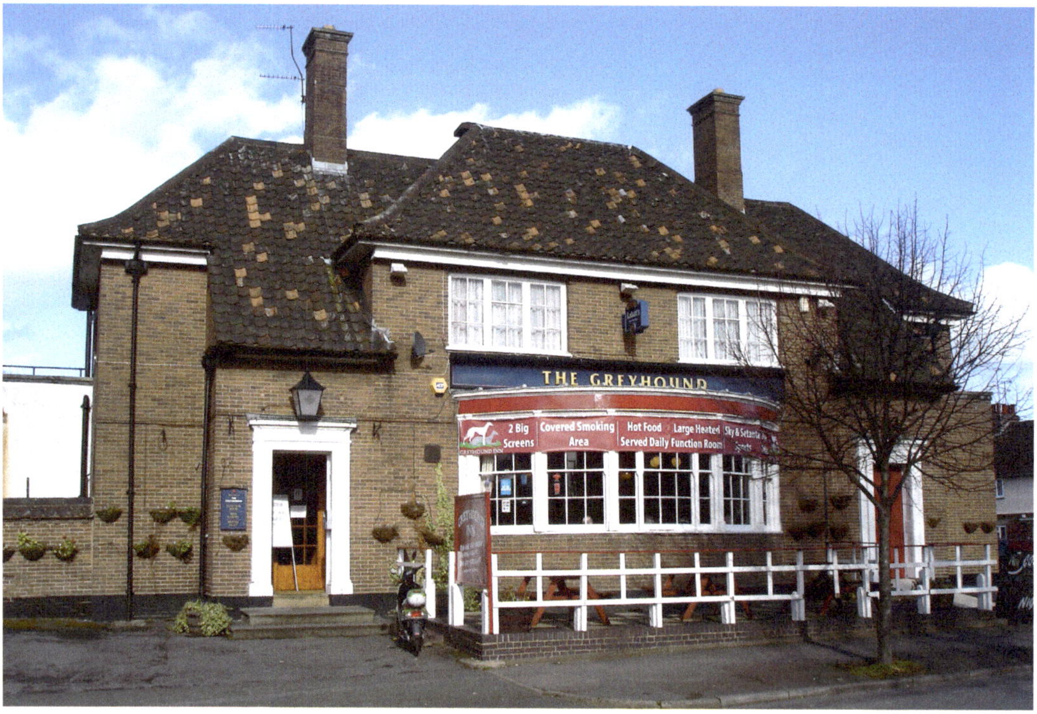

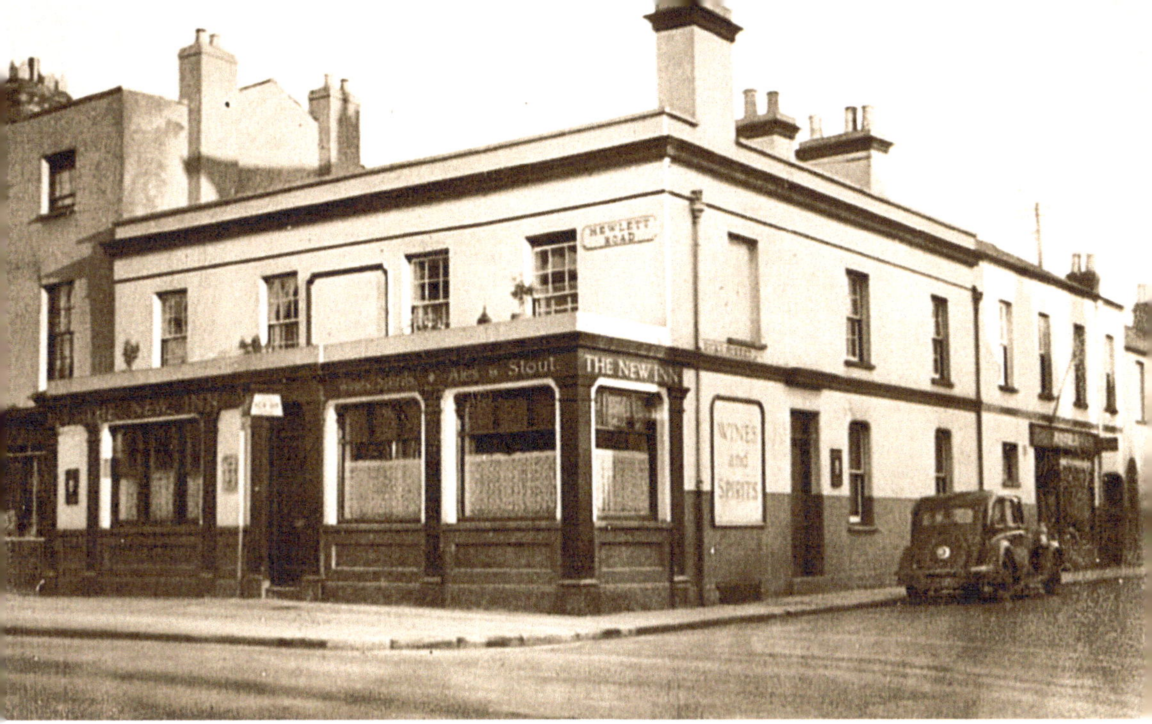

New Inn, Hewlett Road

Now called the Fiery Angel, the pub had a previous incarnation in the 1980s and 1990s as the Pump & Optic. However, for at least 150 years it traded as the New Inn and it was originally owned by Dowles' Carlton Brewery, whose premises was located less than a quarter of a mile away. Through a series of takeovers the Anglo-Bavarian Brewery in Somerset were the new owners of the New Inn in 1903. Beers were certainly less interesting in the 1970s when the pub was tied to Whitbread!

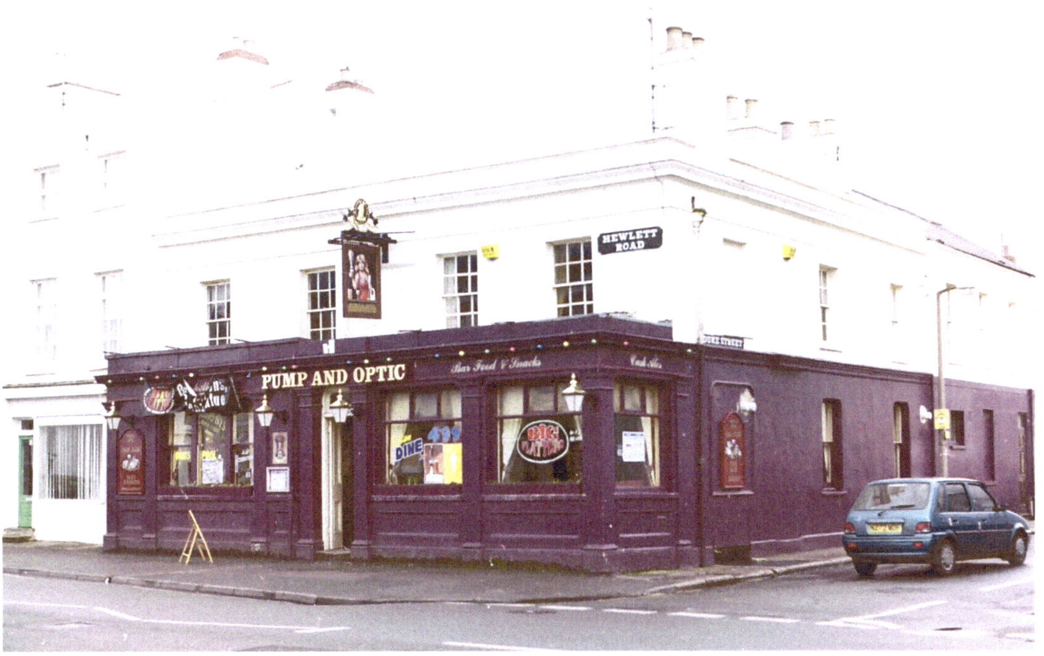

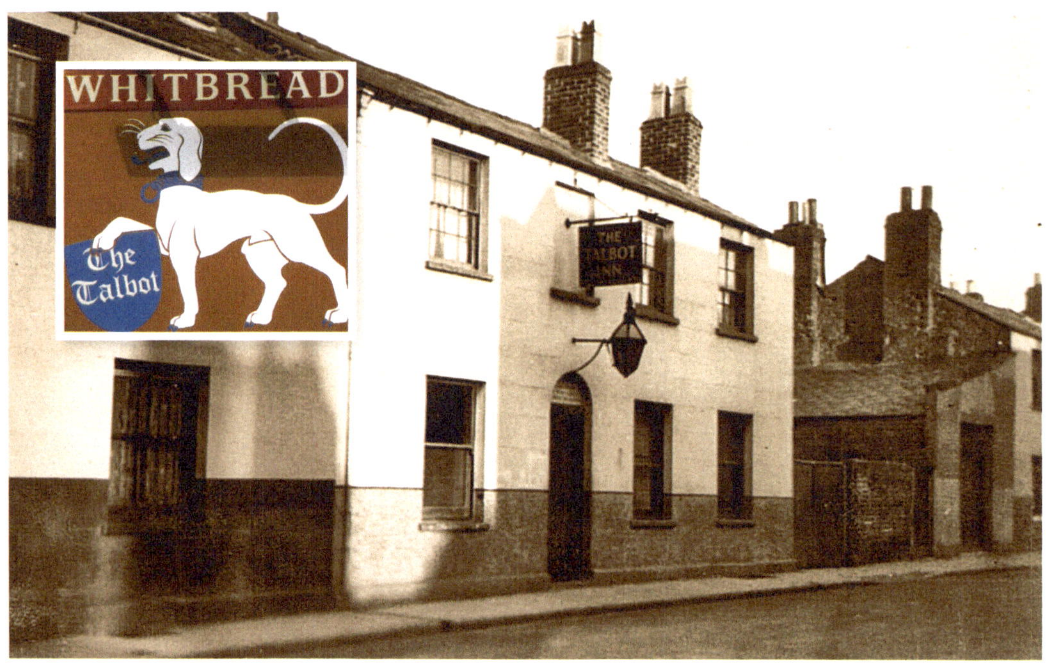

Talbot Inn, Duke Street

The Talbot Inn, on the north side of Duke Street, a few yards from the New Inn (now Fiery Angel), closed in February 1984. It had a reputation as a cider drinkers' pub. The favoured tipple was Bulmer's Traditional Cider served from a 5-gallon plastic barrel for about 34 pence a pint. No 'ice and a slice' or foreign 'pear' ciders in those days!

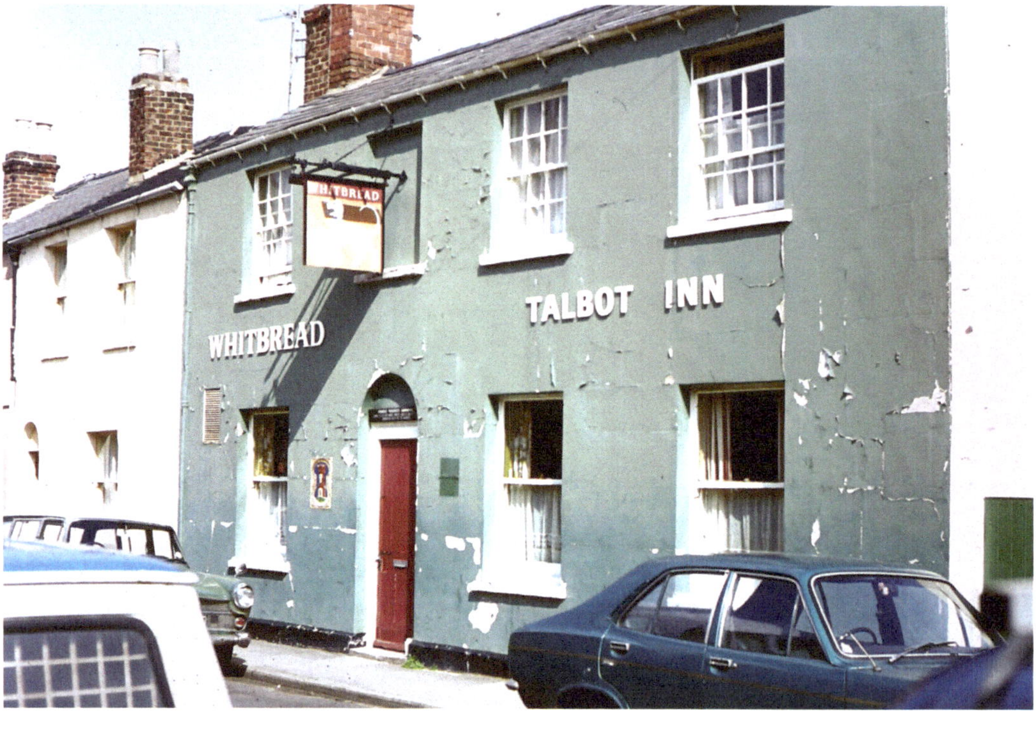

Princes Plume, Princes Street

The Princes Plume was an end-of-terrace pub on the western side of Princes Street near Cheltenham Cricket Club's Victoria Ground. Nailsworth Brewery owned the pub in 1897, the year when the formative CCC played W. G. Graces' X1 at their ground – perhaps William Gilbert himself had a pint at the Princes Plume after the match! The Victoria Ground held first-class county games in the 1920s and 1930s, a time when Cheltenham Ales were on tap at the pub. The Princes Plume closed in the early 1970s.

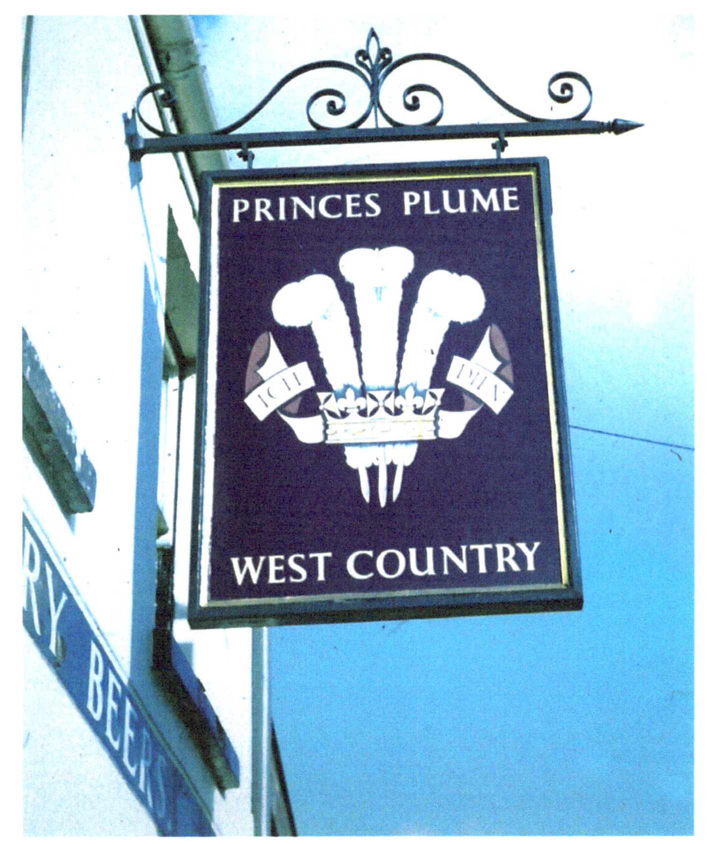

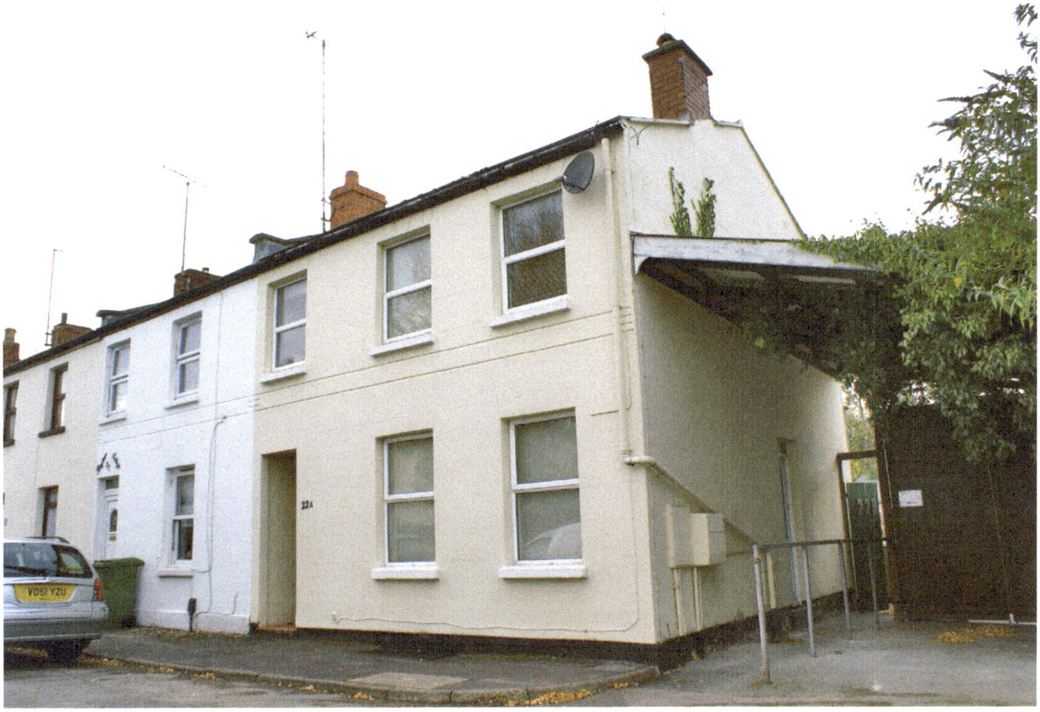

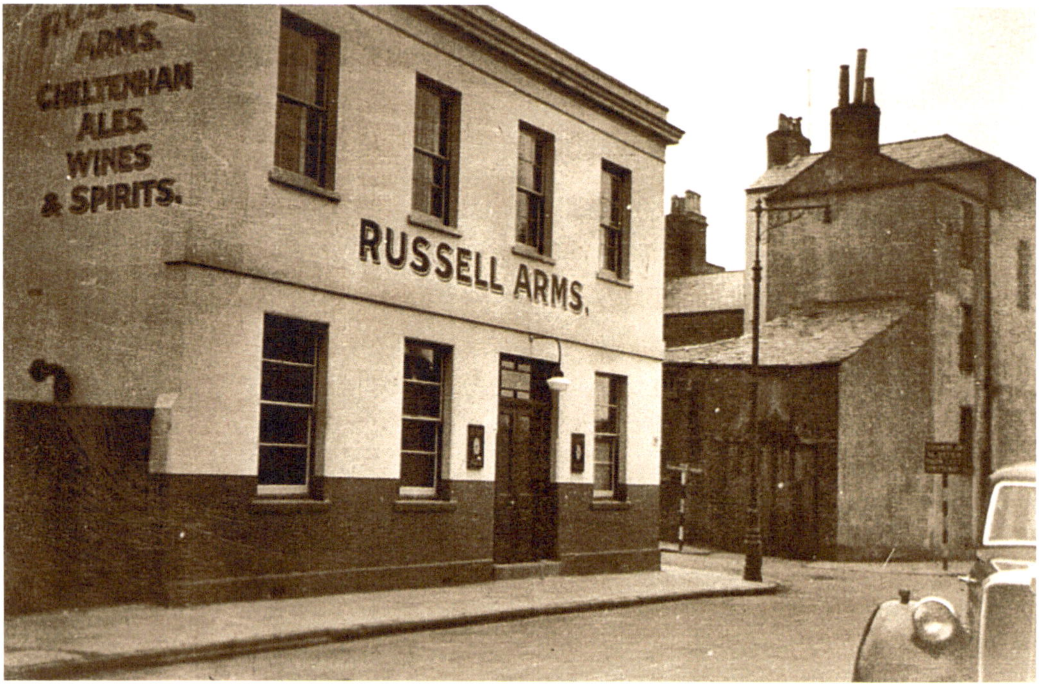

Russell Arms, Hales Road

The Russell Arms is located on the corner of Hales Road and Upper Park Street, close to the junction with London Road. Note the colourful ceramic plaque to the right of the door in the 1970s photograph. These West Country Breweries 'Best in the West' signs are becoming increasingly rare, having mysteriously disappeared in recent years from the Five Alls in Bath Road and the Royal Well Tavern. Thankfully the plaque at the Russell Arms is still *in situ*.

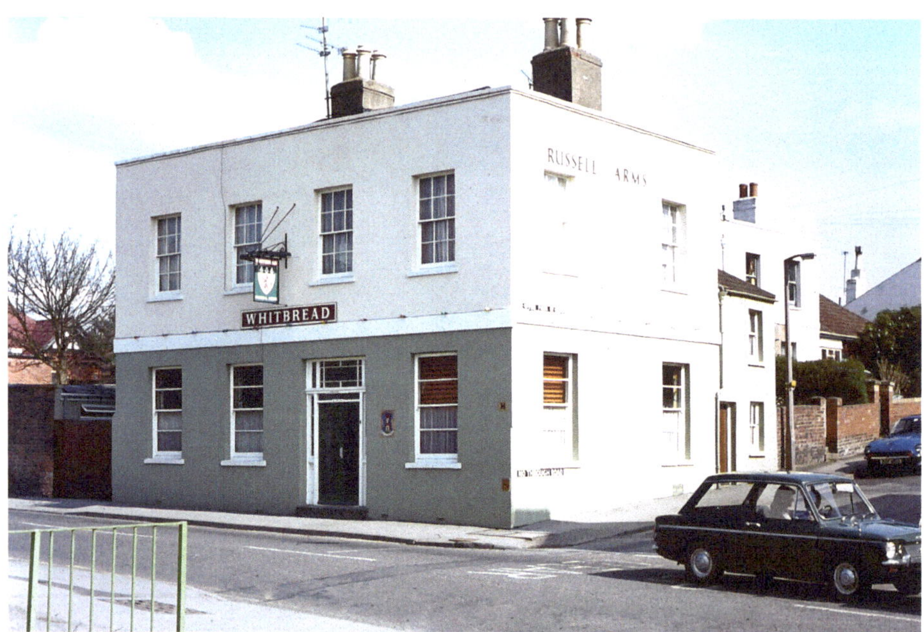

Crown Inn, Upper Park Street

The Crown Inn was known by regulars as the 'Little Crown', a 'hard to find' pub just off the London Road. The Crown is still licensed but now trades privately as the Cheltenham Motor Club. The club sells real ales and was nominated by the Campaign for Real Ale (CAMRA) as one of the finalists for National Club of the Year 2007.

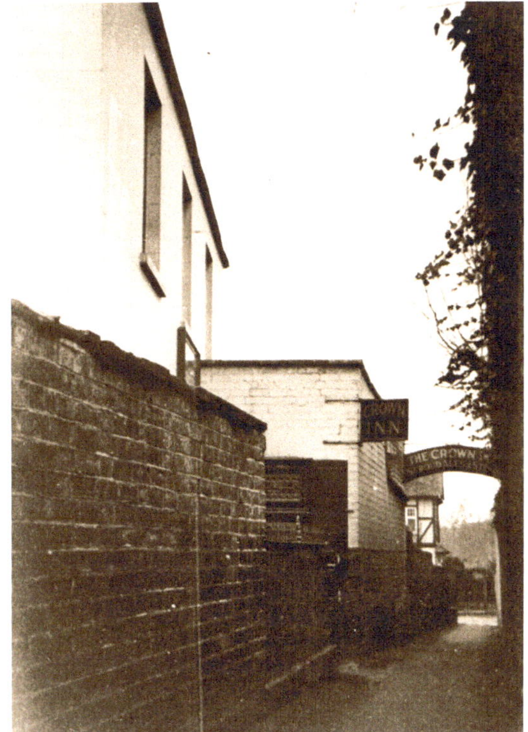

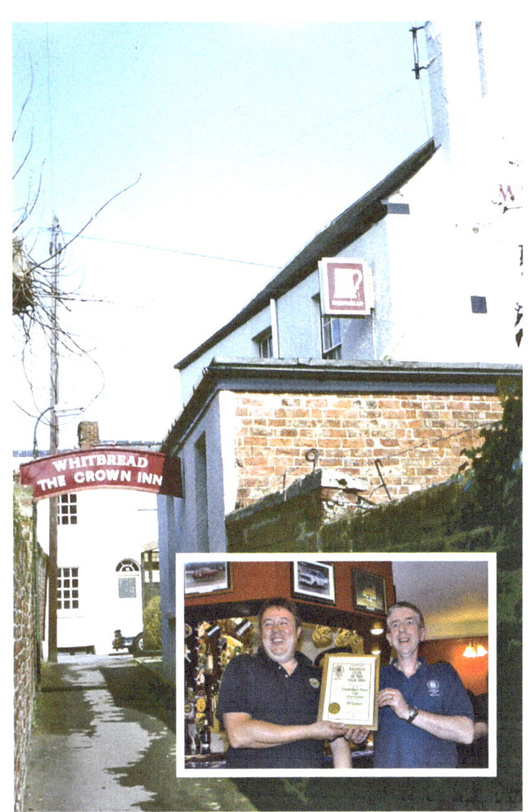

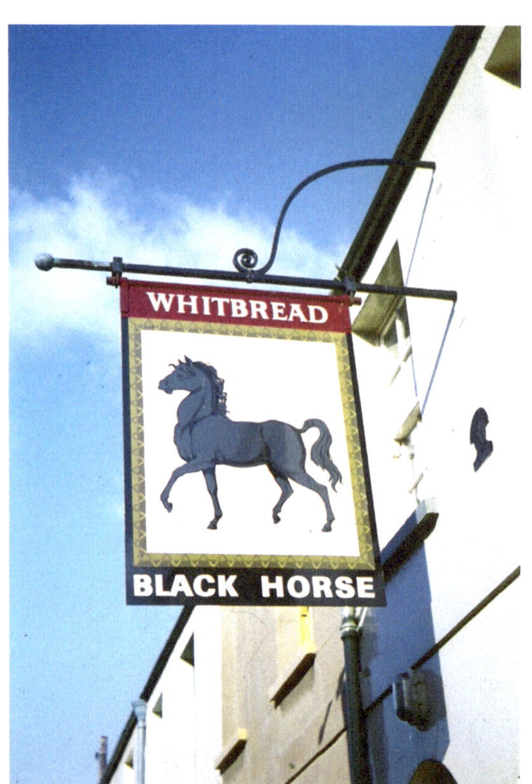

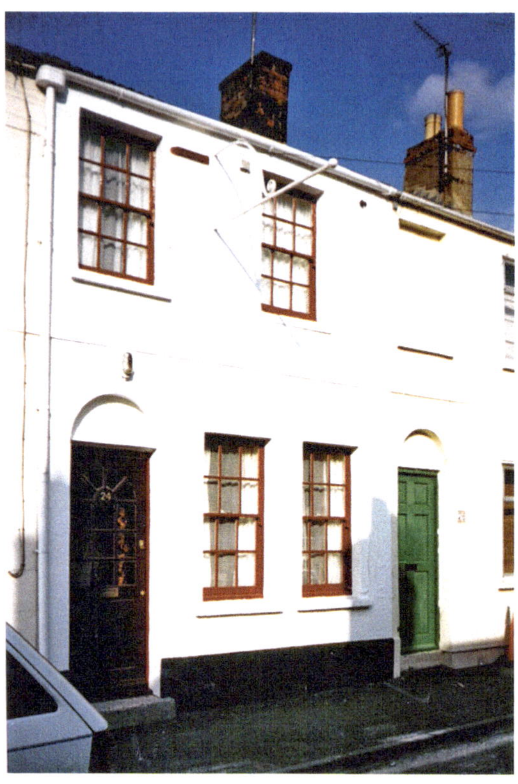

Black Horse Inn, Rosehill Street

The Black Horse must have been a strong contender for the title of the smallest pub in Cheltenham. At the end of the nineteenth century it was owned by the Albion Brewery which was located near the town gasworks in Gloucester Road. Ownership later passed to the Cheltenham Original Brewery, and when the Black Horse closed in the early 1970s it was a Whitbread pub. The ornamental metal bracket which once held the pub sign is still *in situ,* some forty years or so after closure.

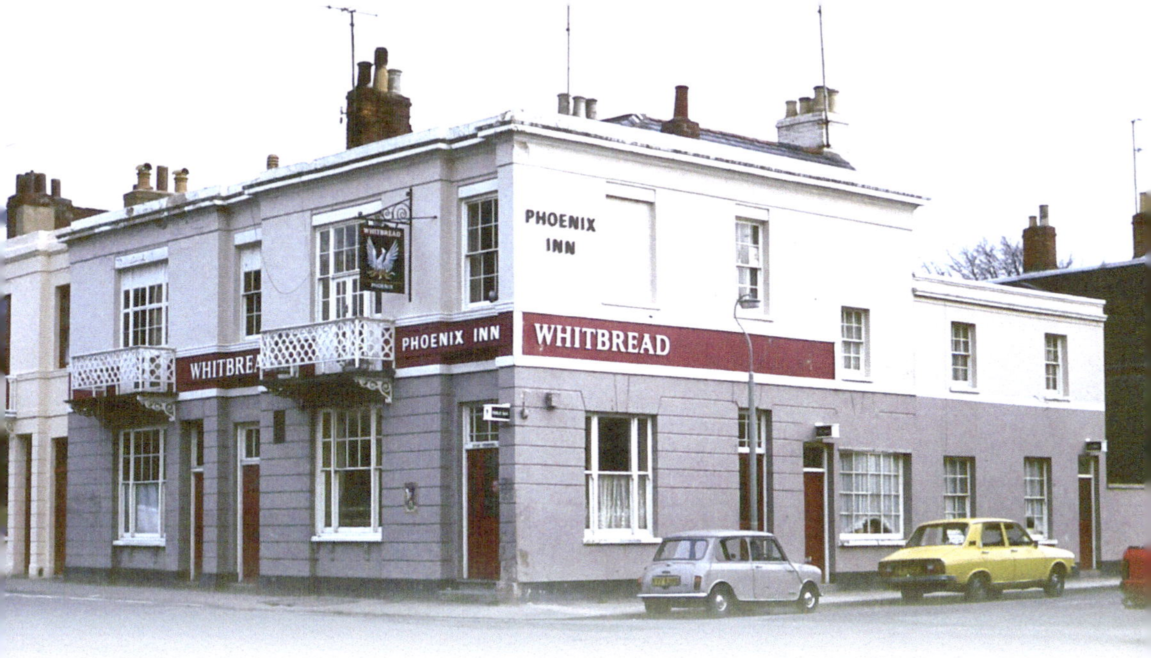

CHAPTER 6

Bayshill, Lansdown, The Suffolks & Montpellier

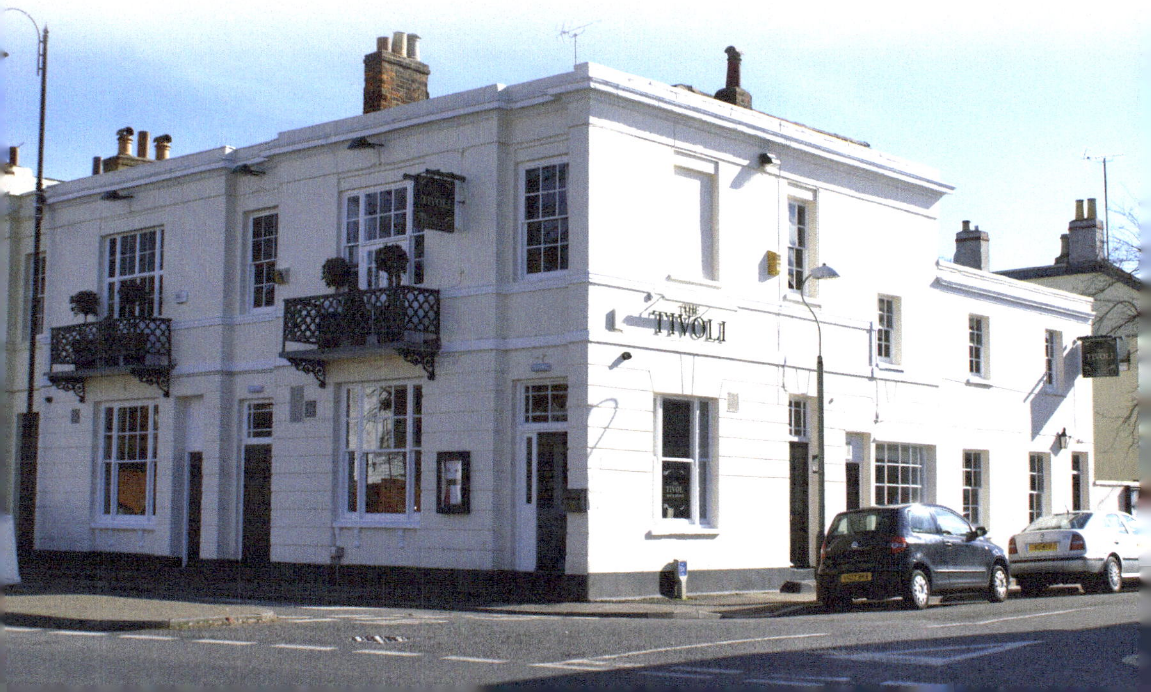

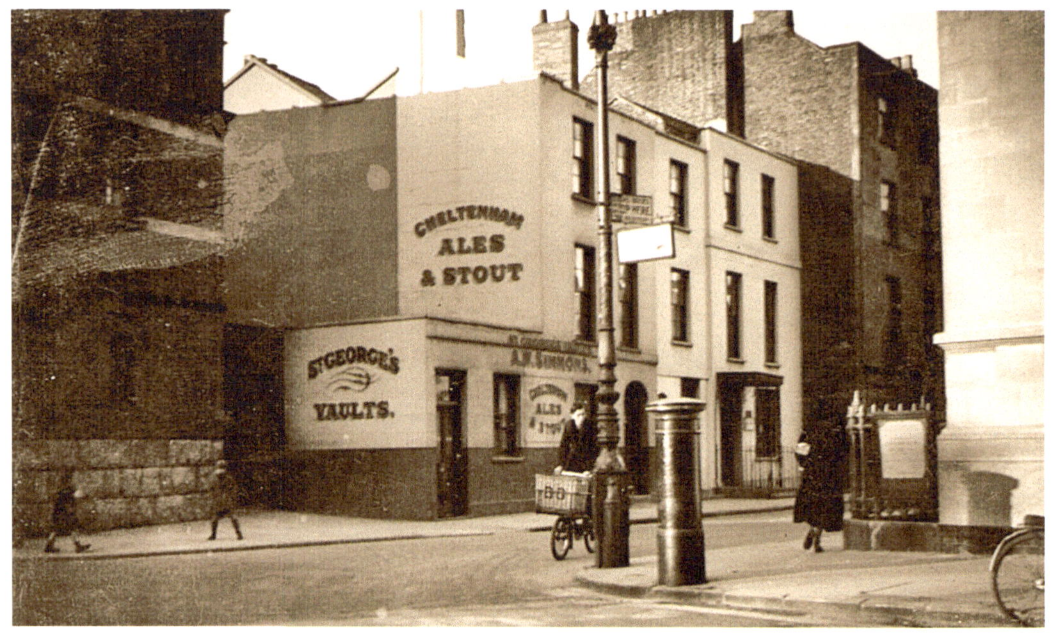

St George's Vaults, St George's Place.

Originally known as St George's Wine Vaults, the pub is still trading. Roger and Sue Bishop, well known for their charity fundraising, were popular licensees at the St George's Vaults from 1983 to 2007. Opposite the St George's Vaults is a building which was once the Horse & Groom pub (the name is still visible, carved in stone). In the 1950s Stroud Ales could be drunk at the Horse & Groom and Cheltenham Ales at the St George's Vaults.

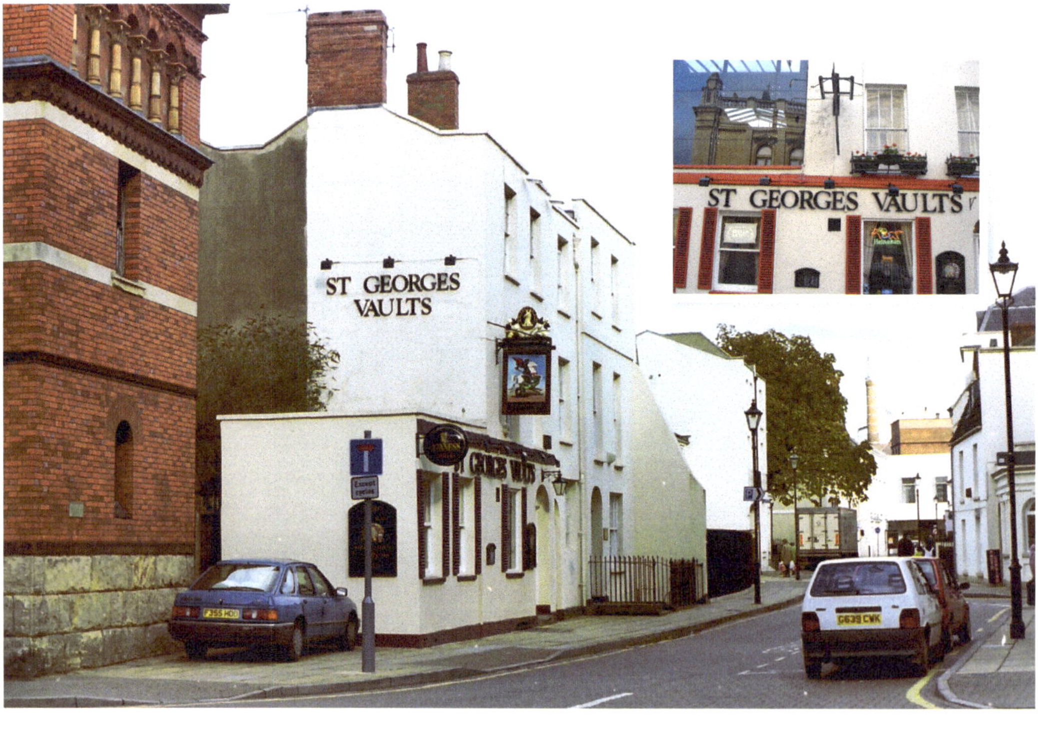

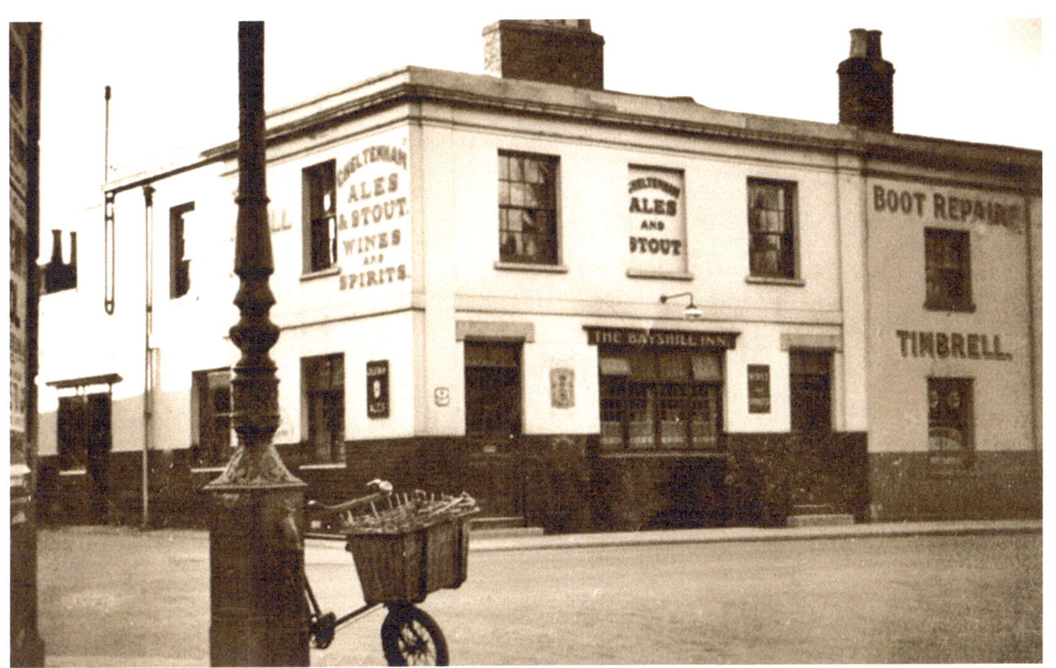

Bayshill Inn, St George's Place

The Bayshill is another Cheltenham pub that once brewed it own beer. An 1874 advert read, 'Bayshill Brewery. Home-Brewed old and mild ales delivered to any part of the town.' Passing into the ownership of the Cheltenham Brewery, the Bayshill Inn later became tied to Wadworth of Devizes. In 1979 a proposal to knock down the pub to make way for a ring road met with strong opposition, but fortunately the plans were shelved.

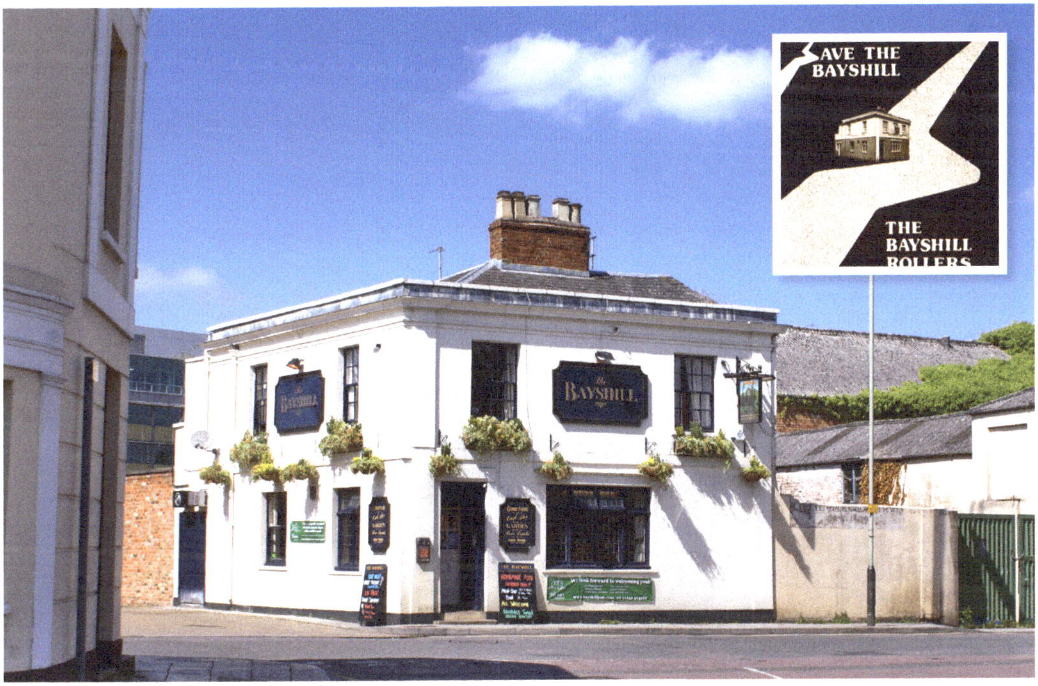

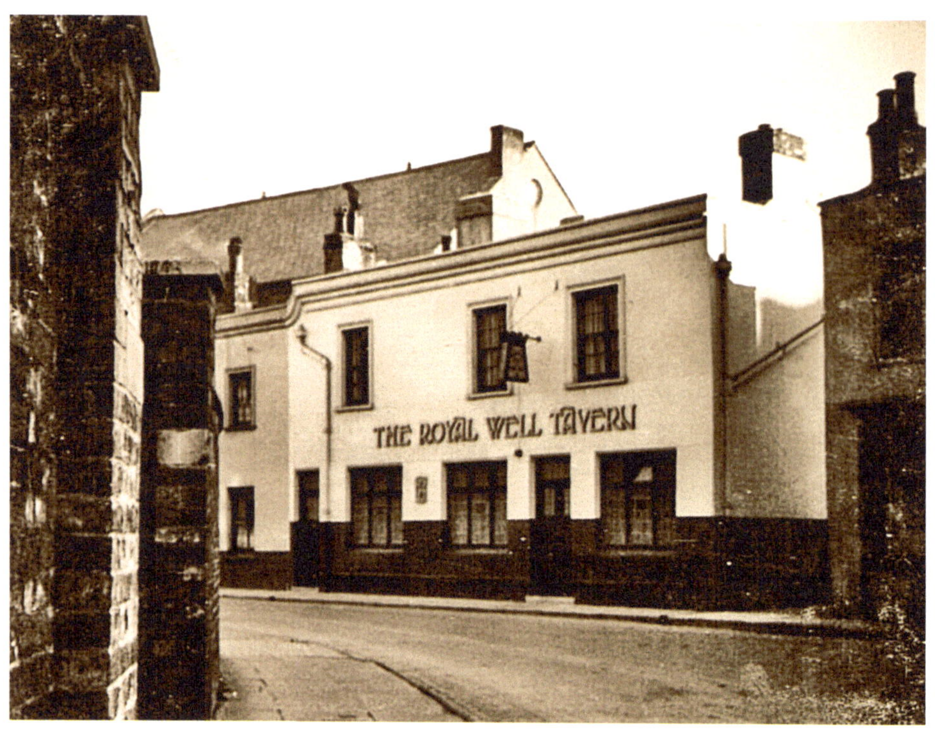

Royal Well Tavern, Royal Well Place

In the summer of 2008 the Royal Well Tavern had a makeover. The pub that just a few years previously had been advertising karaoke nights, open decks and big party DJ nights, was transformed into a gastropub offering such delights as French cured meats with celeriac remoulade and cornichons! During the alterations a West Country Ales plaque was removed. In February 2012 the Royal Well Tavern was due to reopen under new management.

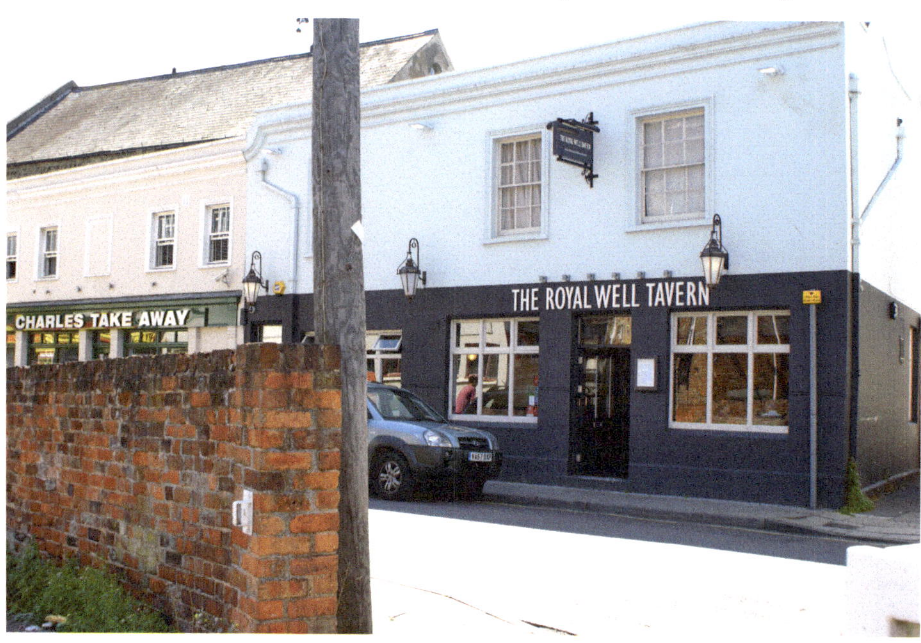

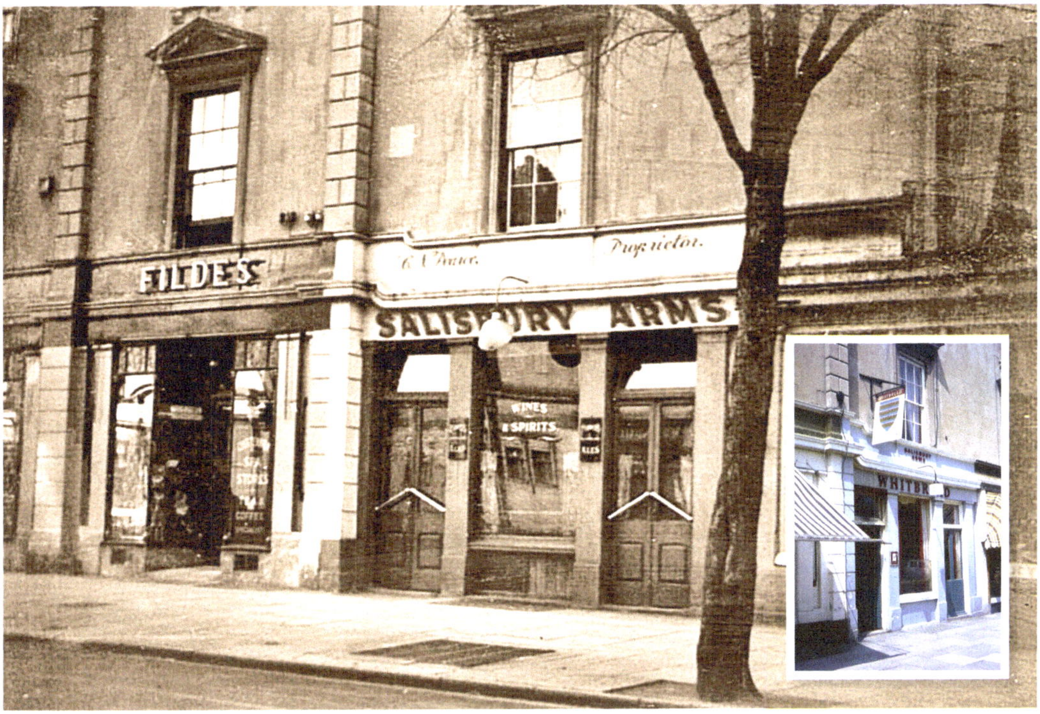

Salisbury Arms, Montpellier Street

After 164 years of trading as a pub the Salisbury closed in 2011. It was named after William Salisbury, the man who first opened the pub in 1847. In the 1990s it changed its name to the Tut & Shive, a real ale bar filled with strange items of junk and bygones. In 1998 the pub had another (clutter-free) makeover as Hydes Bar, eventually reverting back to the Salisbury. Set in a terrace of fine Regency architecture, the building is now a new cocktail and wine bar called Soho.

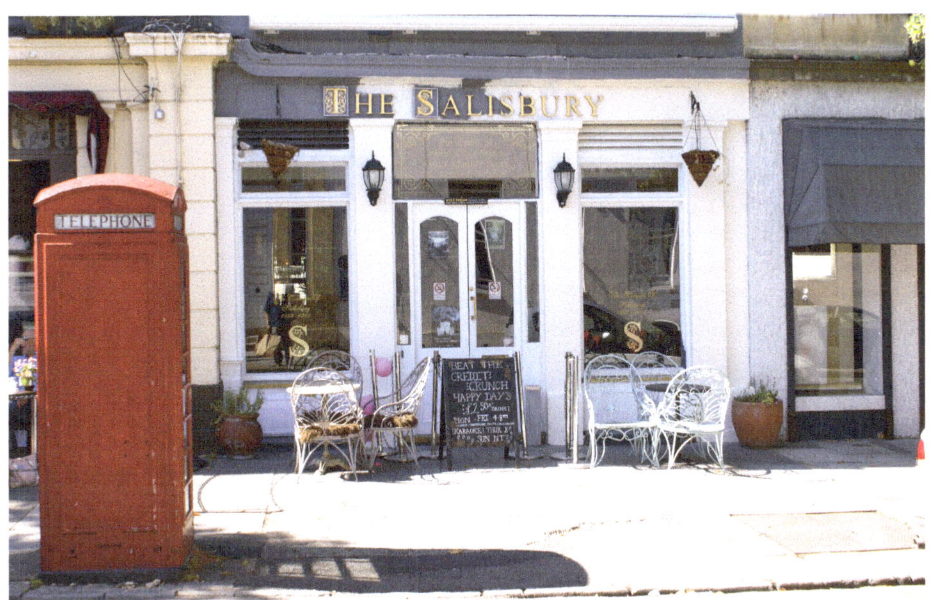

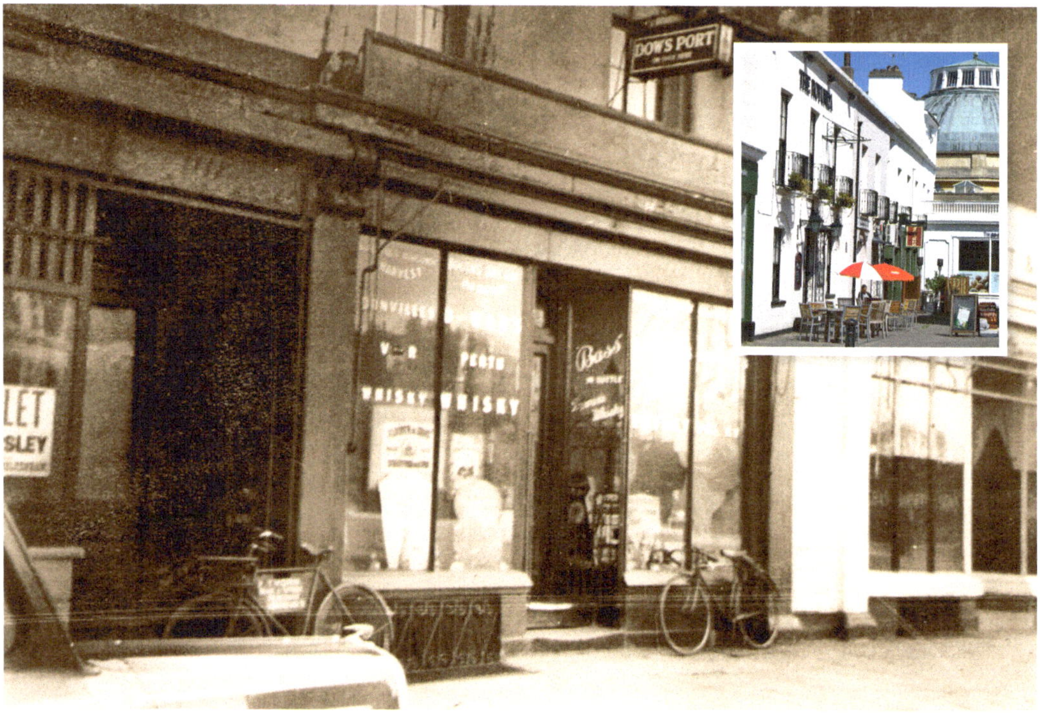

Rotunda Tavern, Montpellier

Built in 1837 the Rotunda Tavern traded as a wine merchant's for over 100 years before its acquisition by Allied Breweries in 1965. The Rotunda was enlarged in the early 1980s when an adjoining butcher's shop was added to the premises. The unusual name is derived from the nearby impressive domed Montpellier Rotunda, completed in 1826 and modelled on Rome's Pantheon, which has been in use as a bank since 1882.

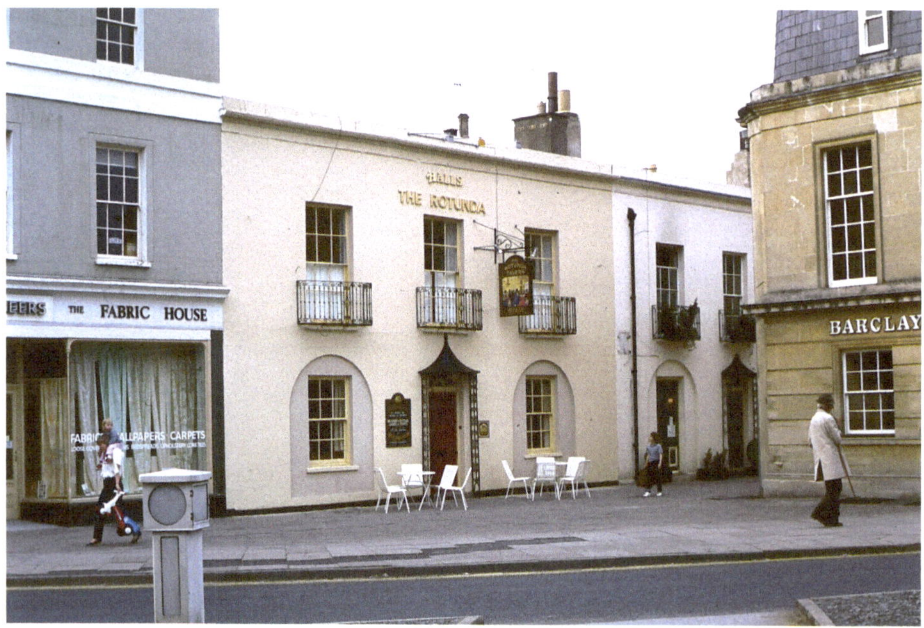

Montpellier Wine & Spirit Vaults, Montpellier Walk

The premises are still licensed today and trade as O'Neill's, an Irish-themed bar owned by the Mitchell & Butlers Pub Company of Birmingham. In the 1980s M&B were part of Bass, one of the 'Big Six' UK brewers, champions of keg beer. At this time the Montpellier pub was called Peters Bar, selling Bass Worthington. 'Worthington Bitter on Draught' is advertised at the Montpellier Wine & Spirit Vaults – they probably sold Guinness as well.

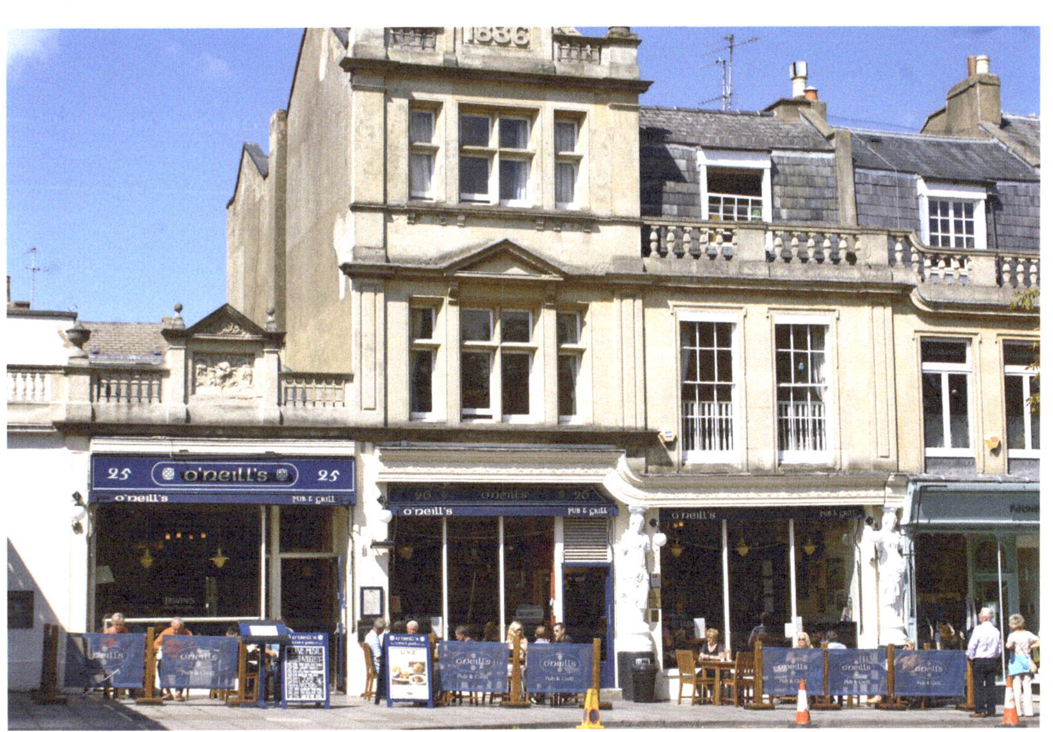

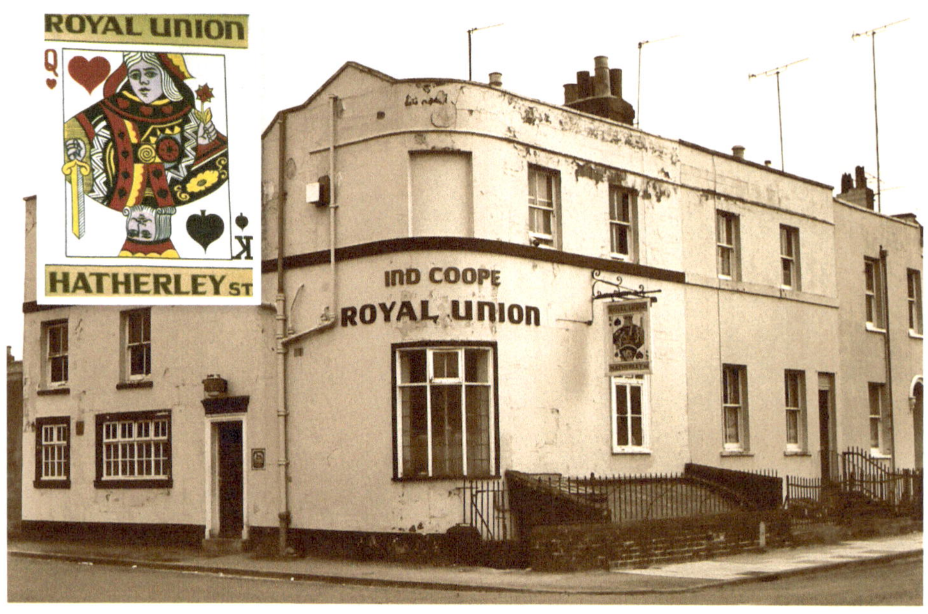

Royal Union, Hatherley Street

The Royal Union had a long association with Allsopp and Ind Coope Breweries. In the early 1980s the pub was branded as a Halls Oxford & West Brewery pub, selling Harvest Bitter brewed at the Ind Coope Brewery in Burton upon Trent. CAMRA Gloucestershire branch had its first meeting at the pub in April 1975 and, thirty-seven years later, the Royal Union still serves excellent pints of real ale.

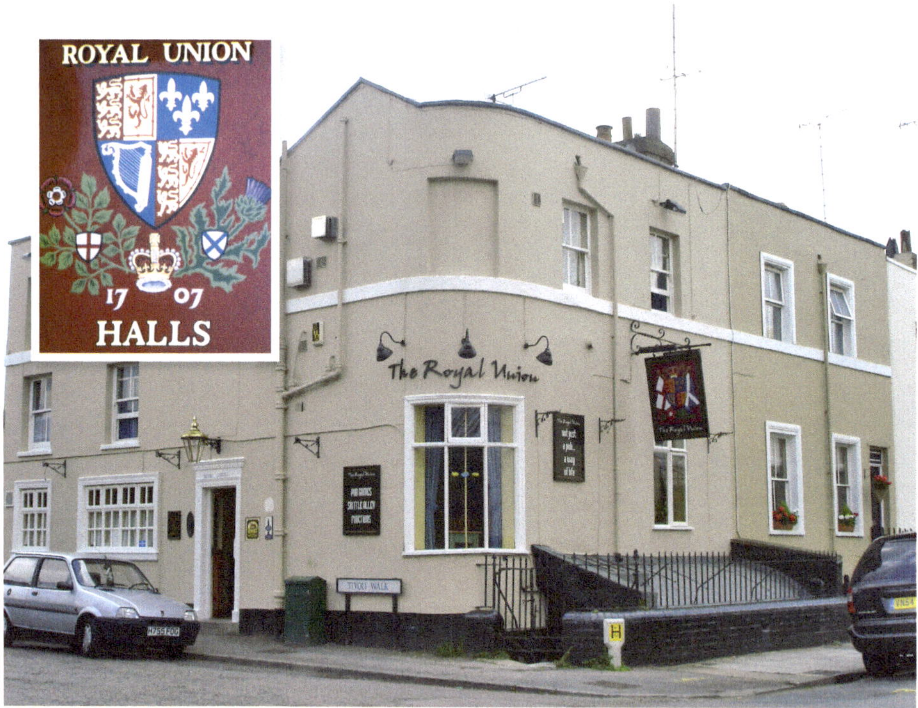

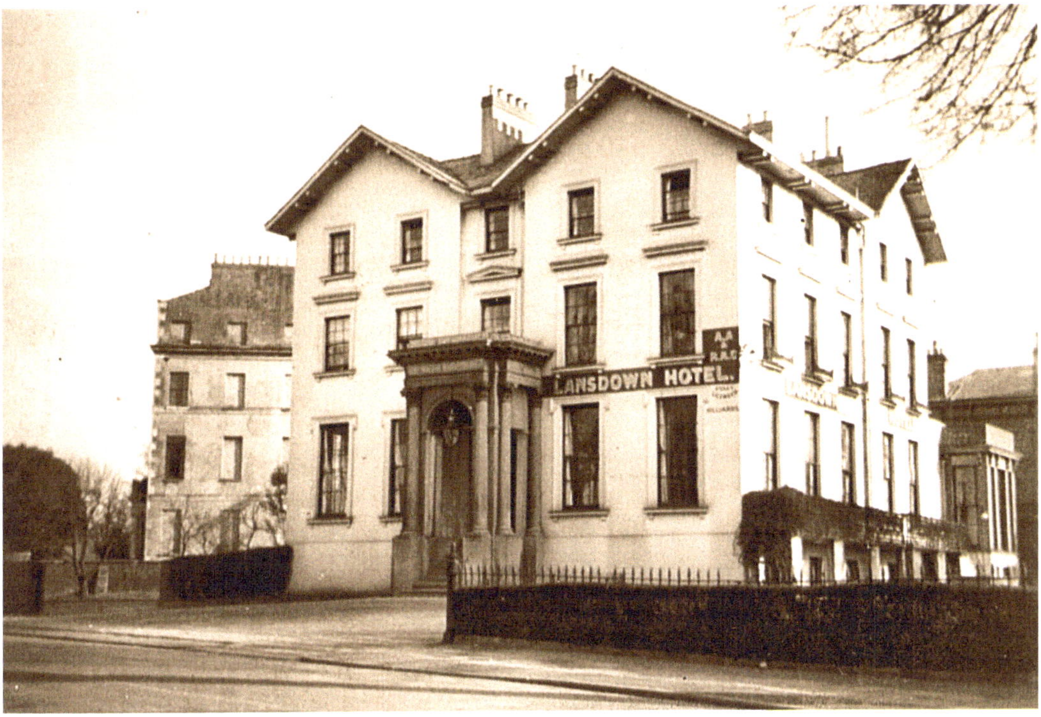

Lansdown Hotel, Lansdown

The exterior of the Lansdown Hotel has remained unaltered over the years. Originally a private residence, the Regency building has been licensed since at least 1856. Today there is a bustling sports bar downstairs featuring 3D and state-of-the-art plasma screen televisions. At least the name has reverted back to the Lansdown – it has previously been called the Rattle & Hum, Dog & Doughnut and the Rat & Carrot!

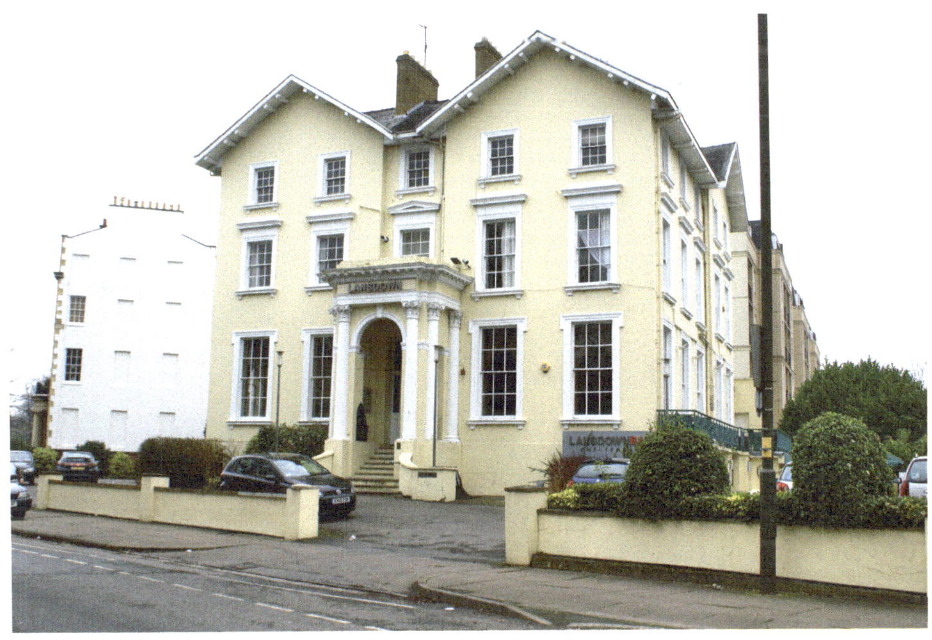

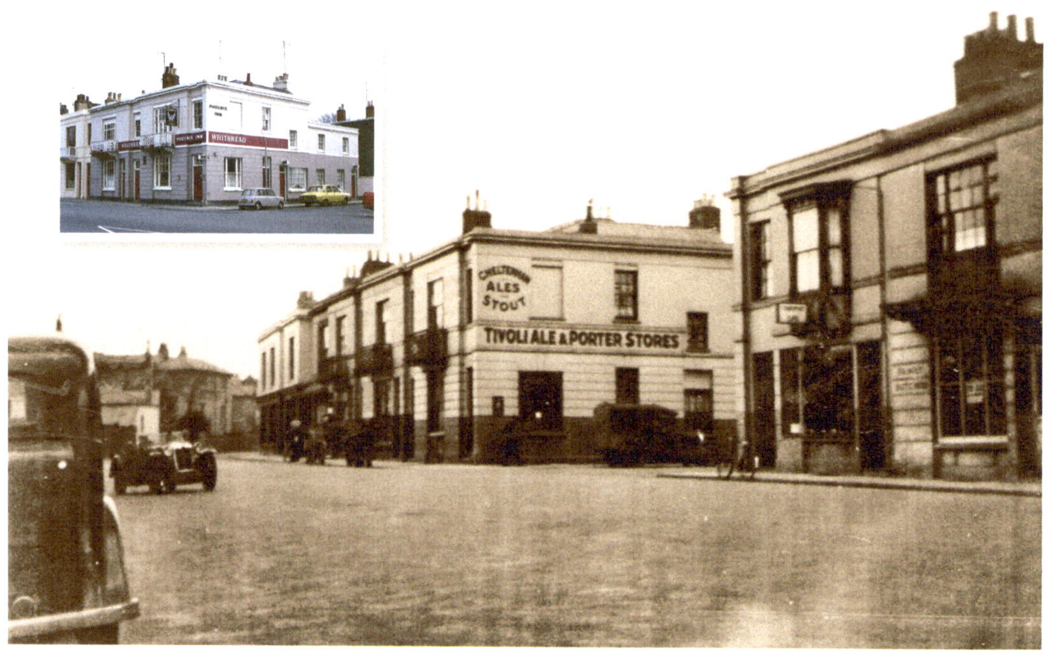

Tivoli Inn, Tivoli Road

Now called the Tivoli, originally the Tivoli Ale and Porter Stores, the pub traded in the latter half of the twentieth century as the Phoenix Inn. To confuse matters there was another pub on the other side of Tivoli Street called the Tivoli Inn (which closed in the early 1980s).

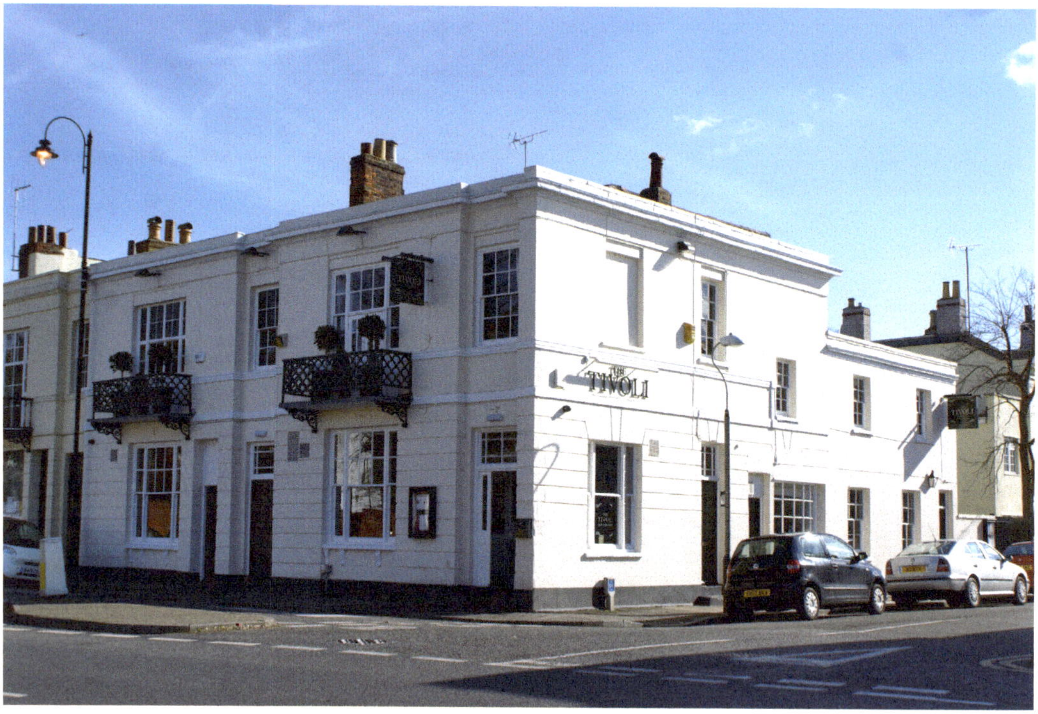

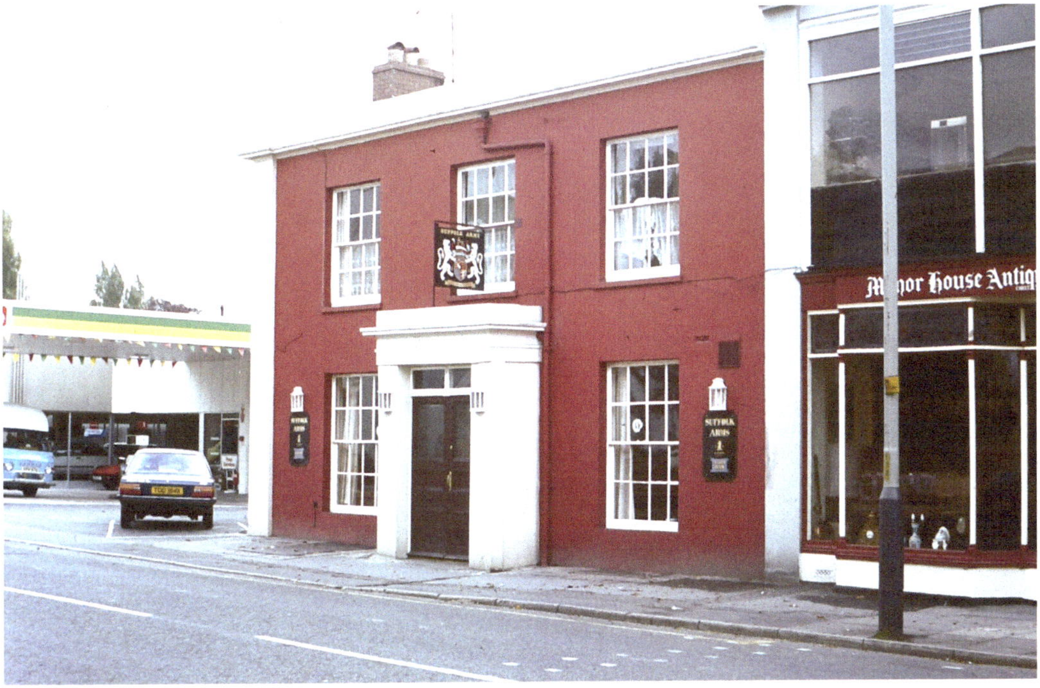

Suffolk Arms, Suffolk Road

The Suffolk Arms is one of Cheltenham's oldest pubs, thought to be continually trading for at least 188 years. Today the Suffolk Arms enjoys a good reputation for Thai cuisine whilst, crucially, remaining a traditional pub. The adjoining garage was Bill Allen's Autos, a Toyota dealer, which closed to make way for the present residential development.

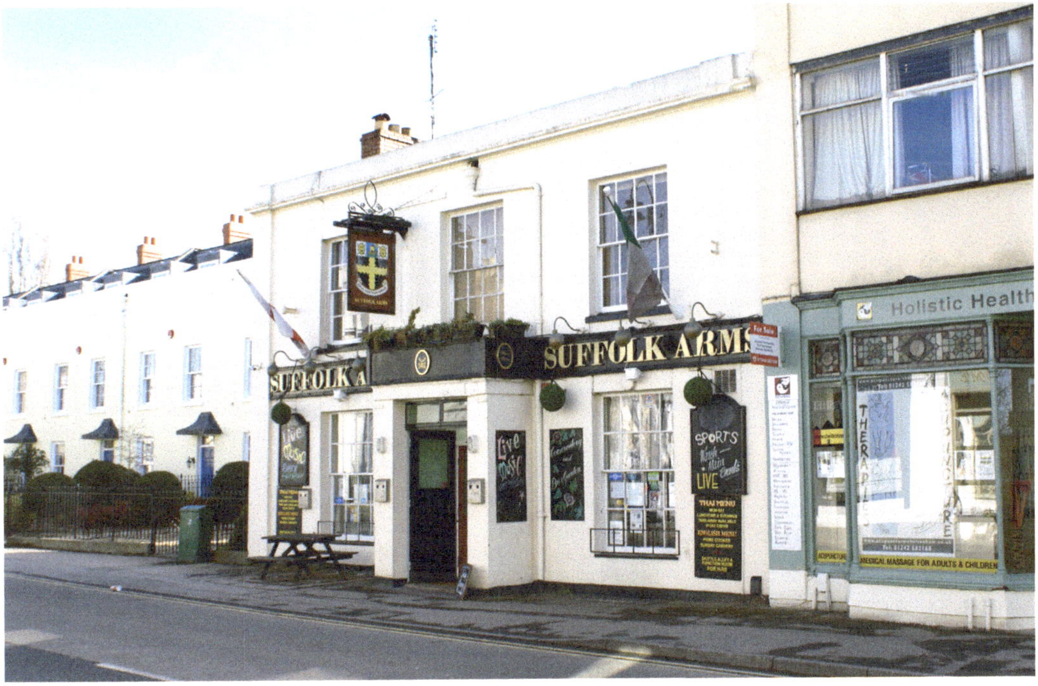

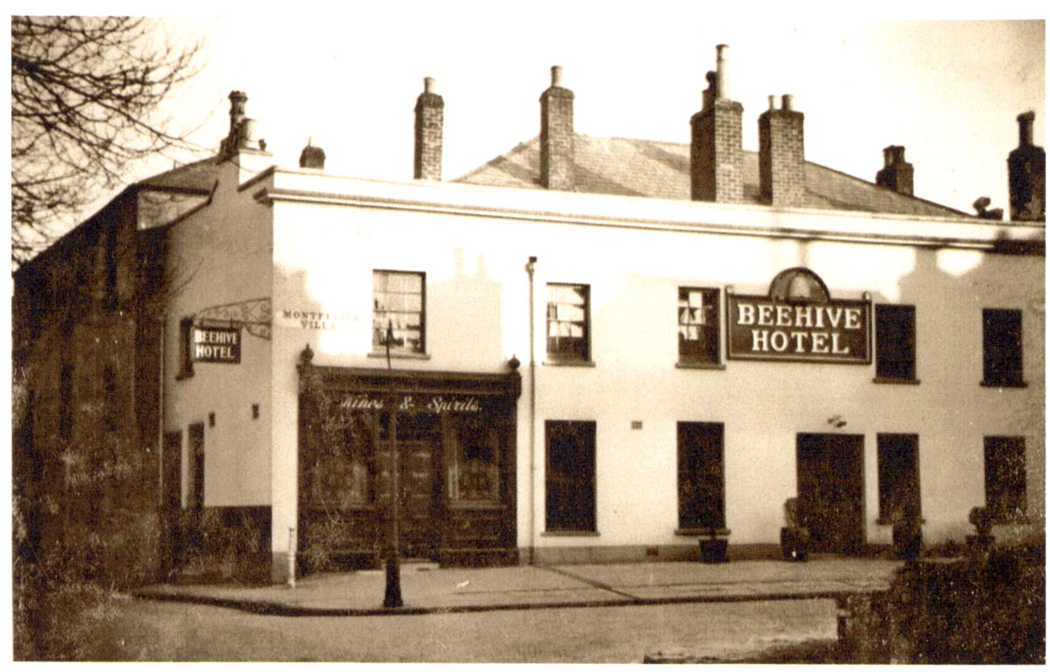

Beehive Hotel, Montpellier Villas

The Beehive Inn is a late eighteenth-century building designed by the architect John Forbes who was also responsible for building the Pittville Pump Room and St Paul's Church in Cheltenham. The Beehive once boasted its own brewery. An advertisement from 1851 reads, 'Beehive Brewery, Cheltenham. J. Carter, Wine and Spirit Merchant and Genuine Ale Brewer.' Upstairs there is a beautiful high ceiling Victorian ballroom featuring a large chandelier.

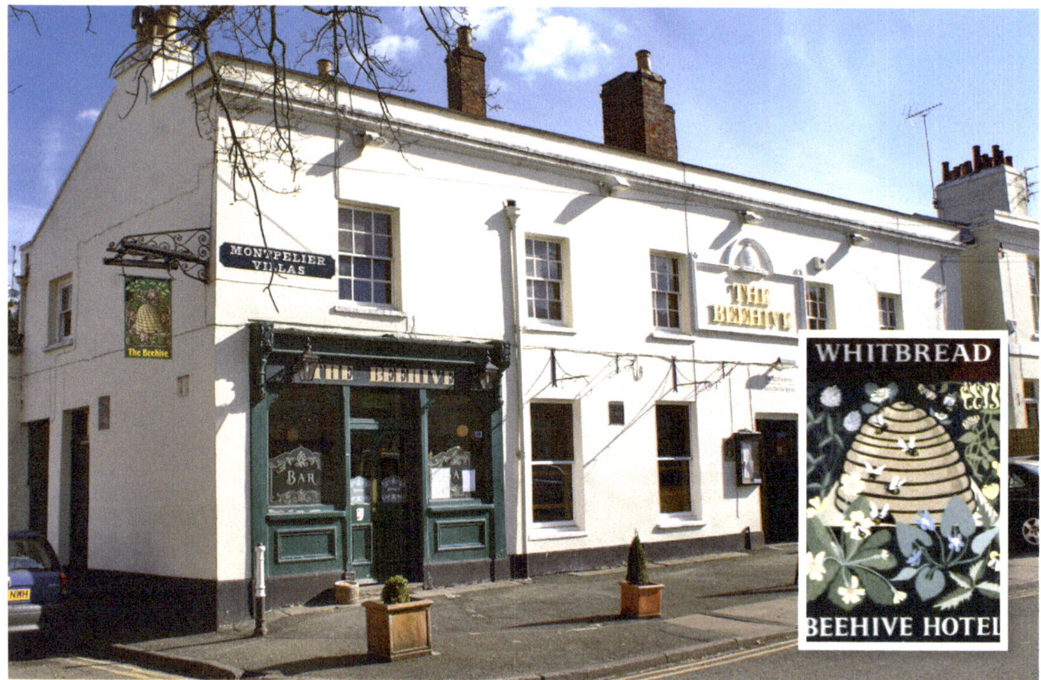

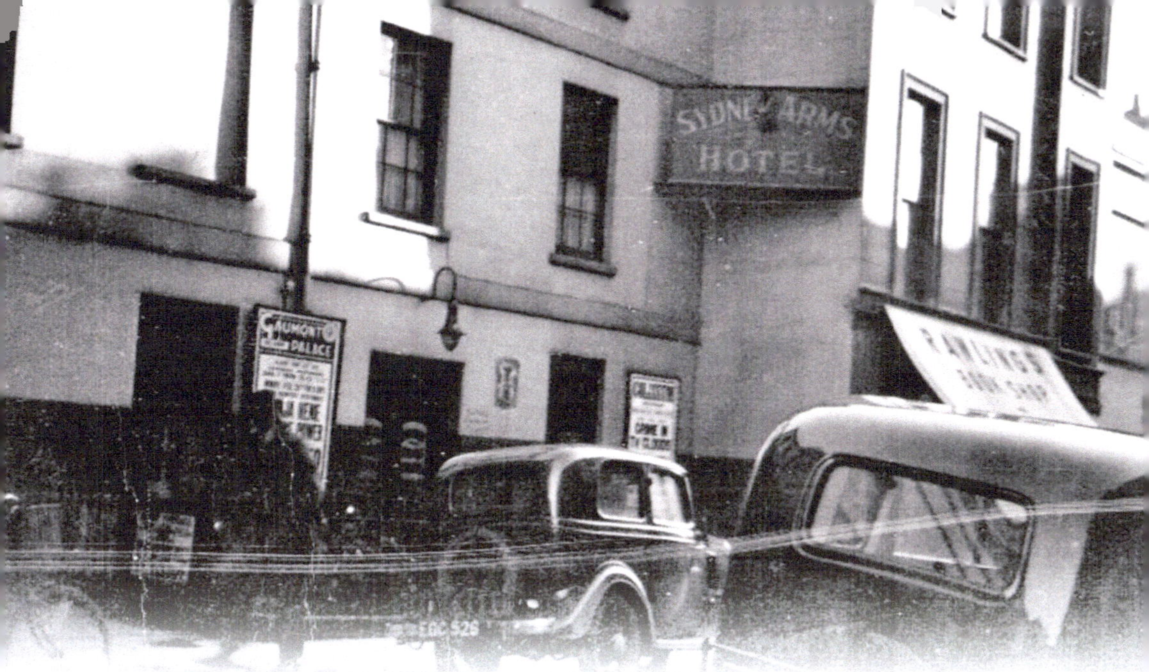

CHAPTER 7

Albion Street, Winchcombe Street & Fairview

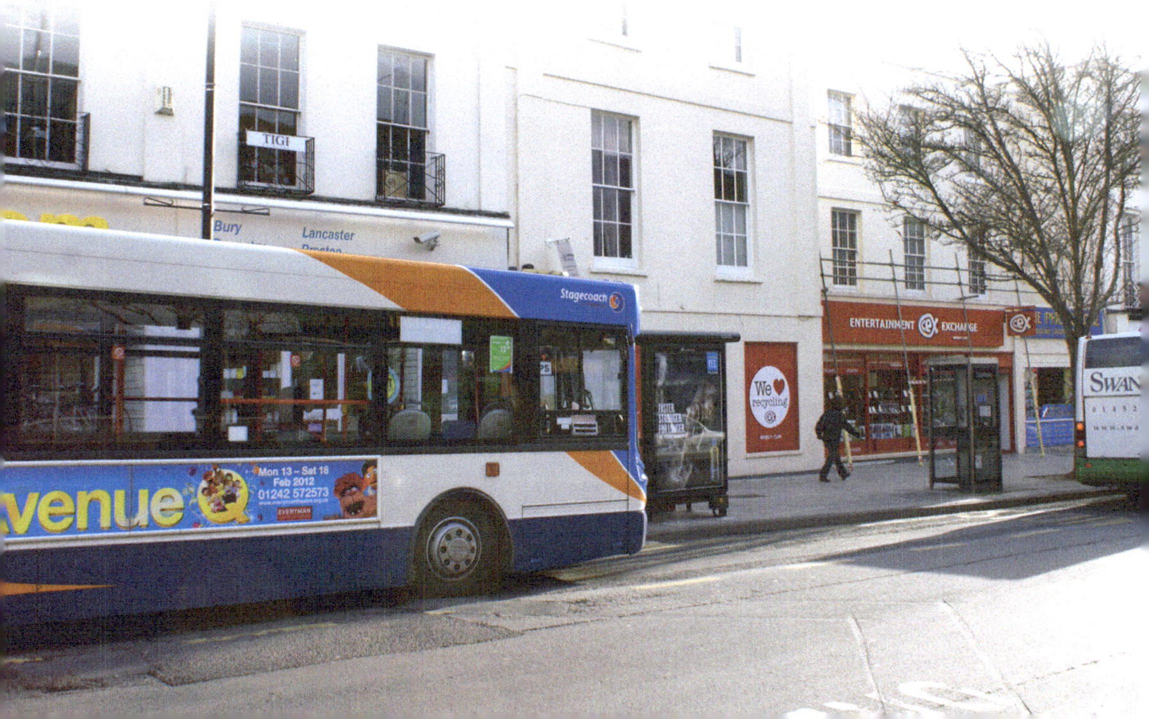

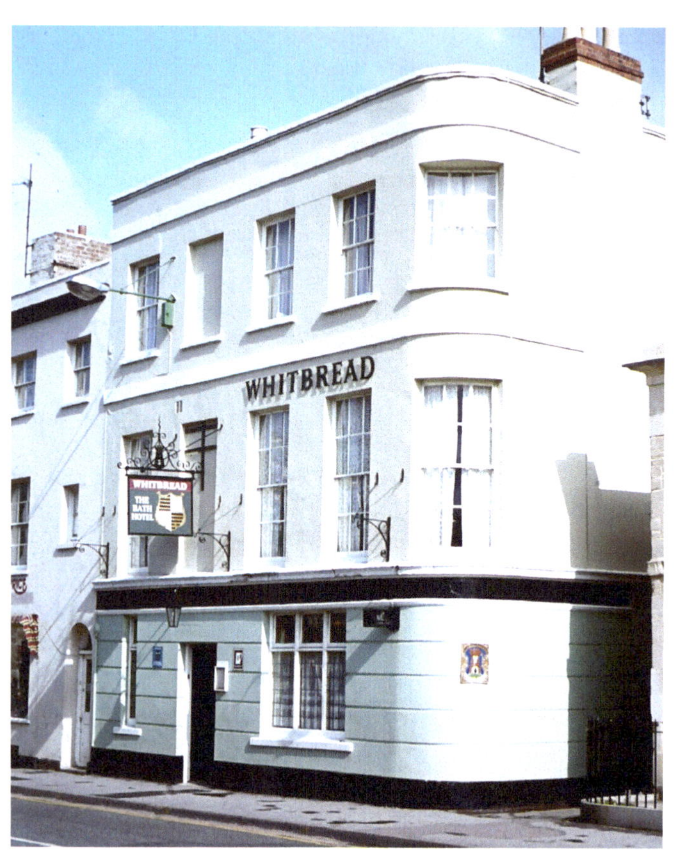

Bath Hotel, Albion Street

In the late 1970s the Bath Hotel sold one of the best pints of West Country PA in the town. Although the Whitbread brewery in Cheltenham brewed vast quantities of the 3 per cent beer, only a handful of pubs sold it in excellent condition. In the mid-1980s the name of the pub changed to the Dawn Run, commemorating the racehorse that won the 1986 Cheltenham Gold Cup. It is now the Turkish Angola Meze Bar.

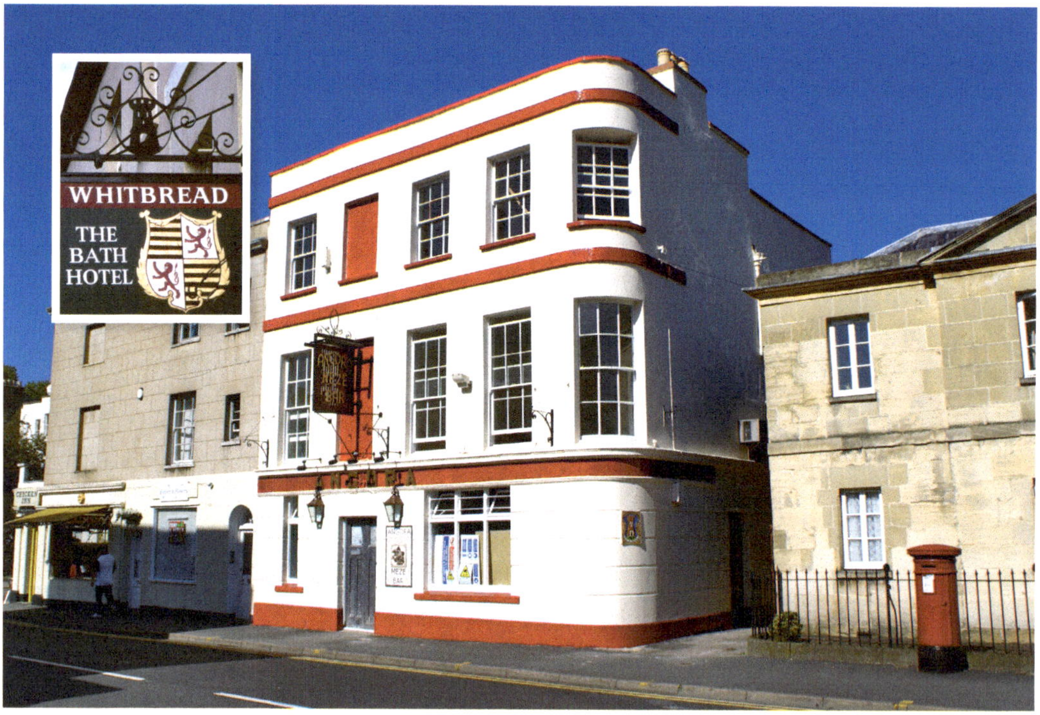

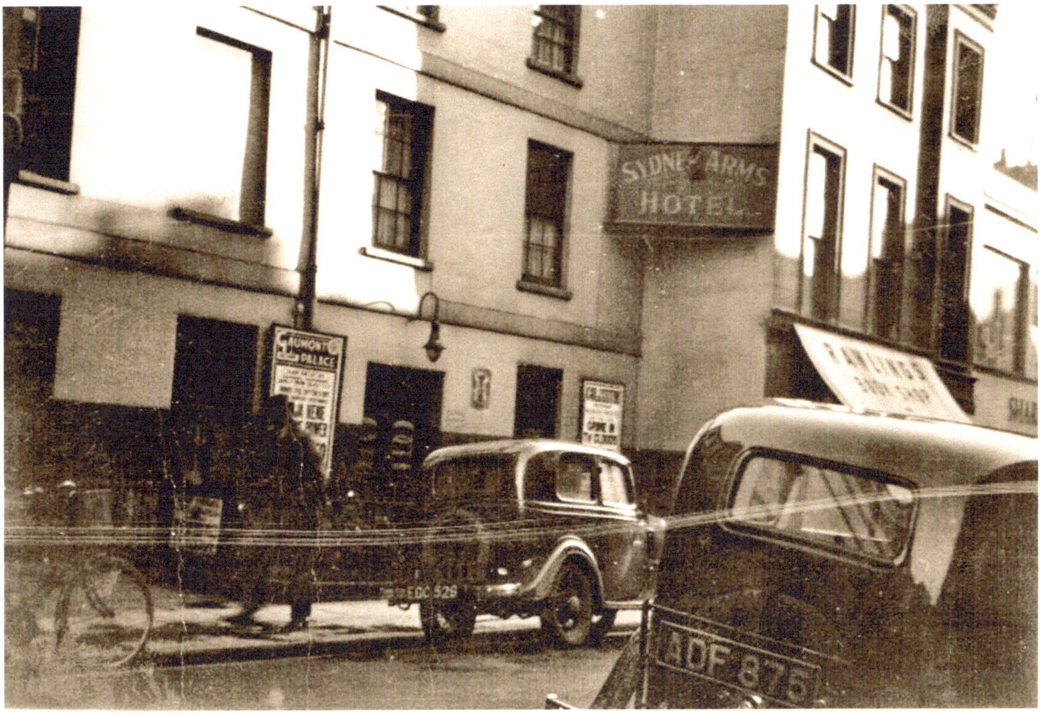

Sydney Arms Inn, Pittville Street

The Sydney Arms was built on a site of a coffee house, where Sarah Siddons reputedly found fame through her performances in an improvised theatre. The Sydney Arms, owned by the Cheltenham Original Brewery, was demolished in August 1954 when the entire western side of Pittville Street was reconstructed. It was replaced by a modern bar, initially called Sarah Siddons but later to become Brahms and Listz and finally Reflections.

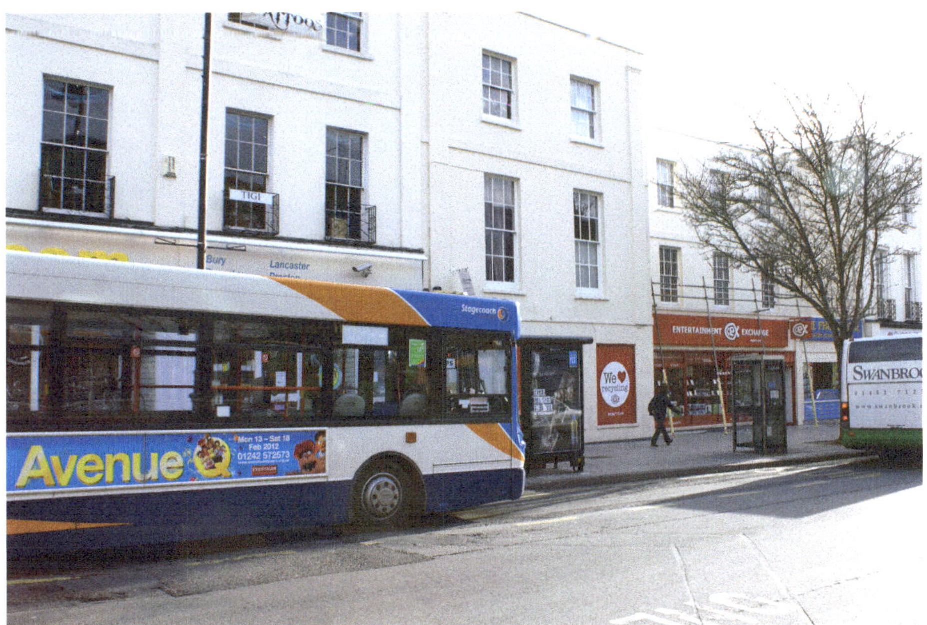

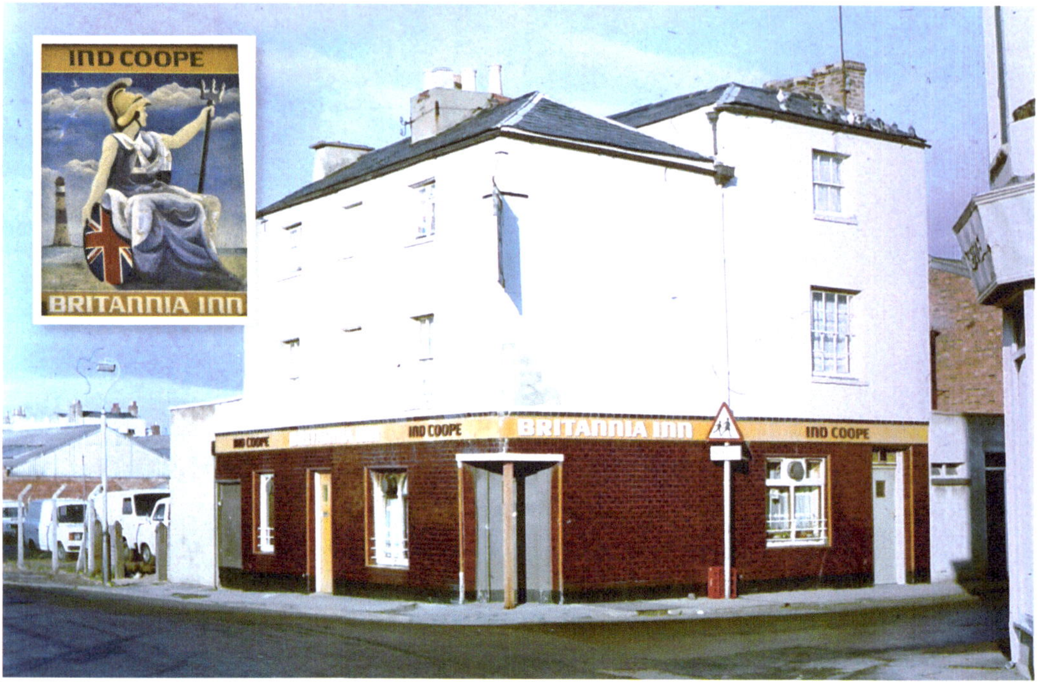

Britannia Inn, Fairview Road

The Britannia, situated on the west corner of Sherborne Street, closed in 1980 and was demolished to make way for road improvements. The Britannia was once owned by John Dobell's Wine & Spirit Merchants (see Restoration Inn, page 16). Apparently when the Ind Coope pub signs were removed from the Britannia just prior to demolition, the original Victorian 'Dobell's' lettering were revealed.

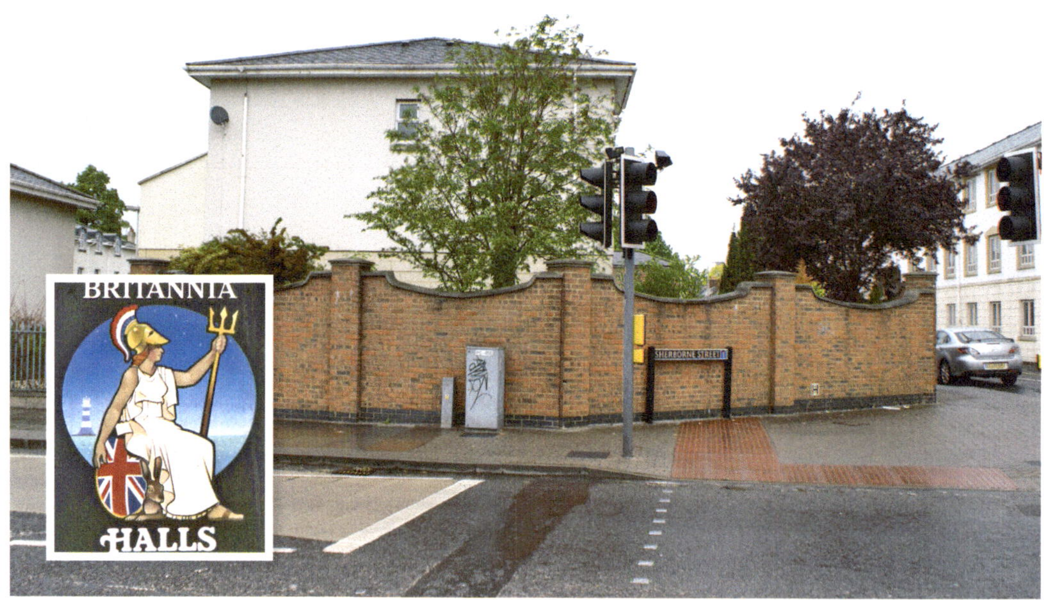

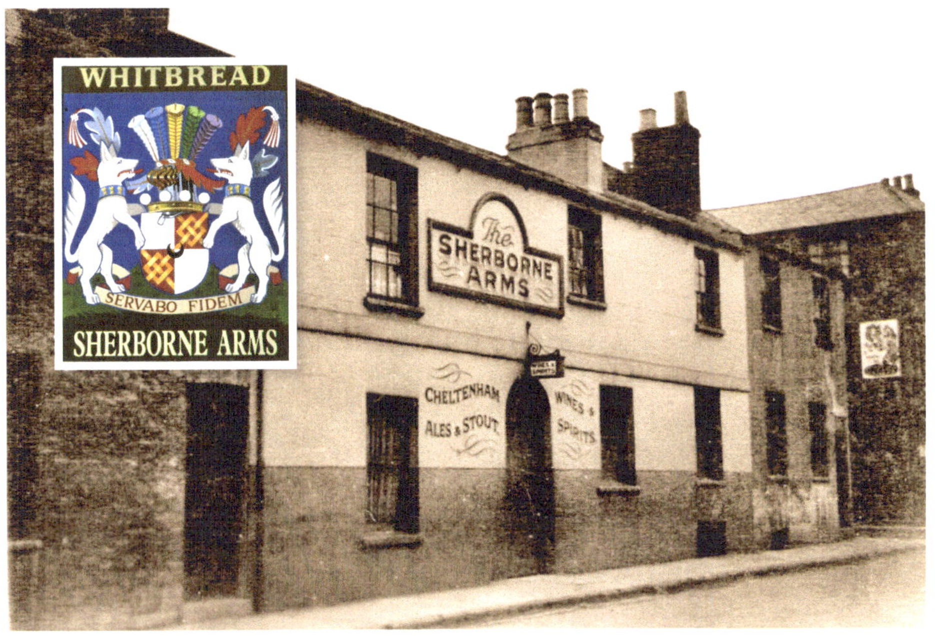

Sherborne Arms, Sherborne Street

After a few turbulent years the Sherborne Arms closed in 2011. A planning application to change the use to residential was apparently unopposed and subsequent redevelopment seemed inevitable. However, in January 2012, Cheltenham Borough Council planning committee refused the application on the grounds that the owning Pub Company had run the premises down deliberately to claim that it was no longer viable as a pub. The developer will no doubt lodge an appeal to rescind the decision.

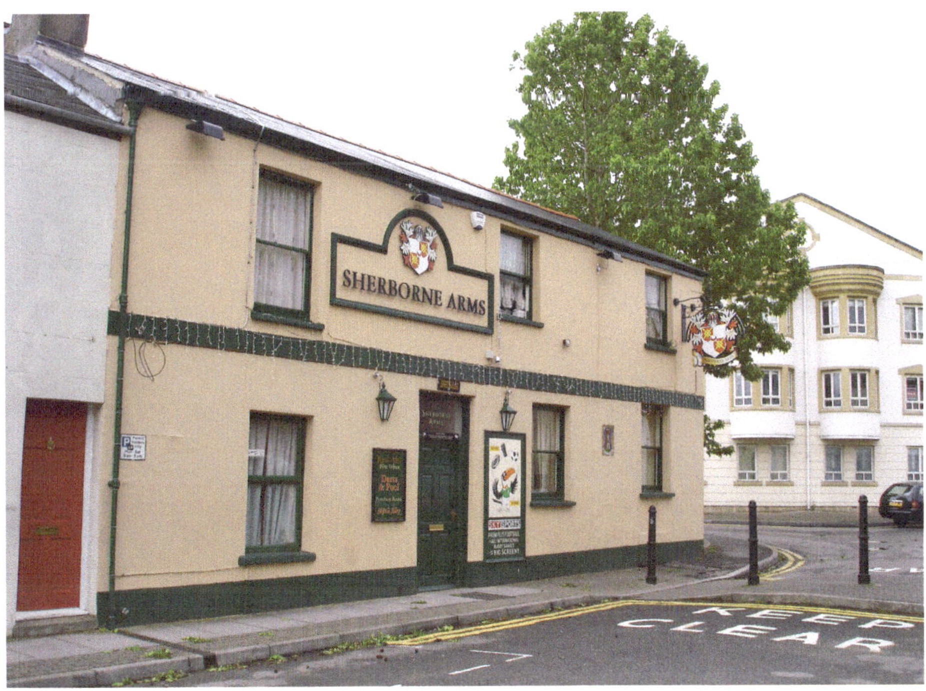

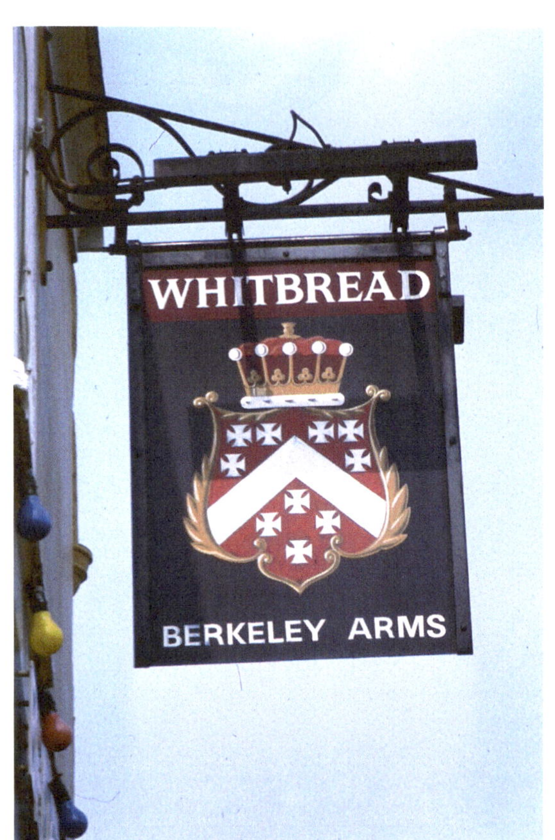

Berkeley Arms, Albion Street

Numbered 89 Albion Street, the Berkeley Arms was situated opposite the old Athletic Ground, now the site of the St John's Avenue and Tom Price Close. The Grosvenor Arms, on the corner of Grosvenor Terrace, was just a few yards away. The Berkeley Arms, popular with motorcyclists, was demolished in the late 1970s and the site was cleared for the construction of a 'superstore' and multi-storey car park.

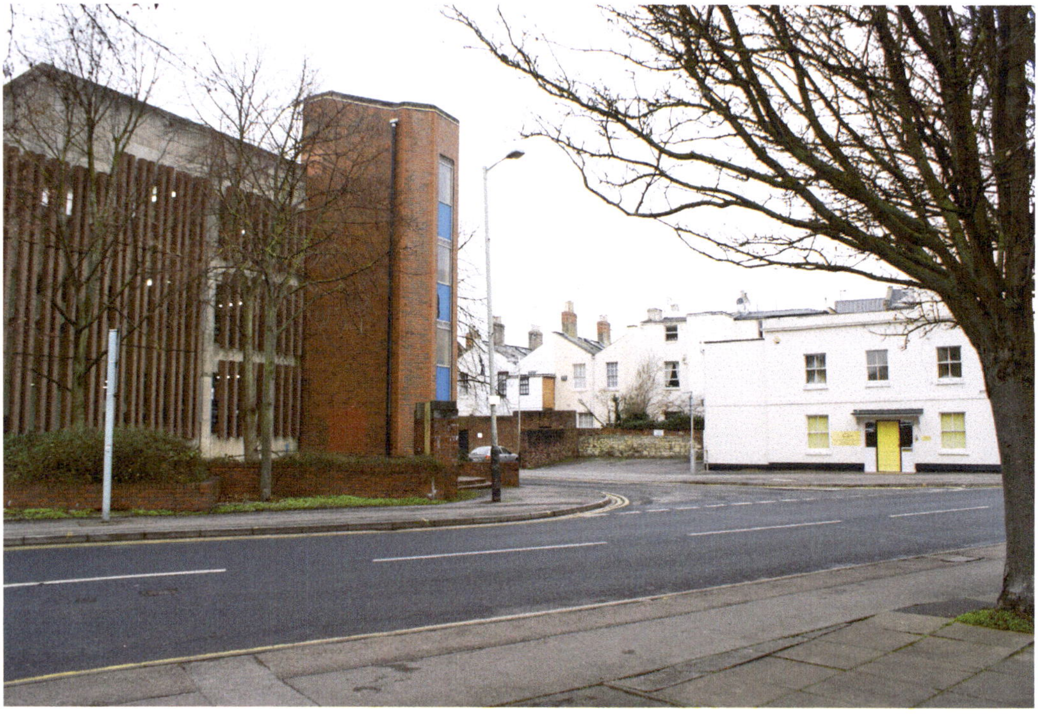

Kemble Brewery Inn, Fairview Street

The building was originally built as a butcher's shop in 1842 and became a pub around 1844/45. Brewing may have once taken place at the pub, but by 1891 beer was supplied to the Kemble Inn by Combs Brewery of Brockhampton near Andoversford. The Kemble Inn eventually passed into the ownership of Ind Coope of Burton upon Trent. The photograph shows landlady Harriet Smith outside the pub in the 1920s. Archers Brewery of Swindon acquired the Kemble in 1988 but it is now a popular free house. (Image courtesy Lynne Hennessey)

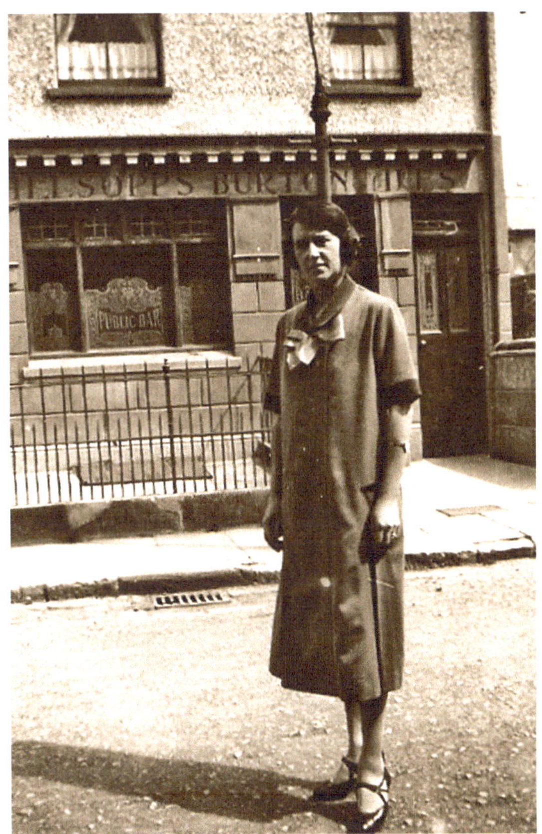

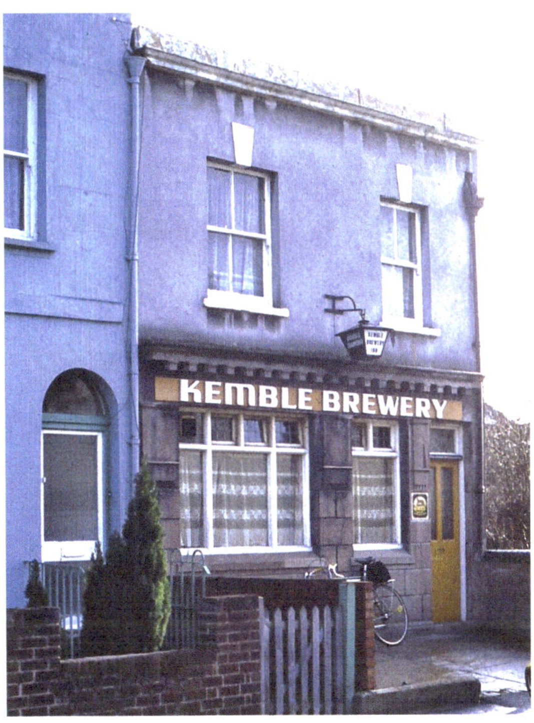

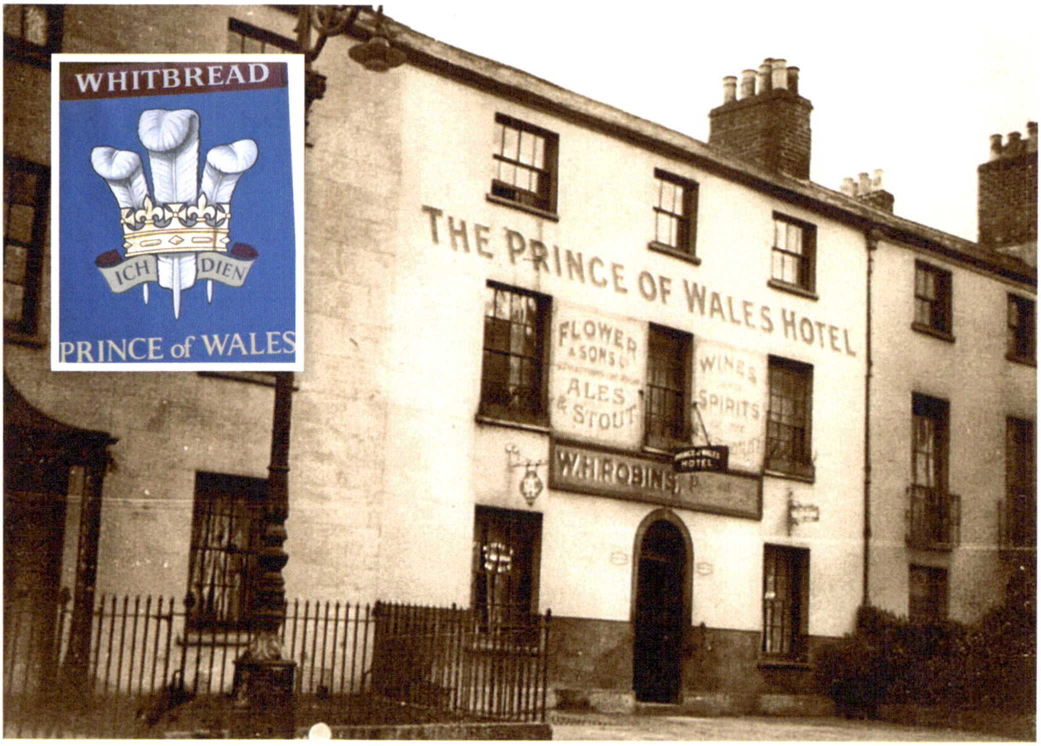

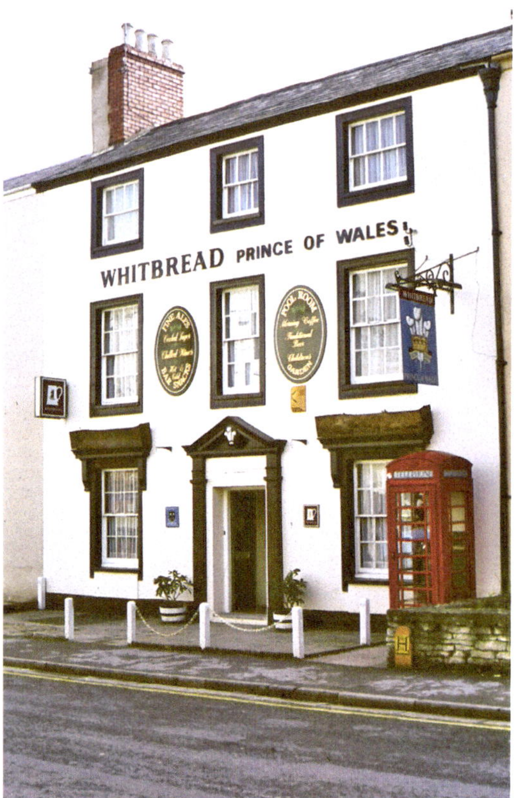

Prince of Wales Inn, Portland Street

The oblique italic lettering on the Prince of Wales is certainly unusual; hopefully not a result of the sign-writer having too many pints of Flowers ales before he started his work! William Harry Robins was landlord at the pub in the late 1930s. In 1980 the pub was run by Terry Paine, an ex-Southampton Football Club player who was a member of the England 1966 World Cup team. The Prince of Wales is still trading.

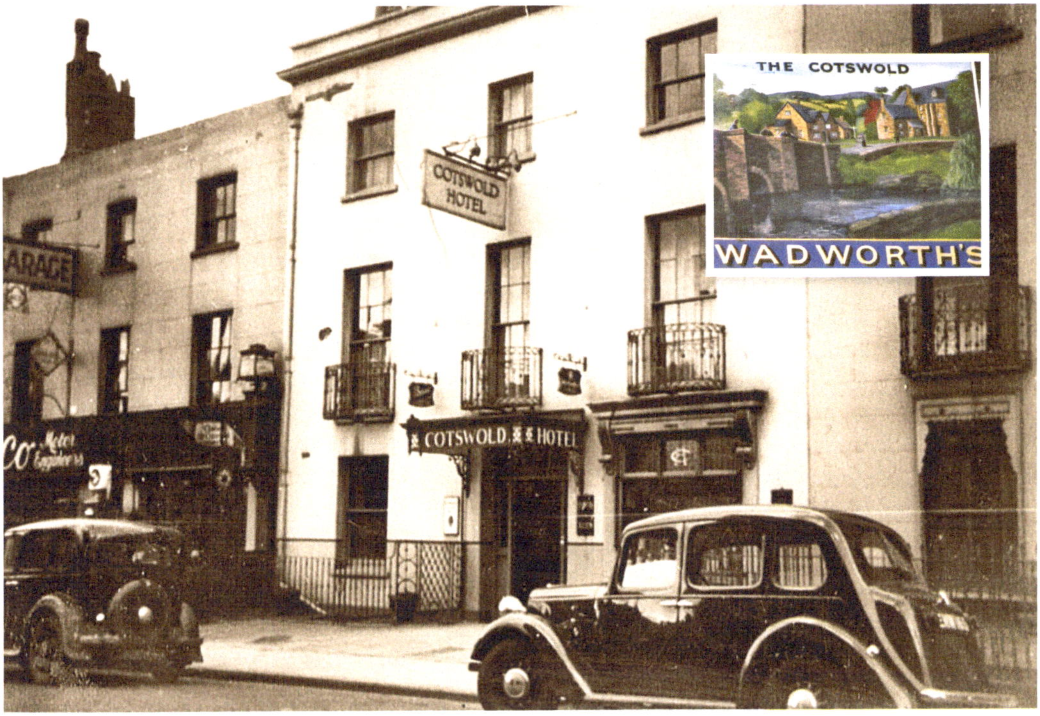

Cotswold Hotel, Portland Street

In the mid-1970s when the pubs of Cheltenham were serving fizzy keg beer like Whitbread Tankard and Double Diamond, the Wadworth ales at the Cotswold Hotel had a cult following. The narrow gas-lit bar was crammed with drinkers enjoying the delights of 6X served from the wooden cask. In those days the pub was in a terrace. The inner ring road now dissects the terrace but the Cotswold remains, still serving Wadworth beers.

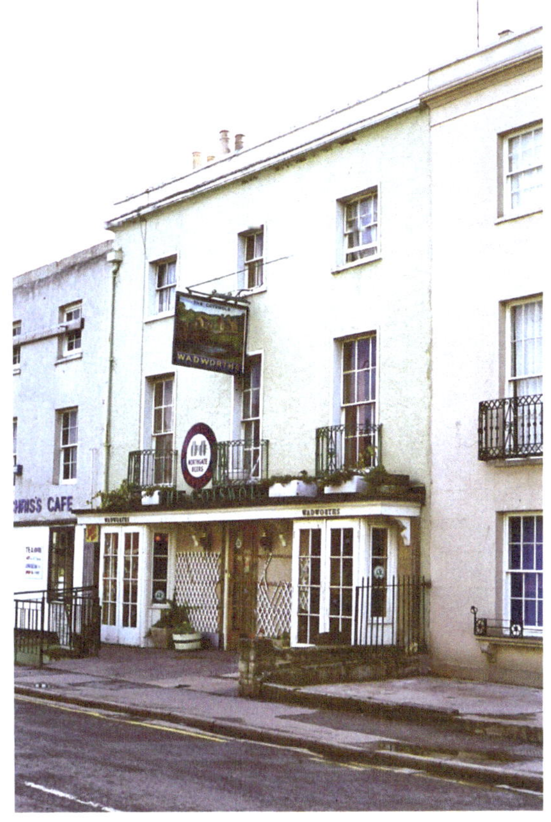

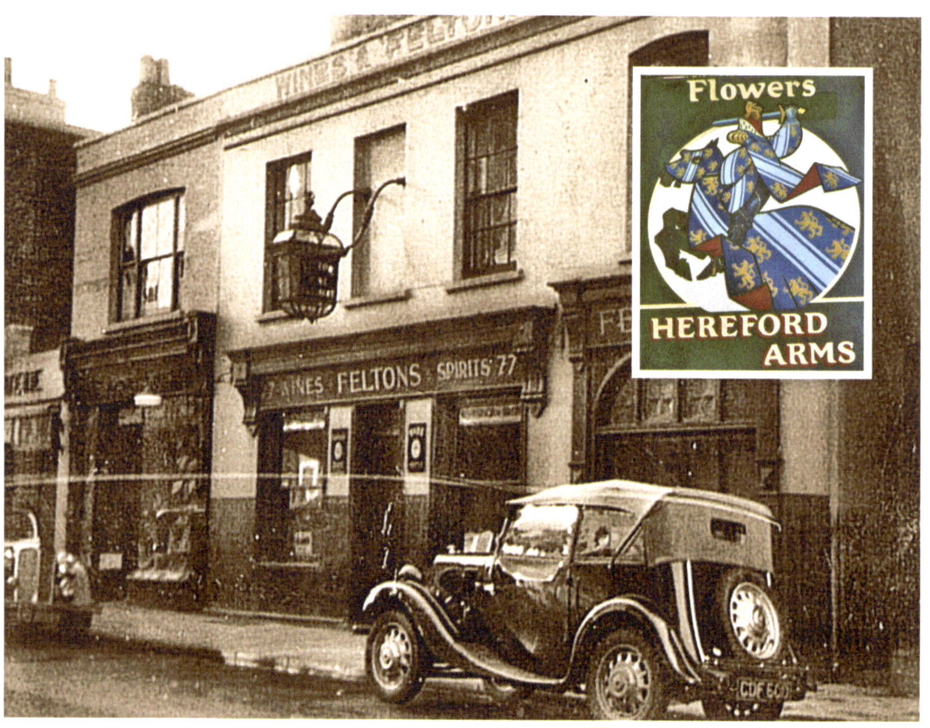

Hereford Arms, Winchcombe Street

Directly opposite the Gaumont Palace Theatre (later Odeon Cinema), several famous actors and entertainers must have popped across the road for a pint or two. The pub was renamed Flicks in the late 1980s, but when Arkell's Brewery of Swindon acquired the premises in 1991 it reverted back to the Hereford Arms. In 2003 the Hereford Arms was converted into a wine bar called Element but it is now a Thai restaurant. The Odeon closed in November 2006.

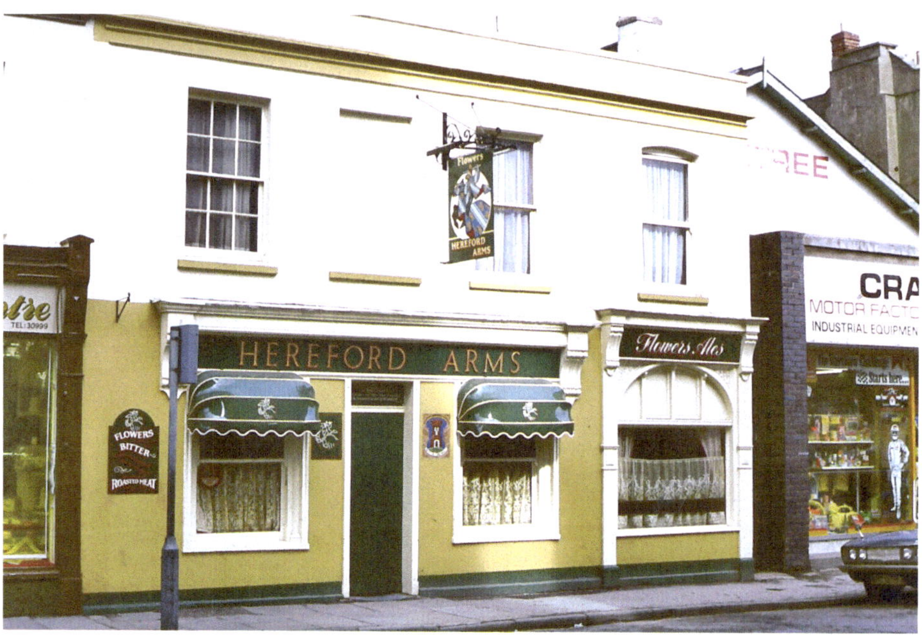

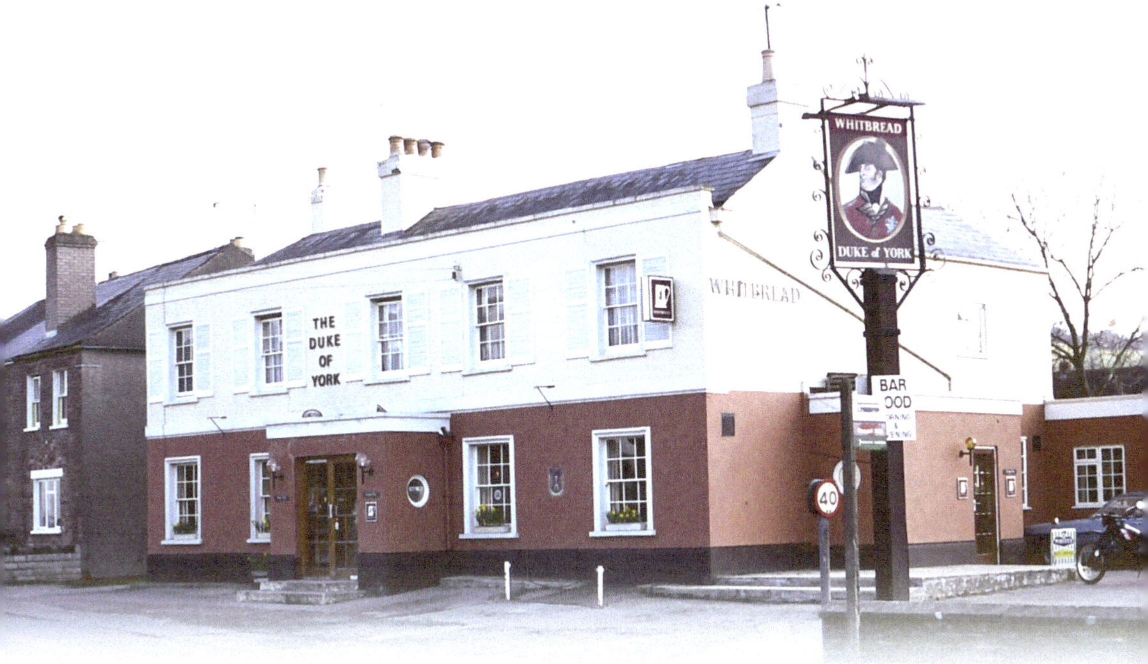

CHAPTER 8

Charlton Kings

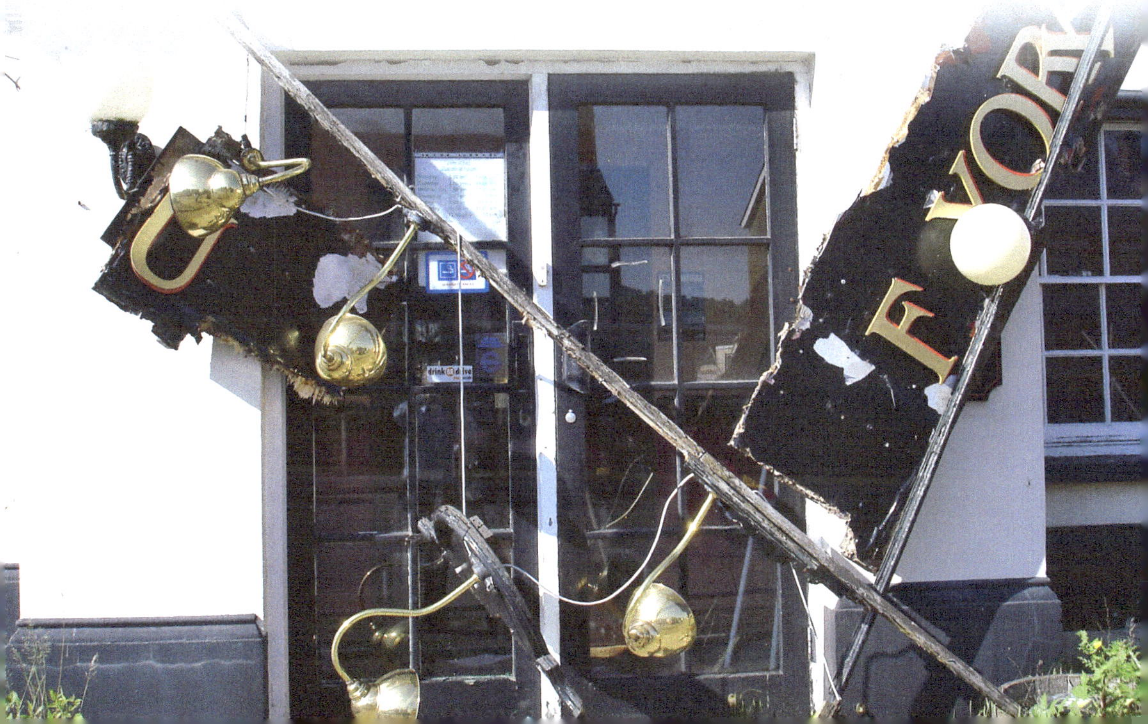

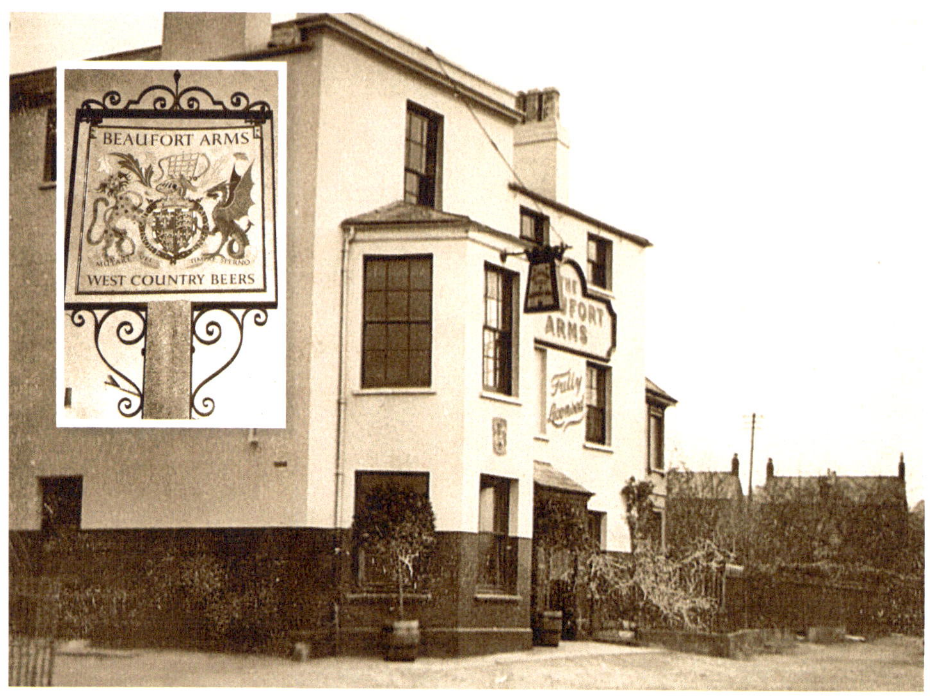

Beaufort Arms, London Road

The Beaufort Arms is owned by the Wadworth Brewery of Devizes, famous for their 6X beer. In September 1999, a 10ft by 4ft mural by artist Rob Russell was unveiled in the pool room capturing the moment when Chetenham Town Football Club, the Robins, scored the winning goal against Yeovil Town on 22 April, which promoted them into the football league. The Beaufort Arms now hosts the Cheltenham Folk Club.

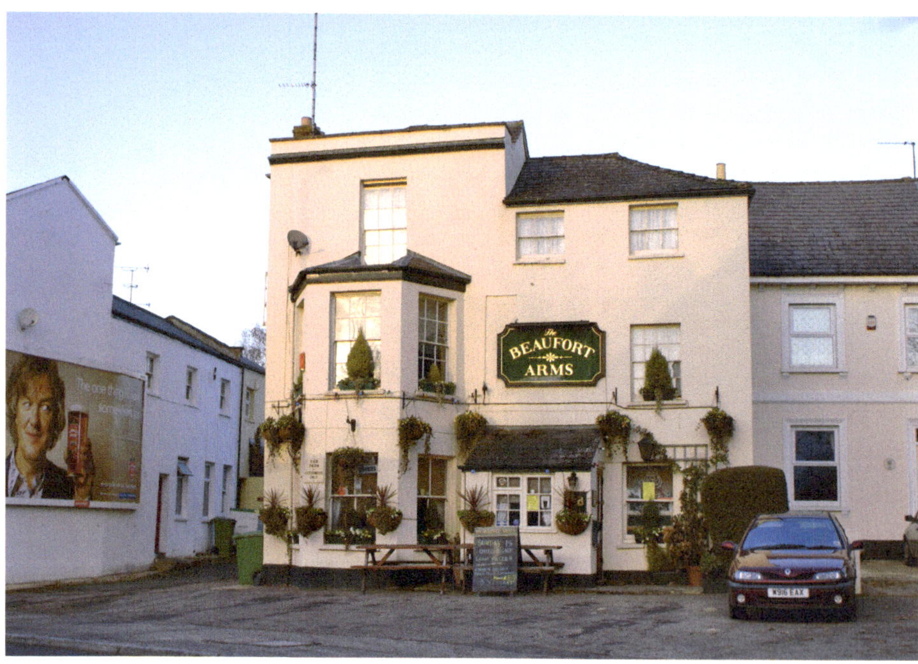

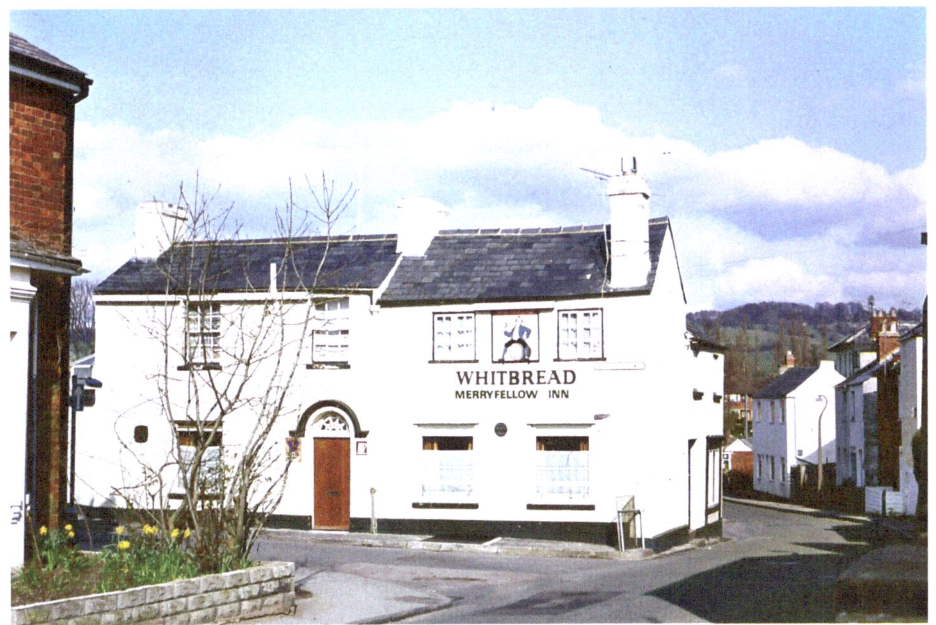

Merryfellow Inn, School Road

The Merryfellow had a long association with the Stroud Brewery Company, being tied to the brewery as early as 1891. Unfortunately, two superb Stroud Brewery etched pub windows were smashed by vandals in 2004. The Royal Hotel in Horsefair Street, a short distance away, was a Cheltenham Original Brewery pub. Stroud Beer devotees at the Merryfellow wouldn't drink the 'inferior' Cheltenham Ales at the Royal, and vice versa.

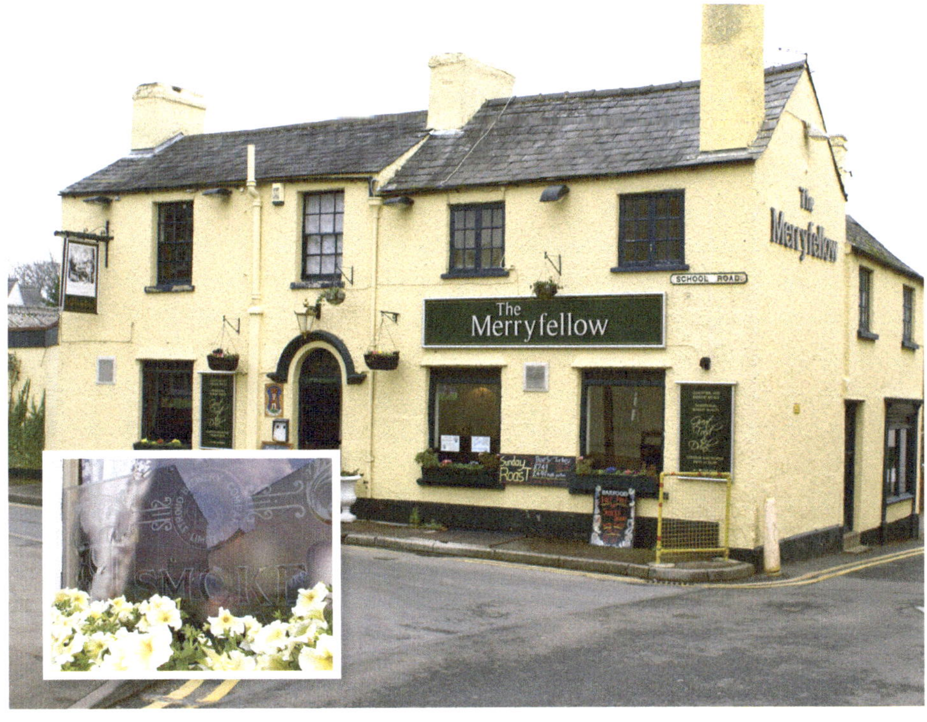

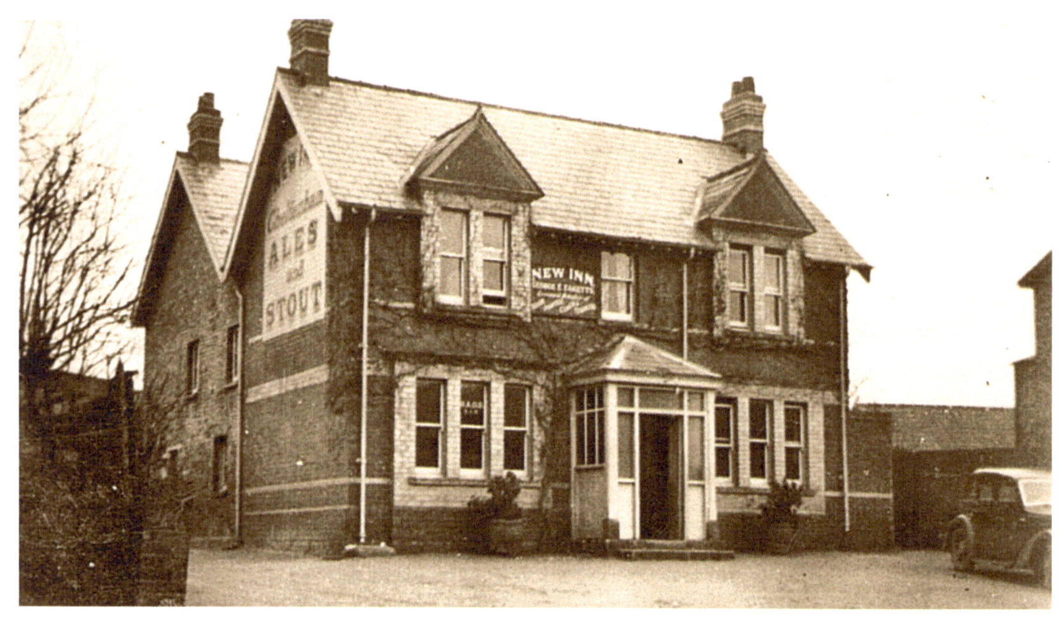

New Inn, Cirencester Road

The New Inn was not far from Charlton Kings railway station and was once a convenient place to wait for a train on the railway line known as the Tiddley Dyke. The New Inn changed its name to the Little Owl to commemorate the winning Irish racehorse in the 1981 Cheltenham Gold Cup. By the late 1990s the pub was simply called the Owl, later to become the Owl at Charlton Kings. It has now reverted back to the Little Owl.

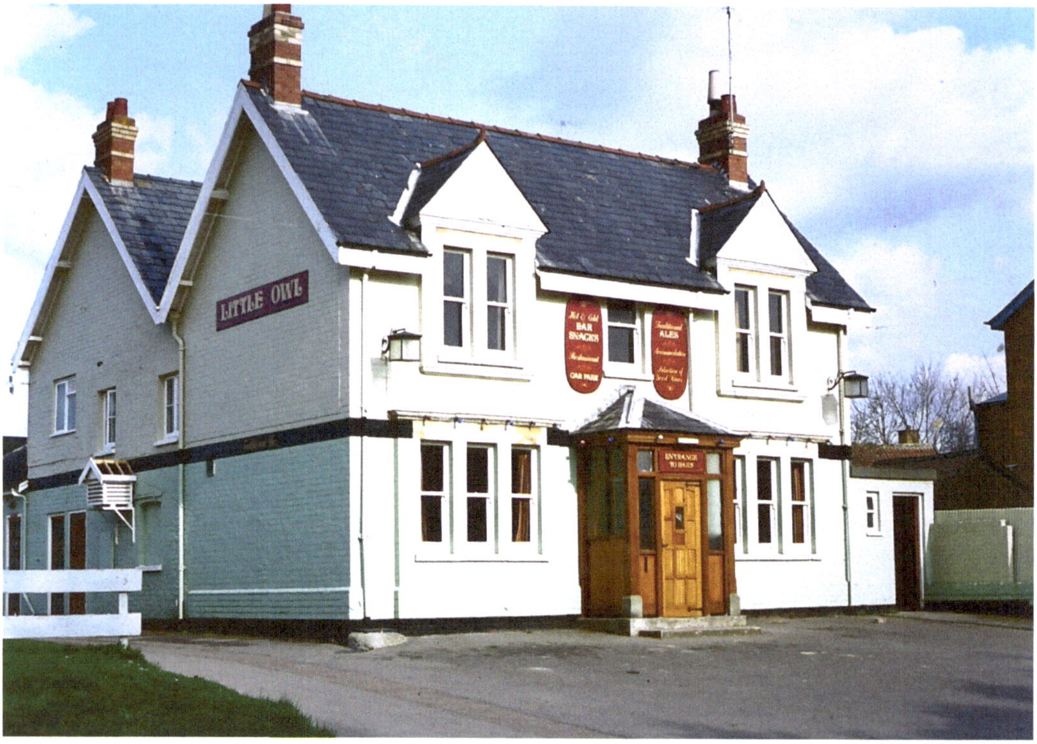

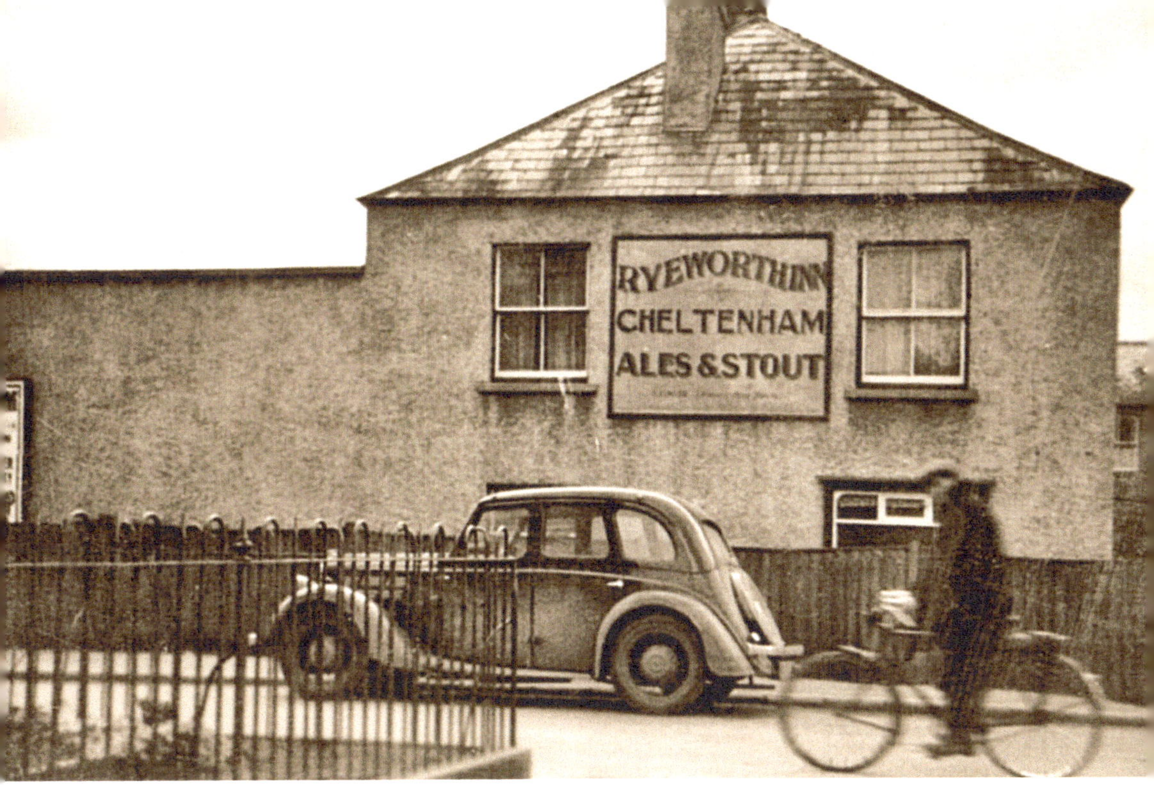

Ryeworth Inn, Ryeworth Road

The advertisement for the Coliseum Cinema is for the 1937 film *Slave Ship* which starred Wallace Beery, Warner Baxter and Mickey Rooney. When the photograph was taken, the landlord of the Ryeworth Inn was Richard Fowler who had been serving pints of Cheltenham Original ales at the pub since the outbreak of the First World War. The Ryeworth Inn is still trading, now dishing up 'sizzling hot skillets'.

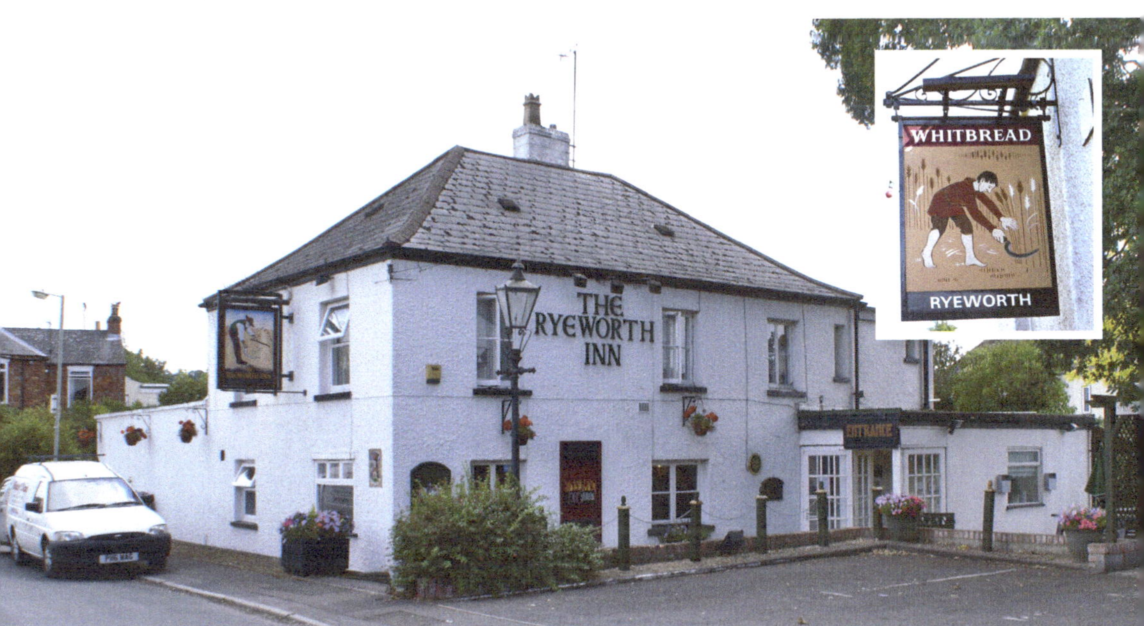

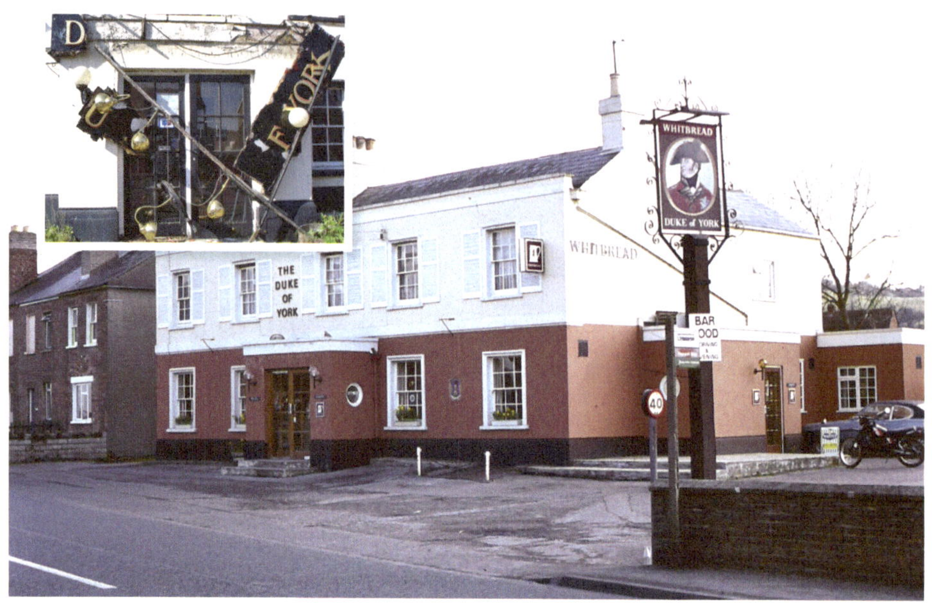

Duke of York, London Road

The Duke of York was constructed in 1848 and records show that Henry Clarke was brewing beer at the pub in 1883. By 1903 it was owned by the Cheltenham Original Brewery who also supplied beer to the Cotswold Inn on the opposite side of London Road. A noise abatement order was placed on the pub in 1999 following complaints. Sedate tea dances had replaced the loud music in 2002 but the Duke of York closed in January 2007 and it is now residential.

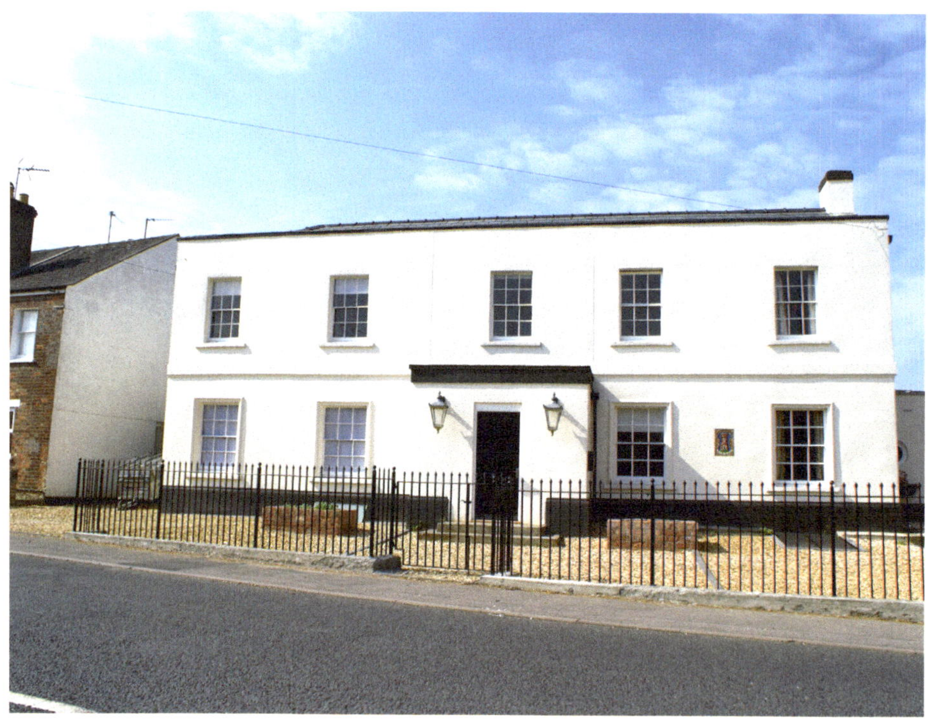

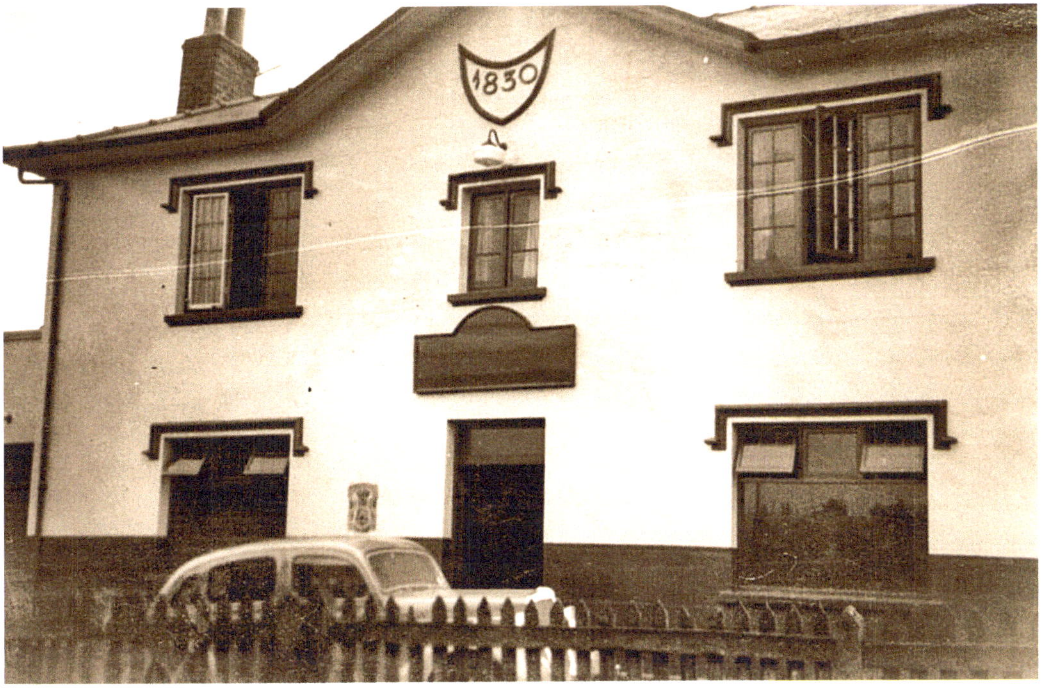

Royal Hotel, Horsefair Street

The Royal Hotel was built in 1830; there is a date stone on the building. A landlord in late Victorian times, Thomas Gosney, is said to have kept a monkey as an attraction for his customers on a pole in the garden. For many years after the locals referred to the pub as the Monkey House. The Royal closed in the summer of 2008 but had reopened by Christmas 2009 after a thorough refurbishment.

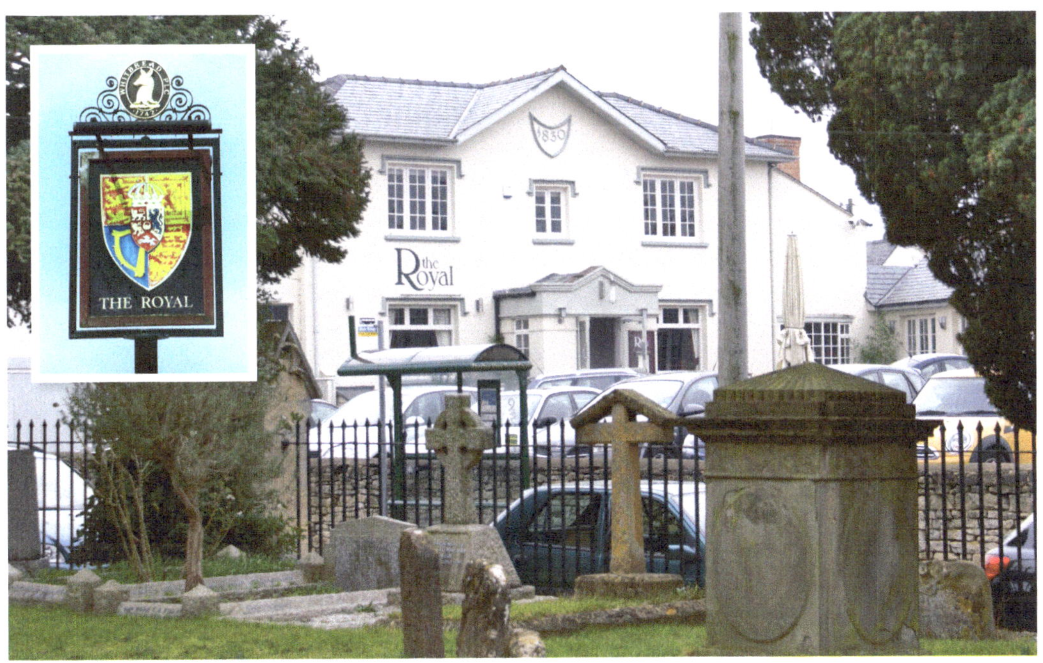

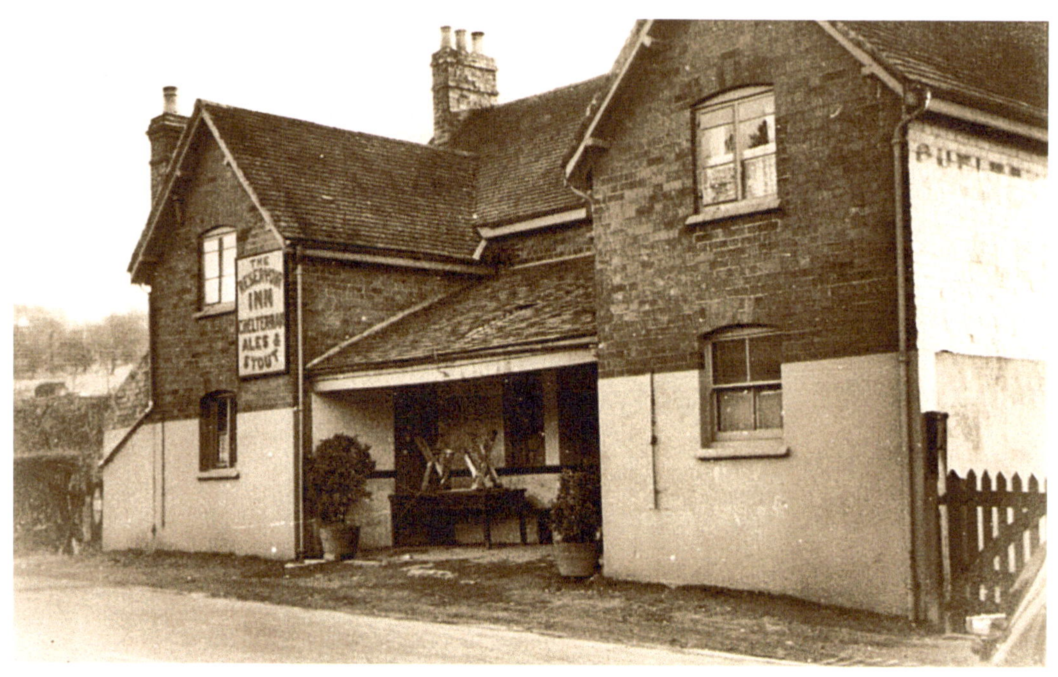

Reservoir Inn

When Cheltenham Corporation completed building the reservoir at Dowdeswell in 1886, the White Swan pub at Dowdeswell Mill was renamed the Reservoir Inn. It traded under this name for over a century until being renamed the Hungry Bear in the late 1990s and then the Waterside Inn. Reverting back to the Reservoir in 2006, it became a short-lived gastropub before closing early in 2011. It is now an Indian restaurant called Koloshi.

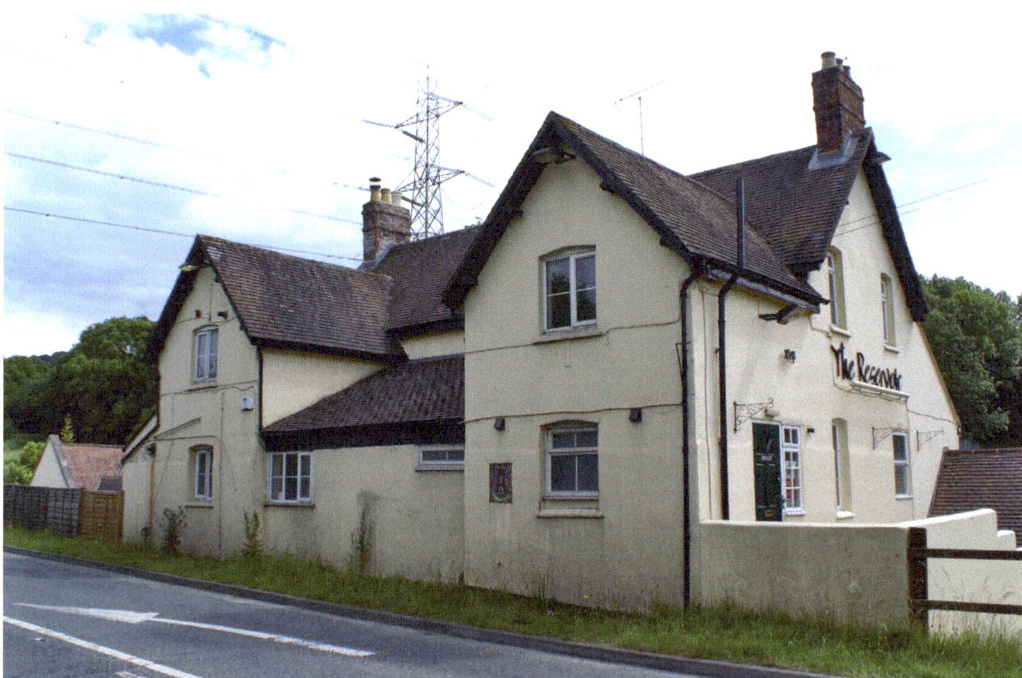

Printed and bound by CPI Group (UK) Ltd, Croydon, CR0 4YY

16/07/2026

02169566-0004